BEND YOUR HEAD, DON'T YOU WISH
THAT YOU WERE DEAD.
BEND YOUR KNEE, ONE, TWO, THREE –
AND OUT GOES SHE.

1920S CHILDREN'S MURDER RHYME

ALSO BY TROY TAYLOR

A SONG OF DANCE AND DEATH
Magic, Murder, Mayhem and the
Diabolical Notes of the Devil's Music

"DON'T YOU WISH YOU WERE DEAD?"

THE HISTORY, HORROR & HAUNTINGS OF AMERICAN MURDER BALLADS

TROY TAYLOR

An American Hauntings Ink Book

"DON'T YOU WISH YOU WERE DEAD?"
The History, Horror & Hauntings of American Murder Ballads

© COPYRIGHT 2025 BY TROY TAYLOR

All Rights Reserved.
ISBN: 978-1-958589-24-3
First Edition

Published by American Hauntings Ink
301 East Broadway - Alton IL - 62002
www.americanhauntingsink.com

Publisher's Note:
No part of this publication may be reproduced, distributed, or transmitted In any form or by any means, including photocopying, recording, or other electronic or mechanical methods, without the prior written consent of the publisher, except in case of brief quotations embodied in critical reviews or other noncommercial uses permitted by copyright law.

Cover Design by April Slaughter
Interior Design by Troy Taylor

Printed in the United States of America

INTRODUCTION

I HAVE A CONFESSION TO MAKE.
The song that first got me interested in murder ballads isn't actually a murder ballad. But it's a song, it's got death in it, and, in this case, there's also a ghost.

Plus, I've always liked it, ever since I heard it on the jukebox of a restaurant in the little Central Illinois farm town where I grew up. I was probably 11 or 12 when I heard it at the "Hog Trough," so it was a fine dining restaurant, as you might imagine.

Anyway, the song was by Jimmy Dean – the singer and sausage guy, not the actor from *Rebel Without a Cause* – and was called "Big Bad John." It told a cool story, and I listened to it over and over again, much to the dismay of other customers, I'm sure.

Jimmy wrote the song on a flight from New York to Nashville because he realized he needed a fourth song for a recording session. When he got to Nashville, Roy Acuff helped him polish it, and Floyd Cramer, hired to play piano on the song, came up with the idea of using a hammer and a piece of steel to keep the rhythm. The song became one of the biggest country songs of the 1960s and, really, of all time.

The song is about a quiet, mysterious coal miner who earns the nickname "Big John" because of his massive size. As Jimmy's lyrics went, "He stood six foot six and weighed 245."

One day, a supporting timber cracked in the mine, and the situation appeared hopeless for the miners trapped inside until John "grabbed a saggin' timber, gave out with a groan, and like a giant oak tree just stood there alone." After he gave the support beam a mighty shove, he opened a passage and allowed the other miners to escape.

Just as a rescue crew was about to enter the mine to save those still trapped inside, the tunnel collapsed, blocking the entrance and sealing the fate of the heroic John. The mine was never reopened, but a monument was placed in front of it, saying, "At the bottom of this mine lies one helluva man—Big John."

The song struck a chord with listeners, especially coal miners, all over the country, but one town in West Virginia knew where the story of "Big John" had come from.

The people of Grant Town, in northern West Virginia, knew about coal mines and the dangers found in them – from tunnel collapses to gas and dust explosions and the black damp – and they knew about Big John.

By the 1960s, they'd been telling John's ghost story for decades – a story about a giant miner who haunted the Federal No. 1 mine, which operated from 1901 to 1985.

The story went that Big John – as the other miners called him – was a Russian immigrant who found his way to the coal mines in Grant Town. At the time, there were immigrants from 14 countries living in town and working for the mine.

Big John became an expert at explosives, but that was his undoing because one day, he was careless and blew himself up. The other coal miners heard the explosion, and they came running, but Big John was dead. They found his body, but his head was gone.

A short time later, one of the miners arrived early for work one day and went down into the mine in the cage elevator. He thought he was alone – but he wasn't. After stepping out of the cage, he heard someone breathing nearby. Then he heard a grunt and turned on his helmet's light to look around.

He was terrified by what he saw – a man with no head was standing just a few feet away. Before he could scream, he happened to look down and see the dead man's head. The figure was holding it under his arm, and he recognized the face – it was Big John. And he was smiling, just as he always was in life.

The miner didn't know what else to do, so he tightly closed his eyes and waited. When he opened them again, his headless old friend was gone.

So, no, it's not a murder ballad, but I've always loved the song, and when I found out it was inspired by a story with a ghost, I couldn't resist including it here.

But from here on, we're going to get into the real murder ballads, the stories – and the songs – that have become an essential part of American culture over the years.

I always like to say that almost every crime from American history I write about seems to have a ghost story behind it.

And it also seems they have a song, too.

TODAY, WHEN WE THINK OF A BALLAD, WE THINK of a love song – or any slow song played by a hair band in the 1980s – but in traditional or folk music, it's really just a song that tells a story. And a lot of those stories – dating back to England, Ireland, Wales, and the rest of Europe in the Middle Ages – are about crime and murder.

Like witchcraft and folk music, murder ballads crossed the Atlantic with the first immigrants. When they got here, they became something uniquely American, even if some of the material used in American ballads was borrowed from English ones. Singers would copy the old ballads and just sort of fill in the blanks with the local killers, victims, and crimes they wanted to talk about.

The way the characters were portrayed in the songs could vary wildly because – I know, big surprise – they were mostly about the murders of women. And the women were usually portrayed as innocent, helpless victims led astray by their lovers who were, more often than not, also their killers. The messages of these songs were meant to be warnings to other young women of the time not to go down the same path.

Oddly, though, the men were often portrayed in a bizarrely sympathetic way, apparently not responsible for their own actions and painted as sort of co-victims in these crimes of passion. Of course, as any woman can tell you, this is because men wrote the songs.

The most famous murder ballads were inspired by true stories, even if, in many cases, the writers and singers changed the storyline to fit whatever direction they wanted the song to go.

One famous murder ballad called "Little Omie Wise," tells the story of the 1808 murder of Naomi Wise, a North Carolina woman who was murdered by a man named John Lewis, the father of her unborn child. Folk singer Doc Watson performed the song's most famous version, but it's been done several times.

American murder ballads began with singers strumming guitars on front porches and in local saloons. Then, they started to be collected by historians who wanted to keep roots music alive. They were eventually pressed into records that told stories about small-town murders to people all over the country.

They became popular in folk music, country music, and even rock 'n' roll.

Remember when Kurt Cobain introduced grunge fans to one of the most famous murder ballads of all time to viewers of MTV's *Unplugged*? Do you think any Nirvana fans watching the show knew that "In the Pines" dated back to at least the 1870s?

My girl, my girl, don't lie to me
Tell me, where did you sleep last night?
In the pines, in the pines
Where the sun don't ever shine
I would shiver the whole night through

Murder ballads might have come to America with the earliest settlers but achieved their greatest notoriety during nineteenth-century America when violence and religiously inspired moralism tried to balance each other out. But even so, they remain with us today – in ways that might surprise you before you finish this book.

So, buckle up. It's going to be a wild ride through American folk history, bloody murder, and darkness and shadows that are filled with vengeful ghosts.

Be sure to leave the lights on while you're reading this one!

Troy Taylor
Spring 2025

1. "STAGGER LEE"

ON CHRISTMAS EVE 1895, A SHOOTING OCCURRED IN a North St. Louis saloon that made history – not because those involved were famous but because the story of what happened that night became one of the most popular American murder ballads ever written, sung, and recorded.

The men involved were two black men – a levee hand named William "Billy" Lyons and a part-time carriage driver and full-time pimp named Lee Shelton. The fight began when Billy snatched Lee's hat from his head, which led to Lee first striking him and then shooting him. Billy died, and Lee was sentenced to 25 years in prison.

These are the bare bones of the story, but a lot of folk tales, legends, and outright lies have been added to them, creating what may be the most widely adapted song in our history.

The song, which sprang up immediately, was called "Stagger Lee." It came to be reinvented as a work chant, field holler, blues, rag, jazz, rock, and folk song.

But why? That's a good question – no one knows. It's impossible to predict what people or events will become legendary and what will be forgotten. However, I can promise that a low-life criminal named Lee Shelton could never have predicted that anyone would still be talking about him more than a century later – or that he'd become the subject of a song recorded hundreds of times.

Four hundred versions of "Stagger Lee" have been released on record since 1895, giving Lee a list of biographers that has included some of the biggest names in American music. Duke Ellington, Fats Domino, Jerry Lee Lewis, and James Brown have all recorded the song, as have Wilson Pickett, The Clash, Bob Dylan, Dr. John, Nick Cave, and Amy Winehouse. Even Elvis Presley took a shot at it in a 1970 rehearsal that later surfaced as a bootleg recording.

All these versions tell the same core story, but no two of them seem to be able to agree on the details. A man named Stack Lee – or Stagger Lee – goes to a bar called The Bucket of Blood – or sometimes The White Elephant – where he kills a man named Billy Lyons – or Billy Lion – for stealing, or winning, or spitting into his Stetson hat. The story takes place in St. Louis – or New Orleans, or even Memphis in some versions – and the year is pretty much any year you want to name. Sometimes, Lee kills the bartender first for disrespecting him and then moves on to Billy, who's done nothing to him at all. He's a sadistic killer in some versions and a wronged innocent in the next.

All these songs are about Lee Shelton, but who was he? And how did he become so notorious?

THE BEST PLACE TO START IS WITH THE CITY WHERE HE lived when the murder occurred. By 1895, St. Louis was a thriving Mississippi River community that had built its prosperity by loading and unloading the hundreds of steamers traveling between Minneapolis and New Orleans. This brought a constant parade of riverboat workers, gamblers, grifters, and thieves, all anxious to raise hell in St. Louis for a day or two before they continued their journey. Itinerant railroad workers joined the party by the 1850s after St. Louis became the fabled "gateway to the west." The end of the Civil War in 1865 caused a huge increase in the city's black population when formerly enslaved people moved north for the new factory jobs and the greater freedoms that St. Louis provided.

Wages for these new workers were predictably low but still gave them more money than they'd ever had before. All they needed was a place to spend that money on a Saturday night.

In 1874, the Mississippi was bridged at St. Louis for the first time, opening the city's riverfront vice districts to the even rougher residents of East St. Louis on the Illinois side of the river.

The population of St. Louis increased sevenfold between 1850 and 1900, and as the new century began, it became the fourth largest city in the United States.

And with all these developments, law and order struggled to keep up with the changes. The city's police department was not fully established until 1846, and its first courthouse wasn't completed until 1862. The infamous Four Courts on Clark Street hosted not only courtrooms but also the offices of the police department, the gallows, and the city morgue.

The Four Courts only stood for 36 years. Its life was shortened because most residents believed it to be "the ugliest building ever erected in St. Louis" and by many structural problems that could not be repaired – including an incessantly leaking roof. Officials eventually gave up trying to fix it, and the building was torn down in 1907.

The infamous Four Courts Building in St. Louis

But not before it gained its reputation for being haunted.

In the late 1890s, stories began to circulate about weird sounds often heard late at night coming from the building's third floor. Mrs. Harris, a matron at the jail, was the first to report what seemed to be footsteps and what sounded like someone moving furniture about. When she and two patrolmen checked the room where the noises came from, they found it empty.

The stories became more frequent toward the end of the building's life. In May 1906, Mrs. Nelson, the night police matron, placed an urgent call to the Central District Station to report footsteps being heard in an empty dormitory that had once been set aside for juvenile offenders. A report in the *St. Louis Post-Dispatch* stated that Patrolman James Dixon climbed the stairs to the third floor and made a search for the cause of the footsteps. He found the dormitory – and the rest of the floor – deserted.

The eerie sounds continued regularly until the jail was closed and the building was torn down.

But let's get back to Stagger Lee.

Near the Four Courts was a red-light district known as the Deep Morgan. It was a place to find blues and ragtime music, gambling, and brothels that operated without interference from the law. Thanks to the many dives that sold "nickel shots" of cheap whiskey, even the poorest customers could find a place to get drunk there.

The Deep Morgan was a part of the city where the normal segregation of the races was forgotten, allowing blacks and whites to frequent the bars and brothels together. Prostitutes of both races staffed the sporting

The Deep Morgan vice district was the place to find blues, ragtime, gambling, brothels, and saloons in the 1890s.

houses, and when business was slow, the girls would try and drum up work by knocking on the windows of each bar they passed. This habit didn't sit well with the prostitutes who worked inside the saloons and would sometimes cause an entertaining catfight in the street outside.

The St. Louis police force was all-white until 1901, and its dealings with the black residents and workers of the Deep Morgan were not always fair and friendly. This is evidenced by the murder of a police officer, which inspired its own murder ballad. The killing occurred at Charles Starke's tavern in October 1890. The two characters often switch roles in this ballad known as "Duncan and Brady," – but a version recorded by bluesman Leadbelly sticks to the facts by making James Brady the corrupt cop and Harry Duncan the black bartender who kills him.

Twinkle, twinkle, twinkle, little star,
Up comes Brady in a 'lectric car,
Got a mean look all 'round his eye,
Gonna shoot somebody just to see them die

Duncan, Duncan was tending the bar,
In walked Brady with a shining star,
And Brady says, "Duncan, you are under arrest,"
And Duncan shot a hole in Brady's breast.

Incidents like this explain how five murders took place in a single night in St. Louis in 1895. Four others occurred on that Christmas Eve night, but only one turned out to matter.

The Deep Morgan was home turf for men like Lee Shelton and Billy Lyons in 1895. Money was flowing, which meant business was booming for a pimp, which makes it strange that Lee would throw all that away over an argument. The lines of the song claim it was about gambling, but according to the newspapers at the time, the argument was political.

Smack in the middle of the district were two of the area's most notorious bars. One owned by Bill Curtis was on the corner of 11th and Morgan, while Henry Bridgewater's saloon was just a block away at 11th and Lucas. The two establishments were bitter rivals, not only because they were catering to the same clientele. Bridgewater was a prominent black Republican, while Curtis' saloon was a frequent meeting place for Democrat activists. Both bars had a terrible reputation. The *St. Louis Post-Dispatch* called Curtis' place one of the "worst dens in the city," calling its customers "the lower class of river men and other darkies of the same social status." Not to be outdone, the *St. Louis Globe-Democrat* referred to Bridgewater's place as "a den of vice."

Billy Lyons had good reason to consider Curtis' bar as enemy territory. He was Henry Bridgewater's brother-in-law and had been involved in disputes with the Morgan Street tavern before – ones he usually started himself. For instance, a few years before, a drunken Lyons got into a fight with Bill Curtis himself, waving around a vicious-looking knife. When a police officer named James Dawson walked in, he found that all the other customers had fled, leaving Curtis and his attacker alone in the bar. Curtis had put a billiards table between himself and Lyons, who continued brandishing the knife.

Dawson later wrote: "I seized Lyons by the throat, and, with the assistance of Curtis, I disarmed him and arrested him. I was obliged by reason of his violence to place the handle of the knife in my teeth and brought him to the station three blocks distant, finally throwing him to the floor of the captain's office."

ON THAT CHRISTMAS EVE NIGHT, BILLY LYONS LEFT Bridgewater's saloon with his friend, Henry Crump, and they walked to Curtis' tavern together. Billy paused at the entrance to borrow a knife from Henry, and then they went inside. He bought himself a drink at the bar, turned around, and saw Lee Shelton walking in.

Lee was a local carriage driver who sometimes moonlighted as a bartender at Curtis' place. He also ran a "lid club" called the Modern Horseshoe for black customers in the Deep Morgan. Clubs like this earned the "lid" moniker because they kept a legitimate tavern in front to keep a lid on the illegal gambling and prostitution in the back room. It's believed that Lee ran his stable of girls out of the Modern Horseshoe.

At some point when he was a boy, Lee Shelton had gotten the nickname of "Stack" Lee – probably after the steamboat the *Stack Lee* that was then well-known on the Mississippi River. He was a streetwise young man – only 30 when he shot Lyons – and was small but dangerous with a left crossed eye that no one dared laugh about. His job as a carriage driver made him a knowledgeable guide for visitors who arrived via the railway station looking for local saloons and bordellos. He directed them to girls whose activities he personally oversaw and to taverns where he would also earn a buck.

Lee was dressed to the nines when he walked into the bar that night – flashy suit, sharp shoes, and a stylish Stetson hat, which all the Deep Morgan dandies considered essential wear. As he stepped through the door, he called, "Who's treating?" Someone pointed him toward Billy Lyons at the bar. He joined him there, and the two men began drinking together in what onlookers later called "a friendly way." In fact, everything was fine until "the discussion drifted to politics."

As we've already noted, Billy was a Republican, like his brother-in-law, and Lee was a Democrat – so active that he was one of the leaders of the 400 Club in St. Louis, which organized Democratic voters in the city.

George McFaro, one of the 20 or so customers at the bar that night, said that words between them became heated, fueled by too much to drink. He later testified before coroner Walter Wait that he'd seen Lee strike Billy's derby hat, crushing its dome. Billy then grabbed the hat from Lee's head and announced he would keep it until Lee handed over six bits to replace the ruined derby.

Lee scoffed. "Six bits would buy a box of those hats!"

When Billy asked him why he'd crushed the derby in the first place, Lee made some unspecified gesture, probably a shrug of dismissal.

McFaro further testified: "They stood and talked awhile. Stack snatched out his pistol and he said, 'If you don't give me my hat, I will blow your brains out.' When he pulled the pistol out, I walked out. I didn't stay any longer."

Another witness told the coroner's inquest that Billy responded to Lee's threat by pulling out the borrowed knife and replying, "You cock-eyed son of a bitch. I'm going to make you kill me!"

And that's precisely what Stack Lee did.

He fired his .44-caliber Smith & Wesson and shot Billy in the stomach. As Billy staggered along the bar, clutching the rail, he dropped Lee's hat onto the floor. Lee picked it up and placed it back on his head. "I told you to give me my hat!" he snarled and then turned and walked out of the saloon.

Henry Crump retrieved his knife to make sure the law didn't find it and recruited another customer, Arthur McCoy, to help him carry Billy outside so he could be taken to City Hospital. When the ambulance arrived there, doctors found the bullet had lacerated his liver and carried out an operation to remove the damaged organ. It didn't help. He'd lost too much blood, and he died at 4:00 A.M. His death certificate showed he was just 31 years old.

A more recent photo of the house where Stack Lee was staying at the time of the murder.

By then, Stack Lee was already in custody. After leaving Curtis' bar, he calmly walked to a house where he stayed on Sixth Street, left his gun with a woman there for safekeeping, and then went upstairs to bed. The police tracked him there and arrested him about an hour before Billy Lyons died.

A few minutes later, they returned to the house and – almost an afterthought – took the Smith & Wesson revolver with them.

LEE'S CASUAL ATTITUDE AFTER THE MURDER suggests that he likely wasn't too worried about the police. He may have assumed, with good reason, that the cops wouldn't take much interest in one black man killing another in the vice district. And usually, that would've been the case, but Lee had killed the wrong black man – he'd killed Henry Bridgewater's brother-in-law.

Bridgewater was the wealthiest African American man in St. Louis in 1895. He owned property all over the city's north side and was a prominent Republican at a time when black Americans' initial loyalty to that political party was fading fast. The Civil War had brought an end to slavery three decades earlier. Since that was achieved by Abraham Lincoln, a Republican president, that was enough to ensure that most blacks voted Republican in the following elections. Few of the party's promises to them had materialized, though, and by Lee Shelton's time, the black vote was up for grabs.

Democrats in St. Louis responded by organizing the 400 Club in the city's black bars, including the one owned by Bill Curtis.

And as Shelton hustled for the Democrats, Bridgwater hosted Republican meetings at his bar. Saloon keepers like him were an essential part of the political machine in St. Louis, just one step down from the ward bosses that both parties relied on to bribe and intimidate voters. A saloon provided a place for political meetings and was a business where party organizers could launder cash they might not want to be traced back to themselves and act as a willing source of muscle when things got rough. On election day, many of the customers' votes could be bought with nothing more than a few free drinks.

Bridgewater's place was a little more upscale than the one owned by Curtis. He often entertained the black celebrities of the day and was able to attract a better – and wealthier – clientele. Even so, it was still in the Deep Morgan and remained as rough as the neighborhood around it. At least two murders occurred there between 1895 and 1902, and it remained a place for drinking, whoring, carousing, and fighting downstairs while hard-nosed political negotiations were happening upstairs.

On that note, it seems possible that Bridgewater might have sent Billy Lyons to Curtis' saloon that night to broker some kind of deal between the Deep Morgan Republican and Democrat factions. That might explain why the initial conversation between the two men seemed friendly and also why it turned ugly when they started discussing politics. Since Billy was married to Bridgewater's sister, Elizabeth, perhaps he decided that only a family member could be entrusted with the task. He'd also know that Billy could defend himself if he ran into trouble – any trouble short of a bullet in the belly, anyway.

When Lee was arrested, officers took him to the Chestnut Street police station and locked him up. The next day, he was taken to the Four Courts to be sworn in for the inquest. Waiting at the entrance were about 300 African Americans from what one newspaper called the "Henry Bridgewater faction." They taunted Lee as he approached, becoming more unruly with every step he and his police escorts took toward the entrance. Finally, they rushed toward them, forcing the officers to fight their way through the crowd with their billy clubs so they could clear Lee's path to the door. There were countless shouted threats to lynch Lee before he ever got to trial.

Even after the prisoner was inside, the crowd refused to leave. The next day, an article appeared in the *St. Louis Post-Dispatch* that described the scene: "Throughout the entire hearing, a large crowd of negroes was in attendance. As many of them as could pushed their way into the coroner's office, while the others crowded the hallway and congregated near the Eleventh Street entrance."

The mob remained after the inquest was over, agreeing to go home only after Coroner Wait had assured them that Lee would be referred to a grand jury pending charges of first-degree murder.

It's unknown how he managed it, but less than 24 hours after the inquest, Stack Lee had already secured one of the top lawyers in the city to defend him. Nat Dryden was a brilliant attorney who had secured Missouri's first-ever conviction of a white man for killing a black man – a conviction which, even more remarkably, led to the white killer being executed. On the other hand, Dryden was also an alcoholic and an opium addict, although these habits did nothing to inhibit his courtroom performance as a brutal cross-examiner and powerful speaker. He had already proven himself capable of winning even the most challenging murder cases, so there's no doubt he didn't come cheap.

Prominent St. Louis attorney Nat Dryden represented Lee in his criminal case, suggesting he had more money than anyone knew or some wealthy friends.

Either Lee was much richer than his lifestyle suggested, or he had some very wealthy friends.

On January 3, 1896, he paid $4,000 bail to get out of jail while he waited for the grand jury to decide if he should be indicted – that's roughly $100,000 today. On February 12, he was indicted for first-degree murder, and he was sent back to jail to await his criminal trial.

The murder trial began on July 13, with Dryden for the defense and Orrick Bishop leading a team of prosecutors for the state. Bishop was every bit as formidable as Dryden, so newspaper readers and courtroom observers eagerly looked forward to the battle to come. As the *St. Louis Post-Dispatch* noted, "The trial promises to develop (into) a very pretty and interesting legal fight."

For some reason, this same newspaper decided to add to the trial's excitement by introducing the idea that Lee and Billy were gambling when the fight broke out that night. There had been no mention of gambling in earlier newspaper reports or any of the statements from the inquest, so either the reporter was confused or couldn't resist embellishing his story with some colorful details.

Whatever the origin of his aspect of the story, gambling became a constant feature in many versions of the song inspired by the murder. In those versions, it's Billy's alleged cheating at craps that prompts Lee to shoot him.

Dryden was forced to accept the idea that his client had shot Billy Lyons but decided to argue that it was done in self-defense. It wasn't a great plan, but it was the only one he had.

The trial ended on May 14, and the next day, the jury returned with a split verdict – seven votes for second-degree murder, two for manslaughter, and three for acquittal. The judge dismissed the jury and ordered a retrial.

Unfortunately for Lee, Nat Dryden went on an epic drinking spree before the new trial date was set, and he died because of it on August 26. His unexpected death delayed the second trial until May 11, 1897. Dryden's old associate, Charles Johnson, replaced him as defense counsel, and while he was a solid attorney, he was not Nat Dryden.

The most dramatic incident at the second trial came when Prosecutor Bishop called Henry Crump – the friend who had accompanied Billy to Curtis' saloon on the night of the murder – to the stand. Before the trial, prosecutors had met with Crump privately and persuaded him to sign a statement saying Billy had never threatened Lee with a weapon before the shooting. But when Henry got onto the witness stand, he told a different story, saying that Billy had pulled a knife on Lee before the trigger was pulled.

Bishop jumped to his feet, cutting off the testimony of his own witness and complaining that his testimony conflicted with the written statement that Henry had already signed. Seeing this new version of events supported the defense's claims of self-defense, Johnson pointed out that the written statement hadn't been produced under oath, arguing that Henry's courtroom testimony must stand. The judge was forced to clear the courtroom while the two attorneys got into an angry and bad-tempered exchange that threatened to turn into a fistfight.

In the end, the judge ruled that Henry had now proven himself to be such an unreliable witness that he should not be allowed to take part in the trial.

Although almost every iteration of the song that was inspired by the murder claimed Stack Lee was executed for Billy's murder – he wasn't.

The jury found Lee guilty of second-degree murder, but the incident with Henry Crump likely created enough doubt in their minds that he was spared the death penalty. Instead, he was sentenced to spend 25 years at the Missouri State Penitentiary.

He didn't have an easy time behind bars, no matter how influential his friends had once been. According to prison records, Lee was flogged at least three times with a steel-tipped leather strap – once for loafing in the yard, once for gambling, and once for stealing a slice of ham from the kitchen. He also spent some time in solitary confinement after sneaking out of his cell one night to shoot craps with other inmates.

But those influential Democrat friends hadn't forgotten him. They continually petitioned for his sentence to be reduced, and by 1899, the Bridgewater family started taking his chances of release seriously enough that they decided to protest. Elizabeth Bridgewater, Billy Lyon's sister, wrote to the governor urging him to force Lee to serve his entire sentence. She wrote, "As a sister, I beg you not to turn a man like him loose on the community at large. If justice had been done, he would have hung."

Judge James Withrow, who had sent Lee to the penitentiary, weighed in on the other side of the argument. He cited Henry Crump's testimony that Billy had pulled a knife on Lee in the tavern that night and wrote, "Lee Shelton had been incarcerated in the jail or penitentiary about six years for this offense. It seems to me that an actual imprisonment of seven or eight years in this case would satisfy the ends of justice."

Henry Bridgewater died in 1904; after that, his family's protests faded away. The support for Lee's release continued, including one petition signed by 10 congressmen arguing that Lyons had been a desperate character and that Lee had only acted in self-defense.

All three governors who held office during the first 12 years of Lee's incarceration – Lawrence Stevens, Alexander Dockery, and Joseph Folk – were Democrats. However, none of them felt able to set him free. Perhaps they feared it would look too much like party favoritism if they commuted his sentence. But Republican governor Herbert Hadley – who replaced

Folk in 1909 – had no such worries. Lee walked out of the prison gates in November 1909 but didn't stay a free man for long.

In January 1911, he robbed a man named Louis Akins, breaking his skull with a revolver before stealing $140 from his house. He was caught, sentenced to five years, and sent back to the penitentiary. By then, he was 46 years old and suffering from tuberculosis. He was released from prison eight months later – this time for health reasons – but he was too sick to be moved. He remained in the prison hospital, where he died on March 11, 1912.

But, of course, that was not the end of Stack Lee's story. The man might be dead, but his legend was just getting started.

WE'LL NEVER KNOW WHY THIS ONE PARTICULAR MURDER gained such notoriety, but it did. The song "Stagger Lee" – because "Stagger" sounded better musically than "Stack" – spread very fast, first appearing a short time after the actual killing.

In the 1890s, Ragtime was the dominant music styler in St. Louis, played by pianists in every brothel and bar in the city's black neighborhoods. By 1895, Ragtime was already taking a turn toward the blues in Deep Morgan, while in the rival red-light district of Chestnut Valley – just a few blocks south – jazz stylings were starting to emerge.

Claims have been made that songs about Lee Shelton's case were being sung in St. Louis within a year of the murder, but the first concrete evidence of such tunes was in an August 21, 1897, newspaper advertising a show by a pianist named Charlie Lee. It was announced that he would be playing "Stack-a-Lee in variations." Aside from the title, nothing is known about the song, but it was clearly popular enough to advertise it. That means that a blues version was likely already going around. Traveling musicians at the time would have kept an ear out for local songs like this to ensure their own sets stayed fresh.

As Ragtime and St. Louis-style blues spread across the country from St. Louis, it took the songs about Lee Shelton along with them. The first collected lyrics of the song – and there were likely earlier ones that weren't written down – showed up in 1910. All the elements were included – the Christmas setting, the bar location, two correctly identified characters, and even the right caliber of the murder weapon. In the song, Shelton was dubbed "Staggalee."

More versions of the song followed, and it seeped into America's popular culture. By 1918, Stack's name had enough commercial draw that a blackface vaudeville duo renamed themselves "Stack & Lee."

But it was through records that the story of "Stagger Lee" really made its mark. Record players started to gain popularity in the late 1870s, and by 1895, they were being mass-produced. To convince people to buy them, companies like RCA and Victor quickly figured out that they needed to press some popular songs onto vinyl for people to play.

But back then, music for white audiences was performed by white people and sold in white record stores. So, if you had popular black songs like "Stagger Lee," they had to be re-recorded by white musicians.

This meant that the first records to exploit the legend were instrumentals by white dance bands. Frank Waring's Pennsylvanians and Frank Westphal's Royal Novelty Orchestra released competing versions of a foxtrot called "Stack O'Lee Blues" in 1923. Ma Rainey recorded a jazzy version with the same name in 1926, and Duke Ellington added his own version of the song the following year.

Also in 1927, bluesman Frank Hutchinson put out "Stackalee," and the Down Home Boys followed with their own "Original Stack O'Lee Blues."

It was the Down Home Boys that started changing the basic elements of the story. They cast Billy as a white policeman who tries to arrest Stack on a trumped-up vagrancy charge. This was a far too common practice among southern cops at the time – the Down Home Boys were from Mississippi – to snatch up black men to boost the local prison farm's workforce at harvest time. It was a reference that didn't escape most of their audiences.

In the Down Home Boys song, it's clear that Billy is afraid of Stack, who taunts the white authority figure to his face. When the cowardly, unjust policeman forces Stack to kill him, it seems like an excusable crime, and Stack returns to his "misunderstood bad man" ways in the final verse.

The song was released on a "black label" at the time, aimed almost exclusively at African American audiences, offering them a strong black man who stood up to a racist white authority that they could root for. In

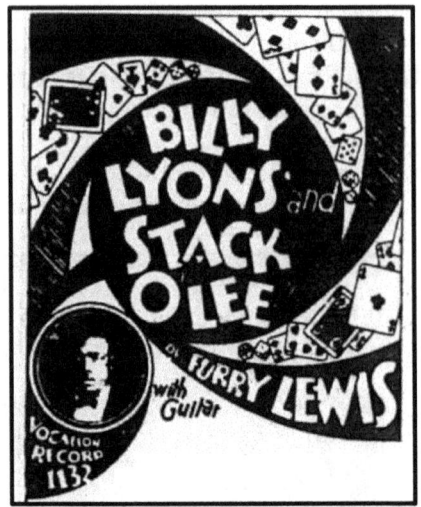

some versions of the early work songs – sung by levee workers, chain gangs, saloon and street singers, and even children – Stack had already been portrayed as an anti-hero, and most versions that followed the Down Home Boys recording took the same route.

But not all of them. In 1927, Furry Lewis recorded a unique and unusual version of the story called "Billy Lyons and Stack O'Lee." He depicts Billy and Stack as two gamblers and attributes the murder to Stack being a bad loser. His chorus goes after Stack for bad behavior, saying, "When you lose your money, learn to lose." This was the first version of the song to claim that Billy and Stack had been gambling when the fight happened, but it has since become a fixture in the song. In the years following Lewis' recording, though, performers gradually shifted the blame for the gambler's disagreement from Stack to Billy himself.

Mississippi John Hurt, who recorded one of the most enduring recordings of the song in 1928, delivered bone-weary sad lyrics – accompanied by skillful guitar playing – about the violence poor black communities like the one in St. Louis had to endure from the killers and thugs among them. He began by berating the police for refusing to arrest Stack Lee earlier and reminded listeners just how cruel this bad man was. Stack may have felt that Billy's theft of his hat justified him to kill the man, but Hurt strongly condemned him for it. He did allow Stack a moment of dignity on

Mississippi John Hurt

the gallows, though – "head way up high" – but gave no sign that he regretted his demise.

There was a steady flow of "Stagger Lee" covers in the years that followed Mississippi John Hurt's recording, including versions by Woody Guthrie, Cab Calloway, Memphis Slim, Fats Domino, and Jerry Lee Lewis.

The first artist to make the song a number-one hit in America was Lloyd Price, a black New Orleans native with a considerable musical background. He'd written "Lawdy Miss Clawdy" and, with it, scored his own number-one R&B hit five years before Elvis Presley covered it. Price racked up four more number ones and then was drafted for the Korean War. He spent the next two years touring Army bases in Korea and Japan, entertaining the troops. Looking for ideas to spice up his sets, he adapted a 1950 version of "Stack-A-Lee" by a New Orleans singer named Archibald and put together a routine based on the story, making soldiers act out the song while he sang it on stage.

On a side note, the Archibald version of the song began a tradition among New Orleans performers that continued the story of Stack Lee after his death – when he descends into Hell. When he arrives, he terrifies the Devil and puts himself in charge. In some of the versions that followed, Billy ends up in Hell, too, allowing Stack to inflict more punishment on him in the afterlife. This aspect of the story first appeared in an unlikely place – a song released by country crooner Tennessee Ernie Ford in 1951. In his version, the Devil flees in panic when he sees Stack Lee at his door, and then Stack takes over and rules Hell himself.

In other similar versions, we learn that Stack's Stetson hat was originally a gift from the Devil and gave magical powers to its owner. There was no limit to the embellishment this detail offered, including the claim that the hat was constructed from the "rawhide of a man-eatin' panther that the Devil had skinned alive."

Another detail also appeared in New Orleans' versions of the story, claiming that women mourning Stack's death should come to his funeral "dressed in red." Both Archibald and Dr. John used that line in their versions.

But back to Lloyd Price...

Price got out of the Army in 1956 and resumed his recording career. He was back on the charts almost immediately with "Just Because" in 1957, and then he released his raucous version of "Stagger Lee" in 1959. It's a loud, wild record, backed by blaring horns and roars of encouragement from the backup singers. Thumping drums accompany

Price's powerful vocals, and an abrasive saxophone erupts whenever he pauses to breathe.

Even without the backing vocals singing the constant refrain – "Go Stagger Lee! Go Stagger Lee!" – it's clear where the song's sympathies lie. All of Mississippi Jonh Hurt's doubts about the killer's code of honor are gone. In Price's version, Billy refuses to admit that Stack had won at dice, making him fair game. There's a moment of sympathy for Billy – "that poor boy" – but Price soon returned to cheering on Stack Lee.

By making "Stagger Lee" a hit, Price introduced the story to large white audiences for the first time. Casual white listeners could have easily missed the Woody Guthrie and Jerry Lee Lewis versions of the song, but Price got enough radio play to make the song inescapable. Everyone knew Stack and Billy's story now, and Price's success invited white audiences to embrace the story, too.

For many, this was an exciting experience. They could get a vicarious thrill of imagining themselves freer and more frightening than they'd ever be in real life while still enjoying the comforts of their safe, white, middle-class lives. It was a foreshadowing of white suburbia's embrace of gangsta rap that would come decades later but was far too dangerous for American television audiences in the 1950s. Dick Clark insisted that Price cut a sanitized version of the song if he wanted it to be played on American Bandstand, and Price reluctantly agreed. In those lyrics, Stack and Billy argue rather than gamble, regret the harsh words between them, and then part the best of friends.

Price's "Stagger Lee" remained on the charts for three months, making it the template for many new cover versions and luring artists from new genres to give it a shot. Until 1959, "Stagger Lee" mainly belonged to folk and blues musicians, with occasional jazz and country versions tossed into the mix. Price's hit prompted soul and reggae performers to give it a shot, too.

Ike and Tina Turner were the first soul singers to take a crack at it in 1965, placing Tina in a dance club, where she watched Billy beat Stack to a pulp for kissing Billy's wife. The song faded out before Stack had the opportunity for revenge.

James Brown funked the story up in 1967, the same year Wilson Pickett offered his version. Both stuck close to the same storyline that Lloyd Price did.

Meanwhile, in Jamaica, artists listened to R&B from America on the radio, adapting the plot and the rhythms for their own use. Prince Buster liked Price's tune enough to create a rude boy version of "Stack-O-Lee" in 1966. For those who don't know, "rude boy" is a term that originated in Jamaica as slang for a young man who is hardened by the streets. It was also a subculture of young men who were known for their fashion, music, and sometimes violent behavior. The Prince Buster song prompted what was effectively an answer record the following year.

The Rulers had already produced a couple of records warning about the consequence of rude boys' delinquency and saw the Prince Buster record as a chance to drive their point home. They open "Wrong 'Em Boyo" with a couple of lines from Lloyd Price's song to remind listeners that Billy cheated at dice and then spend the rest of the tune pointing out that it was the wrong way to live. Most importantly, the lyrics are just vague enough to suggest both parties were cheated in the altercation – Stack lost his money, and Billy lost his life.

When The Clash recorded their 1979 album *London Calling*, it was only natural that "Wrong 'Em Boyo" came up as one of their covers. Paul Simonon, the band's reggae aficionado, made sure that a copy of The Rulers' single found its way onto the jukebox in The Clash's rehearsal rooms. Joe Strummer knew Price's version of "Stagger Lee" very well, so he was thrilled to turbo-charge The Rulers' hit into a piece of what was called "tense, jumping ska" and make it one of the album's standout tracks. Predictably, the band's unique additions to the song made a hero of Stack at Billy's expense. They amended Price's opening verse to make Billy the aggressor, kicking off the violence by coming at Stack with a knife – the implication being that our hero was forced to shoot Billy in self-defense. Their addition to The Rulers' lyrics also painted Stack as the wronged party in the whole affair. Billy was still the one who ended up dead, but the song's warning about bad behavior was aimed at him alone. When it ends, it leaves the listener feeling that getting shot was Billy's fault.

The Lloyd Price version, from which both The Clash and The Rulers quote, takes Stack's side, too, but not with the ferocity that The Clash does. Never slow to celebrate an outlaw, the band used their version of the old hit to put Stack on a higher pedestal than anyone else had ever done.

AS "STAGGER LEE" MOVED FROM ONE GENRE OF recorded music to another, shifting as it went, one part of the story remained largely untold. No version of Stack Lee's story sanctioned by the professional recording industry would ever be intense enough for those who lived in America's ghettos and poor neighborhoods to accept, so they came up with their own versions of his legend.

These were spoken-word accounts of Stack's life, chanted at listeners with percussive force and driving their points home through rhyming couplets. They were sexually explicit, usually told in the first person, and filled with inventive swearing. Like the rappers who followed them, the performers used the tales to portray themselves as charismatic, dangerous gangsters who were feared by the white police. This attitude leaked into real life, as proved by a 1908 Kansas City burglary case when the black defendant proudly told the court his name was "Stack Lee." The real Lee Shelton was still in jail at that time but was already notorious enough for that defendant to use his name for a little borrowed glory.

The first "Stagger Lee" spoken-word account was collected for history in 1911. For the next 50 years, it was taken for granted that the language and descriptions in these accounts were far too volatile ever to be featured in a commercial recording. Isolated from every respectable genre of music, they retained their unique take on Stack's story. The Stetson hat was only mentioned in passing, and Billy slipped into the background. Instead, Stack's primary victim is the bartender at a place called The Bucket of Blood. Sometimes, the bartender deliberately served Stack rancid food. In other versions, he first refuses to recognize him and then treats him with contempt, prompting Stack to shoot him.

The bartender's name was never given, but it was clear he represented Henry Bridgewater, the saloon owner responsible for getting Shelton arrested and jailed after the murder.

The first commercial recording of a spoken-word account that was released in anything near an uncut form appeared on the 1969 album *For Adults Only* by Snatch and the Poontangs – an alias for R&B veteran Johnny Otis and his band. The album offered a string of uncensored spoken-word accounts delivered by road-hardened performers. There's a great deal of swearing, springing mostly from the fact that everyone in Stack's life seems to be a "motherfucker."

Another side note I'm reminded of is that there is even a version of "Stagger Lee" by actor Samuel L. Jackson. Look it up.

Like most "Stagger Lee" spoken-word accounts, the track on the Poontangs album can be traced to verses that appear in a 1976 book called *The Life: The Lore and Poetry of the Black Hustler* by Dennis Wepman. The author includes a "Stagger Lee" account performed by a black inmate called Big Stick at Auburn Penitentiary in New York.

When Nick Cave and his band, The Bad Seeds, recorded an entire album called Murder Ballads in 1996, they used lines from Big Stick's account. Bad Seeds percussionist Jim Sclavunos brought a copy of Wepman's book into the studio, and Cave had the band improvise a backing for the Big Stick verses on the spot. The deep bassline, scratchy guitar, and pounding piano chords provide a menacing background for Cave's low, brooding vocals. He growls the words almost verbatim, drawing every bit of drama from them.

OVER THE YEARS, EVERY SERIOUS VERSION OF "Stagger Lee" can be seen as a strong black man doing whatever it takes to make his way in an unjust white man's world. Rich or poor, bad man or hero, he's always in charge and ready to exact a terrible revenge on anyone who doesn't treat him that way. Stack might not be the best of role models, but he has remained a strong symbol of black pride – serving as the influential badman grandfather of gangsta rap. Comparisons have been drawn between his ballad's story and NWA's 1988 track, "Fuck Tha Police," which opens with a scene putting the white police on trial for brutality. As author Eithne Quinn wrote, "The rebellious intent – pushing at the boundaries of what was permissible in its historical moment – matches that of 'Stackolee.' Stackolee meets the LAPD, as it were."

Thousands of young people trapped in poor black neighborhoods saw Stack Lee as a folk hero, whether they knew his origin story or not. Maybe that's why Bobby Seale, the leader of the Black Panthers, decided to name his son Malik Nkrumah Staggerlee Seale. In 1970, Seale explained, "Staggerlee is Malcolm X before he became politically conscious. Living in the hoodlum world."

Drawing a line from "Stagger Lee" to the Black Panthers brings you to Tupac Shakur. In October 1993, Shakur came across two off-duty Georgia cops who he believed were harassing a black man by the side of the road. He got into a fight with them and ended up shooting them both,

After an arrest in 1993, it was suggested that Tupac Shakur had stood up like a "black hero in the tradition of Stagger Lee."

one in the leg and the other in the buttocks. Charges against him were dropped when it was revealed that the officers were drunk at the time and carrying weapons that had been stolen from an evidence locker.

When journalists asked why he would sabotage his lucrative career for what he called the "thug life," it was suggested that he was "a black hero in the tradition of blues archetype Stagger Lee." While the line of heritage seems clear, it's also clear that the true story of what happened between Lee Shelton and Billy Lyons in St. Louis in 1895 has been largely forgotten.

I guess that just goes to show that while the lowlife pimp and murderer, Lee Shelton, has been largely forgotten, the righteous killer Stagger Lee has become an icon – a character who defied authority and showed strength in the face of adversity.

This has resulted in over 300 versions of the song from black and white artists. We've come a long way from Mississippi John Hurt's sad version of Stack's violence that came out in 1928. Each successive generation has darkened the story, stepped a little more into the killer's shoes, and lost whatever pity remained for Billy Lyon.

But as Nick Cave said in 1996, "Just like Stagger Lee himself, there seems to be no limits to how evil this song can become."

2. "TOM DOOLEY"

IN 1866, A WOMAN NAMED LAURA FOSTER WAS murdered in Wilkes County, North Carolina. The man convicted and hanged for the crimes was named Tom Dulla, which was pronounced "Dooley" in the local dialect and would later be spelled that way when the murder inspired a song.

The murder – and the name Tom Dooley – should have been forgotten, but instead, it gained a new life as another of America's classic murder ballads.

The traditional version of the story casts Tom as a dashing, handsome Confederate veteran. When he returns from the war, he meets Laura Foster, a young woman being courted by a Yankee schoolteacher named Bob Grayson. Laura fell in love with Tom, but so did another woman, Anne Melton. Anne was married, wealthy, beautiful, and – as you soon will be aware – more than a little crazy. Learning that Tom was in love with Laura, not her, she stabbed Laura to death in a jealous rage.

Tom was blamed for the murder and ran off, heading for Tennessee. Bob Grayson headed a vigilante group to hunt him down and dragged him back to North Carolina. Tom then realized that it was Anne Melton who had committed the crime, but his sense of chivalry wouldn't allow him to see a woman dishonored and hanged, so Tom confessed to the murder he didn't commit to save Anne's reputation.

He was executed for Laura's murder on May 1, 1868. Bob Grayson left town, and Anne Melton slowly went insane from guilt and years later, as she was on her deathbed – the song goes – the trees around her house filled with black cats, and the air was filled with the smell of burning flesh as demons came to take her soul to Hell.

It's this version of the story – ending with the death of an innocent man – that became the murder ballad that circulated in North Carolina for

The Kingston Trio

nearly 100 years before it was made famous by the Kingston Trio in 1958. "The Ballad of Tom Dooley" made it to number one on the Billboard Country and R&B charts, although I'm not clear how a group that sounds as white as Kingston Trio ended up on the R&B charts.

The song is performed as if Tom Dooley wrote the ballad himself, strumming his banjo as he sat on top of his coffin, riding in the wagon on the way to his hanging.

But sometimes, it's not what's included in the song that's important but what it chooses to leave out.

"The Ballad of Tom Dooley" sold six million copies worldwide, topping the charts in America, Australia, Canada, and Norway. Dooley's ballad and the murder that inspired it have been cemented in the public imagination ever since, making its way into film, theater, and every other medium.

The singer clearly sympathizes with Tom and invites the listener to do the same. But that's hard to do when the lyrics don't tell us who he killed, why he committed the murder, or what the circumstances were surrounding the crime. When did it happen? Who was Grayson, and how did he ruin Tom's planned escape to Tennessee?

And why did those dorky white guys with their short hair, slacks, and striped shirts release such a violent song?

A quick look at other songs that came out around the same time as "The Ballad of Tom Dooley" includes the sugary songs of the era, making Dooley's tale of bloodshed and despair a strange partner to tunes like "Rockin' Robin," "Queen of the Hop," and "The Chipmunk Song."

Columbia Pictures, anxious to exploit the song's success, released a 1959 adaptation called *The Legend of Tom Dooley*. It starred Michael Landon – then best known as Little Joe from *Bonanza* – but it cheerfully made up its own story from scratch. In the movie, Joe and his Confederate army pals are framed for murder after what they take to be an honorable wartime shooting, and Tom kills his unlucky girlfriend in a tragic accident.

However, none of this brought us closer to discovering Tom Dooley's true story. The folk music covers that started to appear over the next few years, taking folk music from a few Greenwich Village cafes onto the national stage, took a more serious approach. However, most were content to copy what the Kingston Trio had done, and when they did manage to slip in some extra information – like Lonnie Donegan's reference to "Sheriff Grayson" – it usually turned out to be untrue.

Mike Seeger's New Lost City Ramblers returned to an earlier folk version of the song in 1960, adding that Tom had been a fiddle player, naming his victim as Laura Foster, and offering the dimension of her shallow grave.

Country singer Doc Watson contributed his version in 1964, which claimed Tom was innocent of any crime and was condemned to hang only because someone was determined to persecute him. Watson didn't bother to mention who that "someone" was.

When the Kingston Trio song came out in 1958, no one outside of North Carolina had even heard of Tom Dooley. However, five years later, his name was known around the world, with millions of people only dimly aware that he'd been accused of killing his girlfriend and was later hanged for it. Dedicated fans of folk music also knew the murder happened in Wilkes County in 1866, but for every "fact" about the real story that emerged, another came along that contradicted it. This meant Tom Dooley's story became more confusing every day.

The story of Tom Dooley had been turned into a song by three clean-cut white boys that had somehow topped the charts and sold millions of records – but told a story that left out a great deal.

It turns out that the real story of Tom, Laura, and the murder was very different from how it was told in the song – and it involved a lot more syphilis.

TOM DULA WAS BORN IN 1844 IN THE DEEPLY impoverished mountain region of North Carolina. He grew up among what the *New York Herald* would later refer to as the "ignorant, poor, and depraved hill people" near the mouth of Elk Creek in Wilkes County. Like any family in the area whose last name ended in an "a," Tom's was pronounced with a long "ee" at the end, which made it sound like "Dooley."

About a half mile from the Dula's cabin lived a woman named Lotty Foster, who had a brood of five illegitimate children. Lotty's entire family was illiterate, and she was known for being a "loose woman" and a drunk.

A photograph of the young man generally believed to have been Tom Dula.

Her daughter, Ann, was married by age 15, taking a local farmer named James Melton as her husband.

Not long after the wedding – when Tom was around 15 – Lotty caught Tom and Ann in bed together. She broke things up, but that didn't end their affair. Soon, Tom moved into the Melton home, sharing it with Ann and James.

And that wasn't all he was sharing.

The house had three beds, and James usually slept alone in one while Tom and Ann shared another. Some say that James – a successful businessman much older than his young wife – had lost interest in her. Others claim he was simply too scared of Ann's ferocious temper to make much of a fuss. Either way, Tom and Ann began sharing a bed with her husband's consent.

But Ann – even though she was considered the region's most beautiful woman –was not Tom's only bed partner. The fact that Tom was handsome enough to share Ann's bed allowed him also to bed many of the county's other young women. He was a talented fiddle player, hired for many dances and gatherings, which likely helped him to catch the eye of many of them.

According to the 19860 census, Tom's mother, Mary, was listed as the head of the household, which suggests that his father was either dead or abandoned the family. Tom had little interest in farming the family's patch of rocky ground, deciding to follow his two older brothers to the Civil War instead. In March 1862, he enlisted in the Confederate Army, joining Company K of the North Carolina Infantry's 42nd regiment. By February 1864, Tom had been promoted from private soldier to musician, which wasn't as fun as it sounded. He wasn't entertaining the troops. He was responsible for drumming out the charge or retreat in battle, which put him right in the heart of the battle. He saw much action the following year, fighting at Cold Harbor, Petersburg, and other places. In March 1865, he was captured by Union troops and sent to a prison camp.

The war ended a month or so after Tom was captured, but he wasn't released until June 11. The regional pronunciation of his name almost kept him from being freed. Thanks to the confusion between how it sounded and how it was written, the oath of allegiance to the United States that he had to sign to be released listed him as "Dooley." He put his mark next to that spelling rather than risk his freedom and scrawled "Dula" above it. This document offers the most reliable description of Tom – five feet, nine inches tall, dark brown curly hair, and brown eyes.

Tom returned home after the war and found times there were harder than ever. Old resentments that pre-dated the war continued to play themselves out in the surrounding hills, and starvation was a real possibility for the poorest among his neighbors. Most locals had no choice but to replace the formerly enslaved people at the plantations that lined the Yadkin River, becoming sharecroppers and tenant farmers there.

One of those newly minted sharecroppers was Wilson Foster, who lived with his daughter, Laura. The stories describe Laura as a beautiful girl with light brown hair, blue eyes, and a gap between her front teeth. By age 20, she'd gained a reputation for "round heels" – a mountain term that noted the ease with which she ended up on her back.

Wilson first found his daughter in bed with Tom in March 1866, and he later testified that Tom called on Laura about once a week. Often, he'd spend the night with her, alternating his visits with other activities.

When Tom returned home from the war, he resumed his unusual living arrangement at the Melton home. However, things there soon became more complicated when Ann's cousin, Pauline, moved into the house to work as a live-in housekeeper. Soon, Tom was sleeping with her, too, but Anne didn't object – in fact, she joined in, which seems very progressive for the 1860s.

So that you can update your scorecard -- In the spring of 1866, Tom was sleeping with Ann, Laura, and Pauline. Dividing his time between Laura and the Melton house threesome seemed to keep Tom happy – and probably very tired. Tom was the only bedmate of Laura that can be named, but her reputation suggested there were others.

Ann was also sleeping with her husband and, if rumors were correct, a couple of other men. Pauline also slept with Ann's brother, Thomas, and was said to have also shared a bed with her own brother, Sam.

None of this bed-hopping would have mattered – they were all adults – but none of the others knew that Pauline hadn't just come to the area to be a housemaid.

She was also seeking treatment for her syphilis.

Pauline had contracted the disease before leaving Watauga County, where she'd lived before coming to her cousin's house. Dr. George Carter, the only physician for miles around, lived nearby, and she'd taken the housekeeping job to afford the treatment he offered. Only Dr. Carter seemed to have known that Pauline had syphilis.

It takes about three weeks for syphilis to start showing signs after contracting it. The first symptom is usually a sore on the penis, which is what Tom presented during his visit to the doctor on March 31. Dr. Carter later testified, "He had the syphilis. He told me he caught it from Laura Foster."

That's undoubtedly what Tom believed since he knew nothing about Pauline having the disease – and she wasn't going to volunteer the information to anyone.

Pauline arrived in the area on March 1, and assuming a week or so passed before she and Tom started sleeping together, the timing was right for him to have contracted the infection from her. And, of course, Tom then passed it on to Laura and then to Ann, who then passed it on to her husband.

Tom, though, was convinced he contracted syphilis from Laura, and he vowed revenge. He told a neighbor in the middle of May that he intended to kill the woman who'd given him the disease. Ann made a similar threat, telling Pauline that she planned to kill Laura for her own infection through Tom.

Throughout the rest of the month, Tom and Laura were locked in a series of private and very intense conversations, ending with Laura telling a friend that Tom had promised to marry her. Some believe this proposal was evidence that Laura was carrying Tom's baby, while others are convinced he was simply looking for a way to lure her into the woods so he could kill her.

On Thursday, May 24, Pauline was alone at the Melton house when Tom stopped by to get some medicine for the sores in his mouth and to borrow a canteen. She handed over the two items, and then Tom visited a man named Carson McGuire, who filled the canteen with homemade liquor.

His next stop was the home of Lotty Foster, Ann's mother, where he borrowed a mattock, a heavy hand tool used for digging, prying, and chopping. It was similar to a pickax with a long handle and a head that combined a vertical ax blade and a horizontal cutter. He told Lotty he wanted to "work some devilment out of himself." Soon after, a woman named Martha Gilbert saw Tom swinging the mattock on a path about

100 yards from the Dula cabin. He told her that he was trying to widen the path.

Around 10:00 A.M., Carson McGuire delivered the canteen with the moonshine in it to Ann at the Melton house. After the noon meal, she took a swig from it and announced she would take it to her mother's house. Tom arrived back at Lotty's – without the mattock – soon after Ann did, and they left together around 3:00 P.M. Neither of them was seen again until dawn the next day.

Ann arrived home at about 5:30 on Friday morning and went straight to bed. Meanwhile, Tom had gone to see Laura at her father's home. She came outside to talk to him, returned to her bedroom, quickly dressed, and bundled some spare clothing together.

A little later that same morning, May 25, Wilson Foster woke up and discovered that both Laura and his horse were missing. When she left home on her father's mare that morning, she was on her way to a meeting place Tom had chosen. About a mile into her six-mile journey, she met Betsy Scott, the same neighbor she'd talked to about marrying Tom a few days before. She confided in Betsy that she and Tom had agreed to meet at "Bate's Place" – a spot in the woods where an old blacksmith shop had once been. Betsy, probably thinking that a marriage proposal from Tom likely had a short expiration on it, urged her to hurry on her way.

At the same time, Tom took a shortcut toward Bate's Place, which shaved a mile off Laura's route. As always, he carried a six-inch hunting knife on his belt.

Along the way, he stopped and chatted with neighbors three times. One of them was Hezekiah Kendall, the man he'd recently talked to about his plan to take his revenge on Laura. When asked if he still planned to pursue it, Tom replied, "No, I've quit that."

He was next seen at the Melton house when Pauline came inside with a milk pail and found Tom standing over Ann's bed, talking to her in low, urgent tones. He left soon after that, taking a route that could lead to either his own home or to Bate's Place.

By then, Wilson Foster had discovered his daughter and mare were missing. Angry, he followed the horse's tracks but then lost the trail, so he stopped at a friend's house for breakfast. After eating, he walked to the Melton house, where Ann was still in bed. Tom had been there and had just left.

All these encounters – from Tom's conversation with Kendall on the road to Wilson's arrival at the Melton home – occurred between 7:30 and 8:30 A.M.

It was noon before Tom was seen again, this time by his mother, Mary, who had returned to the house they shared to find her son lying in bed. They had lunch together, and Tom remained with his mother until about 3:00 P.M. when she went out to care for her cows. Ann's mother, Lottie, and her brother, Thomas, both later testified that they'd seen Tom walking toward Bate's Place while Mary was making supper that evening. Tom returned home in time to eat supper with his mother but then left again just after dark. Mary said he remained gone for about an hour. The distance between the Dula house and Bate's Place was less than a mile so he could have easily walked there and back during that time.

We know Ann was in bed at home around 8:00 A.M. that Friday, but there is no other account of her movements until nightfall, when Wilson Foster returned to the Melton home for a party with her, James, Pauline, Thomas, and three other men. Wilson stayed at the party for nearly three hours, then spent the rest of the night at the home of his friend, Francis Melton.

When he returned home on Saturday morning, he found his horse had returned without Ann. The mare had chewed through her halter rope, about three feet of which was still hanging from its headcollar.

He never saw his daughter alive again – and neither did anyone else.

WHEN TOM RETURNED TO THE MELTON HOME ON Saturday morning, he spent about a half hour talking quietly with Ann. Laura's disappearance had started the community gossiping about how she and Tom must have run off together. When Pauline mentioned this to him, he laughed and said, "I have no use for Laura Foster."

Later that morning, Ann told Pauline she'd slipped out of the house overnight without anyone noticing. This caused Pauline to come to her own conclusions about what had occurred the previous night. "She'd done what she said. She'd killed Laura Foster."

As soon as people realized that Tom was still in the neighborhood, the gossip changed to speculation about Laura being murdered. By June 22, a local family named Hendricks was even openly saying that Tom had killed her. Tom laughed at that, too. "They'd have to prove it," he said. "And perhaps take a beating besides."

But it was hard to ignore the threats that Tom had foolishly made to friends and at least one neighbor and calls for his arrest soon began circulating. There seemed to be one problem with that plan, though – if Laura had been murdered, where was her body?

A search party was organized to look for what everyone assumed would be Laura's remains. They started at the place where she said she'd been going on the day she vanished, and at Bate's Place, they found a piece of rope tied to a tree that was chewed through at its dangling end. It matched the rope that Wilson's horse had trailed home. Nearby, there were a couple of horse droppings, suggesting that the horse had been standing there for some time.

There was also a small patch of discolored grass and dirt that searchers believed was stained by Laura's blood.

Tom went to the Melton's place the following day around nightfall. He spoke privately to Ann outside, then came into the house to retrieve a knife that she'd hidden for him under the headboard of one of the beds. When Pauline asked what was troubling him, he said that the Hendricks family was falsely accusing him of killing Laura, and he was going to have to leave Wilkes County. After a final embrace between himself and Ann, Tom left. He stopped in Watauga County for a few days and then continued across the border into Tennessee.

By the time Tom left Watauga, the local justice of the peace, Pickens Carter, had issued a warrant for his arrest for suspicion of murder. Sheriff William Hix dispatched two deputies, Jack Adkins and Ben Ferguson, to track down Tom and bring him home. He also arrested Ann and two of Tom's cousins on the same charge, but all three were found not guilty by Justice of the Peace Carter during a June 29 hearing and set free.

Meanwhile, Tom arrived in Tennessee on July 2 after a week of hard walking. Passing through, he learned about a job on a farm owned by Colonel James Grayson, a former soldier and current state legislator. Using the last name Hall, Tom took the job as a field hand. A week later, he'd earned enough money to replace his worn-out boots, and he moved on, heading west toward Johnson City.

But the two deputies on his trail were close behind him. Adkins and Ferguson tracked Tom to Grayson's farm, arriving just a few days after Tom had left. When Grayson realized the man they were looking for was his former field hand, he rode off with them to see the Johnson County sheriff, knowing they'd need his authority to arrest Tom on North Carolina charges. When they discovered the sheriff was out of town on business, they continued after Tom anyway.

They discovered him camped next to a creek at Pandora, about nine miles west of Mountain City, and told him he was under arrest. Tom, seeing the men were armed, thought it best to surrender. Legend has it that the two deputies wanted to hang Tom right there on the spot, but

Grayson insisted he be returned home for trial. He tied Tom on the horse behind him, and the party returned east. Adkins and Ferguson locked him up at the Wilkesboro Jail the next day.

Hearing about Tom's capture, Pauline fled Wilkes County on July 14 and went home, but Ann dragged her back a few days later. She explained forcefully that her panic would make them all look guilty. She urged Pauline to help ensure no further evidence against Tom was found.

She told Pauline: "I want to show you Laura's grave. I want to see whether it looks suspicious." She said that she would dig up Laura's body and rebury her in a cabbage patch if necessary. But Pauline, who later claimed she had been absolutely terrified, refused to go with her.

Ann left alone and returned a short time later, apparently satisfied that the grave would draw no attention, and she cursed her cousin for being a coward.

Pauline soon began to fall apart, tormented by the knowledge that she may have given Tom the infection that cost Laura her life. She started drinking heavily, making her more unpredictable than ever.

About a week later, Ann and Pauline were at home when Deputies Adkins and Ferguson stopped by to ask them some questions. Ferguson told Pauline that he believed she'd helped Tom kill Laura, and that was why she'd fled across the county line to her old home. Pauline drunkenly replied, "Yes, I and Dula killed her, and I ran away. Come out, Tom Dula, and let us kill some more! Let's kill Ben Ferguson!"

Seeing the condition she was in, the two deputies ignored her outburst, and Pauline later insisted it had been nothing other than a joke.

But no one found it funny. The authorities decided that a few nights in jail might be enough to convince Pauline to talk. Locked in a cell and told she was going to be prosecuted for murder, Pauline cracked and described Ann's trip up the ridge to see Laura's grave. Pauline agreed to help the next search party to find it.

A few days later, a party of 70 men followed Pauline to the ridge where she'd seen Ann going to the grave. She pointed up the hill in the direction Ann had gone, and the men split up into smaller groups for the search that followed.

One of the groups was headed by Colonel James Isbell and his elderly father-in-law, David Horton. They carefully searched their section of the ridge for an hour, and then suddenly, Horton's horse began to snort and rear up, refusing to go any farther.

Isbell noticed the horse back away, and he called to Horton to see what was wrong. The older man left his saddle and walked across the area that had frightened his horse. He stamped his boot heel into the ground, turned up a piece of grass and soil, and found Laura about two feet under the ground, cramped into a small grave.

The grave was only about 250 yards from the path where Tom had been seen working with Lotty's mattock back in May. James Isbell later testified: "After taking out the earth, I saw the prints of what appeared to have been a mattock in the hard side of the grave. The flesh was off the face. Her body had on a checked cotton dress and a dark-colored cloak or cape. There was a bundle of clothes laid on the head."

The two men called over Dr. Carter, and he examined the body where it lay in the shallow grave. He found a knife slit in the fabric over Laura's left breast and a corresponding stab wound between her third and fourth ribs. Dr. Carter also later testified: "The body was lying on its right side, face up. The hole in which it lay was two-and-a-half feet deep, very narrow, and not long enough for the body. The legs were drawn up."

After three months in the ground, Laura was too decomposed for Dr. Carter to tell if the knife wound had penetrated her heart, but he was certain it could have done so. Such a wound would have killed her instantly. If he saw any sign that she was pregnant when she died, he seems to have kept that discovery to himself.

The body was taken to the local general store, where it was formally identified by Pauline and by Laura's father, Wilson. They recognized her from what was left of her clothing and the distinctive gap between her front teeth.

Ann was soon arrested and locked in the same Wilkesboro jail cell that Pauline had recently occupied.

LEGAL PROCEDDINGS BEGAN AGAINST TOM AND ANN on October 1, 1866. When the North Carolina Superior Court met at Wilkesboro under Judge Ralph Buxton, Tom was charged with the murder of Laura Foster. Ann was charged with encouraging him to commit the crime and with harboring him after the deed had been committed. The prosecution later dropped the second charge, leaving only the first against her.

A surprising turn of events soon occurred that earned the case widespread notoriety. Former North Carolina governor Zebulon Vance stepped in and offered to defend Tom. Vance had commanded an infantry unit during the Civil War – although not the one in which Tom served – and then had spent the remainder of the war as the state's governor.

When the war ended, he spent two months in a federal jail and was nearly penniless when he started his Charlotte law practice in March 1866.

Since then, Vance had earned a considerable reputation as a gifted courtroom attorney, and perhaps he had sympathy for an ex-Confederate soldier in trouble. It's also possible he simply relished the prospect of a fight with the Republican Unionists – who've never served – and oversaw the prosecution. Regardless of the reason, when the press learned of his vow to save Tom from the gallows, as well as about the complicated sexual details of the case, the newspapers went wild. The trial became a national sensation.

Former North Carolina Governor Zebulon Vance, who defended Tom at his murder trial.

The trial began on October 4, and Vance got things started by arguing that feelings against his client and Ann Melton were running so high in Wilkes County that a change of venue was required for them to receive a fair trial. The court agreed and arranged for the proceedings to be moved 30 miles away to Statesville in Iredell County. Tom and Ann were transferred to the Statesville Jail, and eight additional guards were added to ensure they didn't escape.

The trial started again on October 19, with Judge Buxton still presiding. The jury was selected from a panel of 100 local men, and then Vance stood up to address the court once again. This time, he demanded that Tom and Ann be tried separately. Ann had made several incriminating statements since Laura's death, and often those statements were made when Tom was unable to respond to them or challenge their veracity. Allowing those statements to be heard as evidence in a joint trial would make Tom look guilty, too, Vance told the court. The judge agreed, and Tom was tried alone. Ann's trial would have to wait.

With the preliminaries out of the way, Prosecutor Walter Caldwell gave his opening statement. He told the jury that Tom had contracted syphilis from Laura, and he had passed it on to Ann. His own infection had prompted him to take Laura's life as an act of revenge. Caldwell stated to the jury, "I expect to prove that Tom Dula, the prisoner, committed the murder, instigated thereto by Ann Melson, who was prompted by revenge and jealousy."

There were 83 people on the witness list for the trial, but it's unclear how many were actually called. Pauline Foster, Dr. George Carter, James Melton, Wilson Foster, Lotty Foster, Jack Adkins, James Isbell, and Betsy Scott all took the stand, though, and presented evidence against Tom. Despite her questionable role in the case, the prosecution relied heavily on Pauline's testimony. Prosecutors likely told her that if she didn't fully cooperate, she'd end up with charges herself.

Ann was allowed to be in the courtroom during Tom's trial but was not allowed to testify. Even so, Judge Buxton allowed statements Ann had made to witnesses to be admitted into evidence and overruled Vance's objections every time he challenged this.

Vance made the most of Tom's war record throughout the trial, presenting him as a brave former soldier and Laura as the scheming woman who'd seduced him. When the prosecution fought back by invoking Laura's "lonely grave on the hillside," Vance turned it around on them by asking the jury what they'd achieve by sending his client to a grave there, too. Tom maintained he was innocent and refused to implicate anyone else in Laura's death.

When Vance closed the defense case, he asked Judge Buxton to instruct the jury that any circumstantial evidence they used to convict "must exclude every other hypothesis" and remind them that they must be convinced of Tom's guilt beyond all reasonable doubt. The judge agreed and stressed this to the jury, who, after hearing two days of evidence, retired just after midnight on October 20 to deliberate on the case.

The jury returned at daybreak with their verdict – guilty.

The *New York Herald* told its readers, "Governor Vance and his assistant counsel for the defense made powerful forensic efforts which were considered models of ability, but such was the evidence that no other verdict than that of guilty could be rendered."

Judge Buxton set Tom's execution date for November 9, although Vance was already planning an appeal on the grounds that the judge had allowed a great deal of evidence that the jury shouldn't have heard. The judge agreed to refer his request to the North Carolina Supreme Court but rejected delaying the execution, as Vance had also requested.

Vance had 19 days to get his client a new trial, or Tom would swing.

AS IT TURNED OUT, THOUGH, TOM WAS IN LUCK. THE Supreme Court ruled that Judge Buxton had been wrong to allow some of the evidence that had been heard, and Tom was granted a new trial. The new trial was set for April 17, 1867, and Tom had to sit in jail until then.

He ended up waiting a lot longer than that. When the court convened on April 17, three defense witnesses failed to show up. Vance argued that their testimony was crucial to his case and persuaded the new judge, Robert Gelliam, to postpone the trial until October 14. The court then met only twice each year – in the spring and the fall – so this was the next date available.

When October 14 rolled around, though, it was the prosecution's turn to cause a delay. This time, the missing witness was James Grayson, whom the prosecutors were unwilling to continue without. Caldwell won his bid for another continuance, but this time, the state governor decided on drastic action. He ordered a special court be set up to clear the Supreme Court's growing backlog of cases and demanded that the court hear Tom's case on January 20, 1868. There would be no delays or excuses this time.

The special court convened on time with Judge William Shipp presiding. The evidence presented was largely the same as at the first trial – presumably without the inadmissible information that Judge Buxton had allowed – and the new jury found Tom guilty again.

Judge Shipp set his execution date for February 14 but approved Vance's request to appeal the verdict – again.

On April 13, 1868, the North Carolina Supreme Court ruled there had been no errors in the trial, and another execution date was chosen. It would be May 1, 1868, and this time, it would stand.

Eliza, Tom's sister, arrived at the Statesville jail with her husband on the night before the hanging. Ann was still in jail, too, waiting for her own trial, but Tom refused to say anything that would implicate her in Laura's murder or clear her of it. Eliza passed Tom a note through the jail guards. It contained a plea from his mother that he should tell the full story of Laura's death before he died. Only this, Mary told her son, would give her the peace of knowing once and for all if Tom was a killer. Tom asked the jailers if he could speak to Eliza in person, but he had nothing more to say when the request was denied.

After a last supper, Tom seemed to change his mind about the confession everyone had been nagging him to make. He called for Captain Richard Allison, one of Vance's assistants, and handed him a note. Its letters were scratched out in pencil and were in Tom's crude, unskilled hand. Tom made Allison swear not to let anyone see it until after the execution. The note, it turned out, relayed a simple message:

Statement of Thomas C. Dula.
I declare that I am the only person that had any hand in the murder of Laura Foster. April 30, 1868.

Left alone in his cell overnight, with just hours to live, Tom finally lost the composure he'd maintained for so long. He spent the night pacing up and down – as far as his leg chain allowed – and managed only about an hour of fitful sleep. He'd refused to see any clergymen during the time he'd been in jail, but that changed on the morning of the hanging. Tom allowed the Methodist minister who came to visit to baptize him, and then he dropped to his knees in fervent prayer.

Because Tom's trials had been dragging on for so long and because people from at least three counties had been involved, news of the execution spread throughout the region, drawing massive crowds to Statesville for the hanging.

People pushed and shoved their way toward the pine gallows built near the railway depot – there was no execution site in town – and guards were dispatched to keep the crowds away from it. The sheriff, fearing trouble might arise, ordered all the taverns in town to be closed for the day.

The gallows themselves were far from the "white oak tree" mentioned in the song. Instead, deputies placed two upright poles about 10 feet apart and hammered a crossbar to connect them at the top. The crossbar had been placed high enough to let the wagon they planned to transport Tom from the jail stop directly under it. This would leave him to dangle in place – slowly suffocating in agony – as the wagon was pulled away. This was not the proper method for hanging, but Statesville didn't have much to work with.

A reporter for the *New York Herald* was on the scene that day, moving through the crowd, asking questions, and conducting interviews. He was struck by the number of young women in the crowd and mentioned this several times in his article. He estimated the crowd to number at least 3,000 people of Tom's "own race and color" but did not attempt to estimate the number of African Americans also there.

There were so many people in town that it was inevitable that many with grudges against others would meet. A man named Hub Yount was there that day and later wrote: "Thousands and thousands of people gathered to see the execution. Statesville was a small town then, and there were many fist and skull fights, old enemies meeting. There were several gun battles on the streets that day."

While walking through the crowd, the New York reporter met some of Tom's old army companions and noted their "anxious and singular curiosity" about seeing how their former comrade in arms would meet his end. "Few were those who pitied him dying, as they believed him, guilty without a confession, and none sympathized with him," he wrote.

Tom was led out of the jail just before 1:00 P.M. He was led to the wagon, where he took a seat next to his sister and brother-in-law. His coffin was in the bed of the wagon behind them. The procession then moved slowly through the streets, surrounded by the crowd. Many walked along next to the wagon, stood at the edge of the road to watch, or followed behind the wagon on foot and horseback.

While on the way to the gallows, Tom looked cheerful but spoke nervously to his sister, who did her best to comfort him. At the gallows, throngs of people were already gathered, talking amongst themselves before becoming quieter as the wagon arrived.

The legend about Tom's hanging claimed that he performed his own self-composed ballad for the crowd's amusement as he was taken to the gallows. Most likely, this part of the story arose from the long-standing habit of claiming that any song about an execution was written by the condemned man. It seems very unlikely that the *New York Herald* reporter would have watched Tom busking on his way to the gallows and failed to mention it in his long, detailed account. He mentioned everything else he witnessed that day – obviously being paid by the word – and if he saw something that strange, he would've written about it.

As the wagon rolled to a stop at the gallows, deputies on horseback pushed back the crowd. This allowed the wagon's driver to halt beneath the gallows' frame. Told by Sheriff Wasson that he could address the crowd if he wished, Tom stood up in the wagon with the noose around his neck and spoke in what the reporter wrote was: "a loud voice that rang back from the woods."

Tom spoke for nearly an hour, telling stories about his early childhood, his family, his time in the army, and the secessionist politics still causing problems in the state. He accused several of the witnesses at his trial of lying about him – especially James Isbell, he said – and claimed it was only those lies that had put him on the gallows that day. His written confession, of course, was still between himself and Richard Allison, who'd sworn its contents would not become public until Tom was dead.

Hub Yount, the other witness who wrote about the hanging, said that when Tom was finished, an older man had pointed out Tom and recited the words of a poem that had been circulating about the affair. Yount didn't remember all the words but did recall part of it:

Oh Tom Dooley, hang down your head and cry. Because you killed poor Laura Foster and now you must die.

Tom's final words were a goodbye to his sister, and then he reportedly said, "You have such a nice clean rope that I ought to have washed my neck." He looked up as the rope dangling around his neck was thrown over the gallows' crossbeam and fastened. The cart then pulled away, and Tom was left there to hang. He dropped only two feet, not enough to break his neck, but he slowly strangled, twisting and jerking at the end of the rope until his last breath was gone from his lungs. After 13 minutes, a doctor pronounced him dead. The body was cut down and given to his family.

Eliza and her husband placed Tom's body in the waiting coffin and took him away. Arrangements had been made for him to be buried on a patch of land then owned by one of Tom's cousins, Bennett Dula.

Tom's confession was made public soon after the hanging. It didn't change anyone's mind. Most already assumed that he'd been guilty.

ANN'S TRIAL FINALLY BEGAN IN THE AUTUMN OF 1868, again with Vance acting for her defense. Thanks to Tom's confession, though, the case was quickly dismissed. She'd already been in jail for two years by then, and as the *Statesville American* noted, "The gallows would have added little to her punishment."

Ann died just seven years later, in 1875, after a long period of illness that had kept her bedridden. Her death has been incorporated into the legend of Tom Dooley. There are various accounts – some of which claim to have come from eyewitnesses – that reported she suffered from the hallucinations, violent rages, and convulsions that syphilis can produce when it reaches the brain.

As she lay dying, it's said that Ann saw the flames of Hell dancing around her bed and even the Devil himself when he came to collect her soul.

Although Ann had maintained her innocence until her death, there were always those who believed that it was Ann – not Tom Dula – who had killed "poor Laura Foster."

A North Carolina highway marker that mentions the true story behind the popular murder ballad about "Tom Dooley."

THE FIRST BALLAD ABOUT THE DEATH OF LAURA FOSTER appeared just after the discovery of her body in that shallow grave on the ridge. It was written by a local man, Captain Thomas Land, who never mentions Tom or Ann by name in the 84 meandering lines he wrote, and there's no resemblance between his effort and the Tom Dooley song that we know today. But it was clear that Laura was murdered by the lover that she'd hoped to marry – and that this man didn't act alone.

His neighborhood audiences would have known full well that Tom was the man he had in mind and were equally sure that his accomplice had to be Ann. Through Lands's verses, he shows the pair acting together in Laura's murder and the disposal of her body, using plural phrases like "those who did poor Laura kill" and "to dig the grave they now proceed." By doing this, he ensured that the ballad implicated Laura in the wicked business.

Laura herself was depicted as a sweet, innocent girl, too full of childish love to imagine that Tom would ever do her harm. Of course, locals knew that Laura was a good deal less innocent than that but swallowed the lie for the good of a wholesome song. The more of a saint that Laura appeared, the more despicable Tom and Laura looked by comparison, delivering the story's disreputable thrill.

Land took the listener – somewhat tediously – through the stages of Laura's discovery, then closed with her ascension to heaven to ensure that he didn't give anyone nightmares.

Once Tom was convicted for Laura's murder – the first time – the balladeers of Wilkes County felt free to name him as her killer – and hint at the execution to come.

Between 1912 and 1943, folk music historians collected at least three versions of a "Tom Dooley" ballad by a North Carolina woman named Maude Sutton. She initially performed the Thomas Land ballad, but her second entry was a banjo tune composed by an elderly black musician named Charlie Davenport. There are some lines that you might recognize:

Hang down your head, Tom Dooley,
Hang down your head and cry,
You killed poor Laura Foster,
And now you're bound to die.

You met her on a hill-top,
As God Almighty knows,
You met her on a hill-top,
And there you took her clothes,

You met her on a hill-top,
You said she'd be your wife,
You met her on a hill-top,
And there you took her life.

Sutton only performed three verses of his ballad, so it's unknown if this was the whole song as he found it or just part of it. The verses, though, dated back to 1867 and have survived almost untouched in many modern versions of the song.

It seemed as though Maude Sutton knew the verses would continue to appeal to listeners because it was just the kind of story that was turned into a ballad and sung for generations. "It has all the ballad essentials," she wrote. "A mystery death, an eternal triangle, and a lover with courage enough to die for his lady."

The third ballad Sutton contributed – "Tom Dula's Lament" – was the one that local lore insisted that Tom had composed himself on the way to the gallows. It opened by giving Tom an instrument that no one in the historical record ever mentioned him playing:

I pick up my banjo now,
I pick it on my knee,
This time tomorrow night,
It'll be of no more use to me.

The remaining five verses – all narrated by Tom in the first person while in jail – offer the lament that Laura used to love to hear him play the banjo and that he was too much of a fool to realize how much she'd loved him.

By 1867, most of the ballads known today had already been written. The chorus the Kingston Trio made famous was mostly complete, and at least one of their three verses was substantially finished, too.

While Tom was waiting in Statesville for news of his appeal, the balladeers were still at work, though, and it wasn't long before they had all the remaining elements of the song in place.

The first version of "Tom Dooley" recorded on vinyl was cut by a duo called Grayson & Whitter in September 1929. Gilliam Grayson, the blind musician who sang and played fiddle on the record, was the nephew of James Grayson, who played a part in the real story. Henry Whitter accompanied him on the guitar.

The lyrics they used included many elements of the versions introduced by Maude Sutton, including a familiar tune and chorus, the reference to hiding Laura's clothes, and Tom's final moments with an instrument – a fiddle in this case.

The record received little airplay in 1929, and the obscurity of their version allowed many rival sets of "Tom Dooley" lyrics to develop at the same time. There wouldn't be a "set in stone" version of the song until the Kingston Trio came along three decades later, and while other variations of the song were never able to compete with the hit version's success, they weren't erased by it either.

One of the best-known creators of alternate versions of "Tom Dooley" was Doc Watson, who was born in Watauga County in 1923. An eye infection blinded him when he was only two years old. However, he grew up to be the most talented member of what was already a very musical family, playing the harmonica as a small child, adding the banjo and guitár by 12, and making his first records in 1961.

Doc Watson

Doc put his version of "Tom Dooley" on his 1964 debut album and assured his audiences it was a "completely different version" of the Kingston Trio's hit. It's more of a party record than a folk song, using Doc's harmonica and vocals that drive forward with barely a breath between one line and the next. Drawing on early sources, he sang six verses that were also used by Grayson & Whitter and then added two fresh ones of his own. The last of them quoted from Tom's supposed declaration of innocence on the gallows, which was widely accepted because many people in North Carolina still like to believe that he was innocent, even today. Watson wrote in 1971 that his great-grandparents had been neighbors of the Dula family in the 1860s and that his grandparents knew Tom's mother. In the story that was passed along to him, it was Ann who had stabbed Laura to death, with Tom's role limited to burying the body.

Doc Watson wasn't the only Watauga County man with a grandmother mixed up in the Dula story. Frank Proffitt also had a grandmother with a role in the tale that ultimately gave the Kingston Trio its hit.

Frank Proffitt

According to family legend, Adeline Perdue was among the crowd in Statesville and watched as Tom's wagon passed by her, taking him to the gallows. When she told the story to her children, she described Tom sitting on his own coffin, singing a ballad he'd just composed. Adeline taught the song to her family, and it was eventually passed down to her grandson, Frank.

Proffitt grew up to become a farmer at the foot of North Carolina's Stone Mountain, supplementing his family's income by making and repairing traditional musical instruments. One day in 1937, a New York man named Frank Warner came to Proffitt to buy a dulcimer, and before he left, he asked Proffitt to sing a few of the Appalachian folk ballads he knew. Proffitt obliged and accompanied his singing with an old banjo.

Warner was back again the following year, this time with an early tape recorder, and asked Frank for a repeat performance. As he later recalled, "His eyes sparkled as I can 'Tom Dooley' to him and told him of my grandma Proffitt knowing Tom and Laura."

Assuming the lyrics Frank sang that day were the same ones he used on his 1962 album, the lyrics that Warner heard were a mixture of the traditional verses that have been included in this chapter.

Warner recorded Proffitt singing "Tom Dooley" in 1938, but Proffitt himself didn't release it as a record until 1962. Warner had recorded his own version of the song a decade earlier, in 1952, but he first passed on the lyrics that Proffitt gave him to song collector Alan Lomax.

When Lomax published a 1946 collection called *Folk Songs USA*, he included the words and music for "Tom Dooley" and credited Warner with adapting and arranging the words and melody. The lyrics were cut to three tight verses, with the opening line in the chorus repeated to add an extra sing-along element. This was the version the Kingston Trio used 12 years later.

At the time, the Kingston Trio was comprised of Dave Guard, Nick Reynolds, and Bob Shane, who sang lead on their "Tom Dooley" recording. They were already using the song in their show when Capitol Records signed them.

When their debut album was released in June 1958, "Tom Dooley" was buried halfway through side one, with no thought from either the group or their label that it would be released as a single. The breakthrough came when two radio deejays in Salt Lake City started giving the track heavy airplay and encouraging other deejays around the country to join them. The only way to get the song was to buy the whole Album, but no one seemed to mind. Once radio stations started playing "Tom Dooley," the record took off.

Even with big sales, it took Capitol Records two months to catch on to the fact that "Tom Dooley" should be released as a single. It was released in August 1958, topped the charts in November, and had racked up more than a million sales by Christmas. The album also topped the LP charts and stayed on the charts for an impressive 195 weeks. The group earned gold records for both the album and the single and walked away with a Grammy award that year.

The first that Frank Proffitt knew of the Kingston Trio's hit was when he happened to hear the band perform a strangely familiar arrangement of "Tom Dooley" on television. On the group's album, he discovered that the song's composition was credited as "Traditional – Arr. Dave Guard." According to Bob Shane, the group had credited the song that way because they'd assumed it must be entirely in the public domain. This was a common habit throughout the music industry at the time since many new groups were scouring folk and blues archives for material. As Shane pointed out in an interview, "There were so many old folk songs we had gone through that were either anonymous or public domain."

In the early 1960s, Proffitt joined with Frank Warner and the publishers of Alan Lomax's book to sue the Kingston Trio over their "Tom Dooley" publishing rights and secure the income those rights were expected to generate. The case was settled out of court, but only after an agreement was made that the Proffitt, Warner, and Lomax families would receive a portion of the record's royalties in perpetuity.

Since the Kingston Trio record, most other recordings of "Tom Dooley" have been one of the other versions of the tune that have already been discussed. Others mix and match their chosen verses from whichever predecessors they prefer. Groups that have recorded "Tom Dolley" since Doc Watson and the Kingston Trip include The New Lost City Ramblers, The Frantic Flintstones, Lonnie Donegan, Lee Kelly, and Snakefarm – who put out a version that sounds more like a spaghetti western soundtrack than a bluegrass song – and, my favorite, Steve Earle.

BUT I DO HAVE A LAST NOTE ABOUT THE KINGSTON TRIO – even though it was the most romantic version of the Tom Dooley story that made them famous, the group members did know the sordid details of the real story and often shared them backstage with crew members – and especially with female audience members – after their shows.

Musicians – even ones who looked as goofy as these guys – know how to appeal to the ladies, no matter what kind of music they play.

3. "THE NORTHWOOD TRAGEDY"

THERE IS NO GREATER INGREDIENT FOR A BALLAD than the notorious "murdered girl," just like Laura Foster from the previous chapter. The history of murder ballads is filled with them, and this book will include many more of them before we finish.

Many of the ballads that have become famous in America started in England, Ireland, Scotland, and Wales and were carried across the Atlantic with the early settlers. Ballads like "Pretty Polly" were based on murders that happened back home and became nostalgic tunes for those who missed the families they'd left behind.

Other songs, like "The Knoxville Girl," also told stories of murdered young women in England and were adapted to fit stories that bloodied the landscape of America.

The story behind this song dates back to 1752 when Anne Nichols became pregnant by the son of a miller who, forbidden from marrying her, killed her instead. A ballad was created and re-created over the next eight decades, adding verses along the way.

By the 1830s, the ballad had become well-known in America, and all it needed was a homegrown murder that could be tied to the song; by the end of the century, it had one.

Mary Lula Noel lived with her parents in the small town of Pineville, Missouri. On Wednesday, December 7, 1892, she was staying with her married sister, Sydney Holly, when a Joplin man named William Simmons came to see her. He was still there on Saturday when the Hollys left to collect Mary's parents for a trip to the town of Noel, which bore her family's name. That meant spending the night away, and the Hollys suggested that Simmons might like to accompany them part of the way and then return to Joplin.

Most likely, they feared what the two young people might get up to if left in the house alone overnight.

Simmons decided he'd rather walk as far as Lanagan and then take a train home from there. Mary said she'd stay with him at the Holly farm until he left and follow her sister and brother-in-law to her parent's house if the nearby Elk River wasn't running too high. If she couldn't cross, she'd stay on that side of the river where the Noels had many relatives scattered around.

The Hollys left home on Saturday morning, leaving Simmons and Mary together – and that was the last time they ever saw her alive.

Instead of returning home on Sunday as originally planned, the Hollys stayed with the Noels for the next few days. Mary never arrived, but they assumed she was safe with a relative across the river. When they finally started asking around, they discovered that no one had seen her – there was no trace of her anywhere. They sent a letter to an uncle in Webb City, about 40 miles away, because they knew Mary often stayed with him, but when he replied that he hadn't seen her, a horrible truth started to dawn on them – something terrible had happened to Mary.

Mary's father and brother-in-law went to Joplin the following Friday to try to track down William Simmons. When they confronted him, they later reported that the man started trembling violently and tried to avoid speaking with them. He asked no questions, but Mr. Noel had plenty of questions for him – had Mary come to Joplin? If not, did he know where she was or where she had gone when she left him?

Simmons dodged their questions before finally making a strange remark of his own: "You don't suppose the fool girl jumped in the river and drowned herself, do you?"

The two men returned to Pineville, and on the morning of December 17, they began a thorough search of the area. The Noels were a well-liked, prominent family, so they had no trouble getting hundreds of volunteers to join the effort. Most assumed that Mary had been deliberately killed, and the search soon gravitated toward the swollen river. The deepest stretches were dragged, and every nook and cranny were searched.

Around 2:00 P.M., something ominous was discovered.

At a large, deep hole along the river, Mary's body was found. It was less than a quarter of a mile from her parent's home and within a few feet of the road that her family had traveled when they returned home. Her clothing had been snagged by a willow branch that extended into the water.

The corpse was examined when she was removed from the river, and it became apparent that she'd met a violent end. There was a bruise on one temple, a scrape on one cheek, and three or four of them on the other as if a hand had been placed over her mouth to stifle her screams. There were bruises on her throat that looked precisely like finger marks. Another bruise – about the size of a man's hand – was on the back of her head, and her neck was broken. She had been dead before she ended up in the water. This was apparent from the lack of water in her lungs.

The searchers also found recent tracks made by a man and a woman between the Hollys' house – where Mary and Simmons had last been seen – to the river's edge and the deep area where the body was found. The conclusion was that the couple must have walked there together to see if the river was passable.

Within hours, Simmons was arrested in Joplin – just as he was getting ready to leave town. It was feared that he'd be lynched if he was sent to Pineville, so he was taken to the jail in Neosho instead. He was tried for first-degree murder in May 1893, but the volatile case ended with a hung jury, and he had to be tried again. The second trial came in November when the prosecutor indicated that he'd accept a second-degree murder plea. He said that it was possible the killing might have been committed on the spur of the moment, without the intent that was needed for a first-degree charge. The new jury accepted this, returned a guilty verdict, and Simmons was sentenced to 10 years in the penitentiary.

In 1927, folklorist Vance Randolph collected a variation of "The Knoxville Girl" from a Missouri woman who called the song "The Noel Girl." It began:

'Twas in the city of Pineville,
I owned a floury mill,
'Twas in the city of Pineville,
I used to live and dwell.

The rest of the song follows the familiar path of the original ballad – a false promise of marriage, a private walk, a sudden attack, a plea for mercy, a river, and everything else. The Pineville reference and the song's title aside, it's the same song brought to America by English settlers with all the details left intact.

Of course, it's inaccurate to suggest that Mary Noel's death is the primary source of "The Knoxville Girl," but it certainly became part of its mythology as the American version of the tune. The actual facts of her murder are an almost uncanny echo of the one described half a world away and 200 years earlier.

But not every "Murdered Girl" ballad had a source that stretched back decades or centuries and came from a distant country. There were killers in America who had their own taste for blood.

WHEN GEORGIANNIA LOVERING DISAPPEARED in 1872, there was no great mystery who had caused her to vanish. And when it was discovered that she had been raped and murdered, there was little doubt that the villain responsible was her 64-year-old great-uncle, a man named Franklin Evans.

But Georgiannia was not his first victim.

It was discovered that he had killed for the first time in October 1850, when the five-year-old daughter of a man named Stephen Mills was snatched from her home, strangled, mutilated, and dismembered in some nearby woods. Her body wasn't found until after Evans was arrested and confessed to the crime.

Franklin Evans

The killer struck again in 1862 when he grabbed a young girl named Lura Libby while she was on her way to church on Sunday morning. When she hadn't returned home by 4:00 P.M., a search began of the fields, pastures, and woods between the Libby farm and the village. Late in the afternoon, searchers stumbled across a shallow grave about a half mile from the farm. When they removed the earth, they found the body of Lura Libby. Her dress had been removed, and she had been raped. Her head was cut and bruised, and her throat was cut so deep that her head was nearly severed from her body.

Evans claimed two more victims in June 1865, when he murdered Isabella and John Joyce, two children found in some woods outside of Boston. Their bodies weren't found until a week later – and the crime scene was a gruesome one.

It appeared that 14-year-old Isabella and her younger brother were playing in the woods when the killer attacked. He went after the girl first, cutting her savagely with a knife, tearing off her undergarments, and raping her. The coroner found 27 stab wounds in her torso and another 16 in her neck. The ground around her body was saturated with blood. She had desperately fought back, grabbing the long blade of the knife and trying to wrest it from the attacker's hands. The index finger of her right hand was completely severed, and the rest of her fingers were mangled, bloody, and hanging loosely by bits of skin. Her clothing was soaked in her blood, and clumps of grass and dirt had been roughly shoved in her mouth to try and stifle her cries.

Apparently, poor John had stood paralyzed for a few moments in terror, watching the attack on his sister. When he finally turned to run, it was too late. He was found lying face down in the dirt, possibly having fallen while trying to escape. Evans had pounced on the boy's back and stabbed him several times. The wounds were so deep that, in several instances, the blade had gone all the way through the young boy's body and pierced the earth beneath him.

But it would be the murder of his own grand-niece that would lead to Evans' capture – and the murder ballad that told her tale.

THE EVENTS OF GEORGIANNIA'S DEATH WERE SET IN motion when Franklin Evans came to live with his sister, Mrs. Deborah Day, at her farm in Northwood, New Hampshire.

Evans was a gaunt, grizzled older man with gray hair, a long gray beard, and dark, piercing eyes that gave him a sinister expression. He had led a shiftless existence for most of his life, traveling about New England and Canada. A contemporary writer later said of him, "He belonged to that numerous class of deadbeats that are always broke."

Wandering the New England countryside, he survived by sponging off his adult children, "borrowing" small amounts of money from relatives and acquaintances, and blatantly seeking handouts from strangers. He had married three times and had a son in Derry, New Hampshire, and a daughter in Lawrence, Massachusetts.

What little honest money he made came from supplying a Manchester physician, Dr. F.W. Hanson, with healing roots and herbs that he scrounged up in the forest. His vagabond life had given the old man a deep knowledge of the land, and "his reputation for obtaining medicinal products of the woods and fields was unsurpassed." Even in this line of work, though, Evans could not keep from betraying his lazy and dishonest nature. Claiming that he himself was a "botanical physician," he peddled worthless cures to rural families.

He also passed himself off as an itinerant preacher. Taking advantage of the religious fervor of the era, he joined the Second Advent Society, declared that he was a minister of the Gospel, and managed to raise a little money from his brethren to support himself while on his "sacred mission." The religious society naturally took offense, however, when he was arrested for consorting with prostitutes. And this incident wasn't his only brush with the law. At various times, he was charged with petty theft, attempting to pass crudely forged $10 bills, and – most seriously – scheming to defraud the Traveler's Insurance Company of Boston of $1,500.

If these crimes were the worst of his transgressions, Evans would have been nothing more than a small-time scoundrel, a snake oil salesman, and a con artist. But as the country would eventually learn – much to its horror -- he was something far worse: a creature so depraved that, to the people of his time, his crimes seemed the work of a supernatural evil – "too horrible," as one newspaper stated, "for anything in human form to have perpetrated."

Four people were living at the Day farm when Evans showed up there in June 1872 -- Mrs. Day and her husband, Sylvester; their widowed daughter, Susan Lovering, and Susan's daughter, Georgiannia. This poor young woman – Evans' grand-niece – immediately became the object of the depraved older man's lust. Within days of his arrival, he began trying to seduce the girl. When she repulsed his advances, he concocted a diabolical scheme. It was, as one account stated, "A deeply laid plan designed for no other purpose than to lure his victim into his lecherous grasp."

Near the Day farmhouse was a deep forest, the largest tract of woodland in the county, covering an area of more than 2,000 acres. Late on Monday, October 21, after being away from the farm for most of the day, Evans returned to his sister's home, explaining that he had been off in the forest setting snares for partridges.

This gave him the perfect excuse to invite his niece to accompany him into the woods to see if any birds had been ensnared in his traps the following day. For reasons unknown, she agreed. The snares were empty, but he showed Georgiannia how they worked – little hoops concealed inside the hedges, designed to snag birds by the throat as they scrambled through the foliage. Georgiannia was intrigued by the snares, never suspecting their true purpose was to trap her.

Early Friday morning, October 25, Evans asked the young woman for a favor. He had agreed to take care of some chores for a neighboring farmer named Daniel Hill and would be gone all day, so he asked Georgiannia if she would mind going into the woods and checking the partridge traps for him. Surely, he told her, they must have caught something by now. She was reluctant at first but allowed herself to be persuaded. Evans left soon afterward, presumably for Hill farm several miles away. A short time later, Georgiannia stuck a comb into her thick brown hair to hold it in place, threw on a shawl, and walked into the forest.

Georgianna Lovering

It was the last time she was seen alive.

When Georgiannia failed to return by lunchtime, her grandfather went to look for her. Unable to find any sign of her, Sylvester returned home and told her mother, Susan, that the girl was missing. She immediately became alarmed. The two of them hurried back into the woods. As they frantically made their way along the forest paths, shouting the girl's name, they spotted her shawl on a tree branch. A short distance away, they discovered her comb, broken in half, with strands of her hair still tangled in its teeth. The earth all around had been trampled with footprints – one made by a man's boots, the other by a girl's shoes – evidence, Sylvester Day would later testify, of a "squabble." Terrified now, Sylvester and his daughter went deeper into the trees but found no other signs of the missing girl.

The two of them ran home, alerting the neighbors as they went. Throughout the weekend, all day on Saturday and Sunday, hundreds of people scoured the woods but found nothing.

By then, however, suspicion had fallen on Franklin Evans. The authorities checked with Daniel Hill and found that Evans' story didn't hold up. The farmer had not asked him to help with chores that day. In fact, Hill hadn't seen him for more than a week. Another witness, a young man named James Pender, testified that he had seen Evans entering the forest at around 8:30 on Friday morning, just a half hour before Georgiannia had disappeared into the same woods.

County Sheriff Henry Drew grilled Evans, but the older man could offer no convincing account of his whereabouts on the day that his niece went missing. He was promptly taken into custody. Inside Evans' pockets, Drew later stated, he found "a wallet, money, obscene books, a bottle of liquor, and a common bone-handled knife with two blades, blood-stained and keen as a razor."

Even after he was arrested, Evans initially denied knowing anything about what had happened to Georgiannia. But when Drew assured him that "no harm would come to him if he confessed," Evans changed his story. Georgiannia, he insisted, was alive and well. He had arranged to have her "carried away by a man from Kingston," a farmer named Webster who wanted her for his bride and was willing to pay for her. Although Sheriff Drew was skeptical, he immediately rode to Kingston, where he quickly confirmed the story was a "base falsehood."

Back at the jailhouse, he continued to badger Evans, plying him with liquor and even telling him that he would help him escape to Canada if he told him the truth. Finally, on October 31, six days after the girl's disappearance, the older man gave in.

Drew leaned in close to him as he spoke, "In the hearing of no persons but us two and the Great Being above, I ask you this question: Is the body of the girl cold in death?"

Evans hesitated for several seconds before he choked out his reply. He said, "It is, Mr. Drew. I have done wrong."

Evans told the sheriff he would accompany him to the place where the body had been left. Even though it was close to midnight – on All Hallows Eve – they left for the woods. Through the dark forest, they silently made their way along, over rocks and logs and along narrow trails. Then, in a clearing at one of the deepest points of the woods, Evans took the sheriff and an assembled group of deputies to a spot underneath the roots of an upturned tree. He pointed a shaking finger at a pile of dried leaves and quietly murmured, "There she is." The sheriff gently brushed away the leaves, and by the dim light of his lantern, he saw the pale face and mangled remains of Georgiannia Lovering.

Two townsmen who were at the scene -- Eben J. Parsley and Alonzo Tuttle -- had brought the local physician, Dr. Caleb Hanson, with them. Gaping in shock at the body of the naked, savaged girl, Parsley couldn't help but speak. He demanded of Evans, "How did you come to do such a bloody deed?"

The old man shrugged as he replied, "I suppose the evil one got the upper hand of me."

Dr. Hanson bent down to examine the dead girl. A glance at her face, with its bulging eyes, swollen and protruding tongue, and dark bruises at her throat, told him that she had been strangled. Her body had been hideously mutilated. Evans later confessed that he had raped her corpse and then had torn open her belly with his bone-handled knife to get to her uterus. He had also sliced away her vulva, which he carried away with him and hid under a rock. When a stunned Sheriff Drew asked him why he had committed such butchery, the old man calmly replied that he did it "to gain some knowledge of the human system that might be of use to me as a doctor."

As he was dragging the man back to jail, Drew had one more question for him: "What did you set those snares for, Frank?"

Evans answered with a self-satisfied smirk: "I set them to catch the girl – and I catched her."

FRANKLIN EVANS' TRIAL OPENED IN THE TOWN OF Exeter, New Hampshire, on February 3, 1873, but it was a perfunctory affair. The outcome was a foregone conclusion to everyone involved, including the defendant. Only one dramatic moment occurred during its three-day duration. Early on the morning of Tuesday, February 5, while his guard was off fetching him a glass of water, Evans took one of his suspenders, tied it around his neck, attached the other end to a clothing hook on the wall of his cell, and tried to hang himself. Just then, the newspapers reported, the guard returned, "seized Evans and disengaged him from the hook."

Most observers believed that the man's half-hearted suicide attempt was nothing more than a ploy to set up an insanity defense. If that was the case, the effort failed. The jury was out for only 45 minutes. He was convicted of murder in the first degree and sentenced to hang on February 17, 1874. For "his unnamable and incredible crimes, he will be swung like a dog," celebrated one local newspaper, which went on to recommend that those wishing to attend the hanging should make "early application in order to secure 'reserved seats,' which will be scarce."

Accompanied by the high sheriff of Rockingham County, J.W. Odlin, Evans was transported by train to the state prison at Concord. A crowd of more than 800 people gathered at the station to get a glimpse of him. One newspaper stated that they were "excited to a remarkable pitch of feeling." This frenzied fascination was not entirely based on Evans' notoriety as the killer of Georgiannia Lovering. By then, he had confessed to other crimes as well – atrocities that marked him as one of the most appalling killers of the era. Further investigations by investigators in neighboring cities and states linked him to the other crimes, which convinced anyone with doubts about his guilt to look forward to his pending execution.

Evans spent the last night of his life quietly, falling asleep around midnight. At 5:30 A.M., he ate a hearty breakfast and drank a cup of tea. When asked if he had any last-minute statements to make, he replied, "I have confessed everything. If the people don't believe it, I can't help it."

A large, excited crowd gathered outside the prison walls as the hour of execution drew near. At 10:50 A.M., they were admitted into the building, where the gallows had been set up in the corridor between the guardroom and the cells. Within minutes, every available space was packed with spectators, some of them standing on the stairways leading up to the cells, others crowding around the scaffold.

At 11:00 A.M., Evans, dressed in a black suit, was led through the crowd by the prison warden. He climbed the scaffold on his own and muttered something under his breath as his arms and legs were tied. He appeared "quite calm and possessed," although the people who were standing closest to the gallows later reported that his knees were trembling. The noose was adjusted around his neck, and a black hood was pulled over his head. After reading the death warrant, Sheriff Odlin placed his foot on the spring that controlled the drop and – at exactly 11:06 A.M., on Tuesday, February 17, 1874 – the killer was "launched into eternity."

His neck didn't break. He dangled in the air, slowly strangling, for nearly 20 minutes before his heart stopped beating, and the attending physician declared him dead.

After the execution, Evans's official written confession was released to the press. In it, he detailed the murder of Georgiannia Lovering but attempted to mitigate the crime by describing the members of the household as intemperate and immoral -- his sister's husband, Sylvester, was drunk and abusive; his niece, Susan, was a woman of loose morals, and even 13-year-old Georgiannia was sometimes drunk and lewd, talking of her "shameful intercourse" with three young men. Evans claimed that he, himself, had consensual sex with Georgiannia, and she threatened to expose him. He stated that he was completely under the young girl's power, and that was why he decided to kill her.

Evans also confessed to murdering the Mills child in 1850. He heard moaning from inside of the house, he said, climbed in the window, and found her sitting on the floor, apparently very sick. He concluded that she would not live until morning, and he wanted a body to examine for "surgical purposes," so he took her to the woods and strangled her. He stopped the examination when he found that she had a deformed hip and spine and buried the body in the woods under a tree stump.

Although he had earlier confessed to the other murders, those were the only two he admitted to in writing. He also confessed to theft, counterfeiting, and attempted insurance fraud. Despite what he'd told Sheriff Drew, other investigators, and reporters, he did not commit the other murders – the Libby and Joyce killings – that he had earlier taken credit for.

Was he telling the truth?

Or rather, which version of his story was the truth?

Evans's confession had been dictated to the warden and the chaplain of the prison. They wrote it down and read it back to him, and he accepted it as correct and signed it. Later, though, the two officials admitted to some creative editing. They explained that much of what Evans said was "too gross and indelicate to be written or read" and cut it out. Thanks to this, we will likely never know the extent of Franklin Evans's crimes.

Whether he committed only the two murders to which he confessed in his final statement or was the killer of several others – as so many believed then and now – he was a monster. Ironically, since he claimed that his murders were committed so that he could gain anatomical knowledge to "aid him as a doctor," his corpse was donated to Dartmouth Medical College so that it could be dissected by the students there. His skeleton still resides in the college's anatomical museum after all these years.

FRANKLIN EVANS WAS STILL IN JAIL, WAITING FOR his trial to start, when a local balladeer named Byron DeWolfe composed and printed a song about the murder of Georgiannia Lovering. Unlike most "murdered girl" ballads – which tend to play fast and loose with the facts – DeWolfe's composition, despite a thick coating of sentimentality, offered an almost journalistic account of the crime.

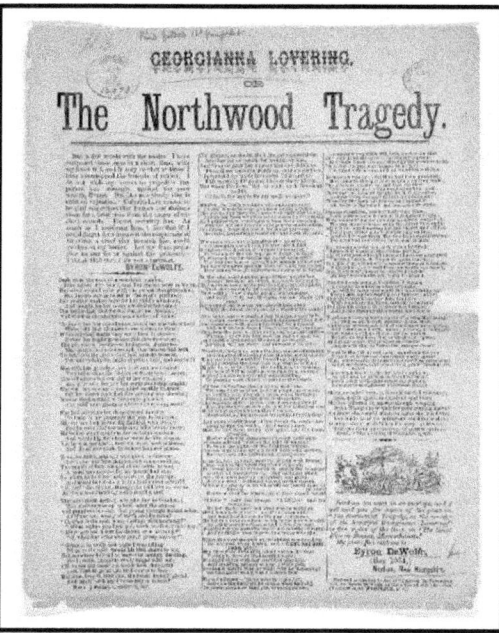

Consisting of more than two dozen eight-line verses, it's much too long to reprint here, but here's a taste of it:

Dark were the eyes of the beautiful maiden,
Like music, her voice and her cheeks were in bloom,
Her mind seemed to be with the purest thoughts laden,
Her beath as sweet as the rose's perfume...

She had an uncle too deep steeped in error,
To learn in her presence the way to improve,
His sinister look would fill children with terror,
Few hearts could towards him affectionate move...

And when Sherrif Drew at last forced the confession
From Evans, the uncle a fiend among men,
That he had done wrong, and great was his transgression,
That search was abandoned, but not until then!
Abandoned! But twas for the sake of another,
To be in the night – in the darkness intense,
For one that would bring a dead child to its mother,
But for a lost idol make small recompense.

And it goes on – and on and on – from there. Unlike other ballads that have come before in these pages, this was not a piece of music that has lived on through the generations. It has elements of other ballads that have stood the test of time, but perhaps the real-life details of this murder are a little more distasteful than most music historians want to remember.

4. "FRANKIE AND JOHNNY"

ON OCTOBER 16, 1899, A SHORT ARTICLE WAS PRINTED IN THE *St. Louis Globe-Democrat* newspaper that told the story of a shooting that had occurred the previous night. It read:

Allen Britt, colored, was shot and badly wounded shortly after 2 o'clock yesterday morning in Britt's room at 212 Targee Street and was the culmination of a quarrel. The woman claimed that Britt had been paying attention to another woman. The bullet entered Britt's abdomen, penetrating the intestines. The woman escaped after the shooting.

It's hard to believe that a story that short gave birth to a murder ballad that has become one of the most popular in American history – but it did.

In fact, just 48 hours after Frankie Baker pulled that trigger, a ballad telling her story was already being played on street corners in the city. Allen wasn't even dead yet – he didn't succumb to his wound for two more days – but the balladeers already had him in the grave. The song has been around ever since.

As an aside, Allen's murder took place only a few blocks from where Stagger Lee had killed Billy Lyons just four years earlier, and this meant that the two ballads often became tangled in each other, with lyrics being swapped with no warning. It should also be no surprise that many of those who sang about Stack Lee also tackled Frankie's story, too, but what might be surprising is how much attention Hollywood has always paid to her story.

From the 1933 Mae West film *She Done Him Wrong* to a 1991 outing with Al Pacino and Michelle Pfeiffer, Frankie has frequently shown up on screen. She could also be found in the theater, often appearing on stage, starting with John Huston's 1930 play about her crime.

However, as we'll soon see, very few of these productions have paid much attention to the facts, although they have managed to firmly link the names of the two lovers together in popular culture.

Frankie Baker circa 1899

FRANKIE BAKER WAS A YOUNG PROSTITUTE, LIKELY AROUND 24 years old when the murder happened, who lived and worked in St. Louis' vice district. A former neighbor named Richard Clay later described her as "a beautiful, light brown girl who liked to make money and spend it. She dressed very richly, sat for company in magenta lady's cloth, diamonds as big as eggs in her ears. There was a long razor scar down the side of her face she got in her teens from a girl who was jealous of her. She only weighed about 115 pounds, but she had the eye of one you couldn't monkey with. She was a queen sport."

Allen Britt, who was only about 17 when he died, shared Frankie's rooms on Targee Street and apparently acted as her pimp. He was known for being a talented piano player and a snappy dresser. But little did Frankie know, he was cheating on her with an 18-year-old prostitute named Alice Pryar. This was certainly not something he wanted Frankie to know. She loved him, bought him everything he wanted, and kept his pockets stuffed with cash. While she was with her "company" at home, he was out playing music in the saloons – and was usually up to no good.

According to Frankie's neighbor, Richard Clay – who also sat with Allen when he was dying in the hospital – Frankie had surprised Allen while he was with his sidepiece, Alice, at the Phoenix Hotel and called him out into the street for a loud and angry argument. Allen had refused to go home with Frankie, so she stormed back to Targee Street alone.

Part of a Thomas Hart Benton mural that shows the murder that inspired "Frankie and Johnny," even though the location for the murder is wrong — not a surprise considering all the songs were wrong, too.

Allen turned up there around dawn, admitted he'd spent the night with Alice, and threatened to leave Frankie for good. Frankie then started crying and stormed out the door to find Alice. Allen threatened to kill her if she took another step, and that was when the fight broke out.

Frankie offered her version of events when she later testified in court. She said that she'd known Allen was at a party with Alice on Saturday night but was determined not to let that bother her. She had gone home and went to bed, hoping to get some sleep. As was her usual habit, she'd stashed a loaded handgun under her pillow.

Allen loudly stumbled into the room at about 3:00 A.M., waking up Frankie with all the noise. He grabbed a lamp and threw it at her. She told the jury:

> I asked him, "Say are you trying to hurt me? I don't want to hurt you, and you don't want to hurt me. Best place for you to go is to your mother."

He stood there and cursed me and said he wasn't going anyplace. I said, 'I'm the boss here, I pay the rent, and I have to protect myself.'

He ran his hand in his side pocket, opened his knife, and started round this side of the bed to cut me. I was standing there, pillow lays this way. Just ran my hand under the pillow and shot him. Didn't shoot but once, standing by the bed.

When she recalled the event years later for a 1935 interview in *Daring Detective* magazine, Frankie added that Allen had beaten her badly a few nights before the incident. The judge had noticed her black eye in court, she added, and he may have taken pity on her because of it.

Even if we assume that both Frankie and Allen were trying to salvage what pride they could when they described what happened that night, there's no real contradiction in their two accounts, aside from when the shooting occurred. Allen just described what happened up to the point when Frankie went home, and Frankie picked up the story from there.

After Frankie shot him, Allen staggered out of the room and made it as far as his mother's house at 32 Targee Street before he collapsed. He told her what happened, and – according to Clay – she began to scream, "Frankie shot Allen! Frankie shot Allen!" By the time he was taken to City Hospital, everyone in the neighborhood knew that Frankie had got her man.

When the police arrived, they took Frankie to the hospital, too, where Allen pointed her out as the one who'd shot him. Doctors found a bullet in his liver, but there was nothing they could do. He died during the early morning hours of October 19. Frankie was arrested and jailed, and a hearing took place on November 13, where the verdict was justifiable homicide in self-defense.

"I ain't superstitious no more," she later said. "I went to trial on Friday the 13th and the bad luck omens didn't go against me. Why, the judge even gave me back my gun."

THE FIRST KNOWN BALLAD THAT TOLD THIS TALE WAS Bill Dooley's "Frankie Killed Allen," which he supposedly wrote on the night of the shooting itself. Dooley, a black St. Louis piano player and songwriter, had a knack for writing tunes about the city's juiciest news stories of the time. By all accounts, this was one of his most popular songs. He printed up crude one-page copies of it when he finished and started hawking them for a dime while performing the ballad on the streets of the Chestnut Valley vice district.

It wasn't long before the local bars and brothels all had copies and were ordering their entertainers to play it, too. Frankie soon began to hate the song. By Christmas 1899, she couldn't go anywhere in St. Louis without hearing it being played by a street musician or blaring from the doorway of a crowded bar.

And she would never escape from it again.

Ragtime musician Hughie Cannon – who'd had a big sheet music hit with his 1902 song "Won't You Come Home, Bill Bailey" – gave the next big boost to "Frankie and Johnny." In 1904, he published sheet music for a song he called "He Done Me Wrong," adding the subtitle "Death of Bill Bailey" to try and cash in on his earlier success. The tune is very similar to the "Frankie and Johnny" melody as it's known today but retains Bill Dooley's "He Done Me Wrong" refrain. Cannon discarded the rest of Dooley's lyrics, though, substituting Mrs. Bailey's tale of her husband's death from cholera.

By 1909, song collector John Lomax found a Texas version of the ballad that brought it back to Frankie's own story, but her victim's name was no longer Allen but Albert. Some sources claim that this was his real name all along, and "Allen" was what he preferred to be known as on the street. Truth or legend, no one knows, but it wouldn't matter because, in 1912, Frank and Bert Leighton's sheet music for their vaudeville song changed his name again. They called the song "Frankie and Johnny," and that's the name that has stuck ever since.

Here's a little from the Leighton Brothers' song:

Frankie and Johnny were sweethearts,
They had a quarrel one day,
Johnny vowed he would leave her,
Said he was going away.

In their version, Frankie begs her lover to stay, saying she knows she'd done him wrong, but she would make it up to him. Johnny, though, tells her that he doesn't want her anymore because he's found another woman.

Frankie then said to Johnny,
"Say man, your hour has come,"
From under her silk kimono,
She drew a forty-four gun.

Johnny dashed down the stairway,

*Crying "Oh Frankie, don't shoot,"
Frankie took aim with the forty-four,
Five times with a rooty-toot-toot.*

*Send for your rubber-tired hearses,
Go get your rubber-tired hacks,
Take lovin' Johnny to the graveyards,
I shot him in the back.*

It's odd to hear Frankie telling Johnny that it's she who's done him wrong there rather than the other way around, but they managed to turn the song into a hit that kept the story alive until it was finally recorded almost a decade later.

It was first pressed onto vinyl by the Paul Biese Trio in 1921, and by the time their vocalist, Frank Crumit, cut the song as a solo record six years later, most of the elements of the song that we're familiar with today were already in place. Crumit's version gave Frankie a better understanding of where the real blame was in the situation with lyrics like, "He was my man and he done me wrong," and he added a couple more verses about Frankie's arrest. He briefly raised the possibility of the electric chair but then explained that the law decided not to punish her at all.

A few other additions were made over the next few years, but essentially, Crumit's version of "Frankie and Johnny" remains the one we know today. Crumit had recently enjoyed a big hit with a tune called "Abdul Abulbul Amir," and after he chose "Frankie and Johnny" as a follow-up, the profile of the song was raised to a whole new level.

Meanwhile, as musicians all over the country continued to put their own unique twists on Frankie's story, John Huston wrote a play based on the story. In the book he published for the play in 1930, the dozen ballads it included not only referred to Allen by a few different names, but he also had six or more different names for Allen's girlfriend, Alice. Even Frankie's name wasn't left alone. She appeared as Amy in two of the ballads and Lily in a third one.

But whatever he decided to call him, Huston's ballads wanted everyone to know that Allen / Johnny had some bad habits:

Albert was a bad man,
He always liked to sin,
The only fault that Albert had,
Was drinking too much gin.

Another set of verses wanted us to know that Frankie found out that Albert was partial to opium, too:

Oh, I went down to the hop-joint,
And I run the hop-joint bell,
And there sat Albert a-hittin' the pipe,
A-hittin' the pipe beat to hell.

The verses that Huston added were interesting, but Crumit's 1927 recording only underlined the fact that an accepted version of the song's lyrics was already in place. Huston made sure that his play stuck closely to the same plot and included the same elements despite all the names and side trips. He also has Frankie kill Johnny with three shots, giving him time to quote a verse from the ballad verbatim before he dies. After that, Frankie goes to the gallows without complaint. Huston left the audience to decide precisely how Frankie earned the money that Johnny stole from her but did nothing to deny she was a prostitute.

Huston's play flew through the entire story in a brisk 60 pages of double-spaced dialogue, saving a macabre touch for the end when Frankie addressed the crowd gathered around the gallows and offered to lead them in one last dance. "I'll show you new stops in a minute," she promised as the hangman placed the noose around her neck.

Huston first staged his play as a – and I can't even imagine this – as a puppet show and it became a big hit at New York's society parties near the end of the Prohibition era. In 1930, gossip columnist Deming Seymour revealed that George Gershwin had paid Huston and his assistant $200 for a recent performance at the composer's home. Jules Glaenzer, the man behind Cartier, and philanthropist Paul Felix Warburg also hired him to stage the show for their own guests. All three hosts likely had plenty of bootleg liquor on hand, which may explain rumors that circulated later about Huston's *Frankie and Johnny* once being interrupted by a police raid.

Just as with "Stagger Lee," Frankie's story also spawned an underground spoken-word version of the song – one that was way too filthy to be published in any respectable journals or recorded commercially. Fortunately, the anonymous compiler of a 1927 anthology called *Immortalia* liked "Frankie and Johnny" enough to include it in his daring book. The verses told the same basic story, although they painted a picture of what the lives of the couple must have really been like.

Frankie, we are told, was a "fucking hussy" whose customers kept her so busy that she "never had time to get out of bed." She gives all her money to Johnny, "who spent it on parlor house whores," but still can't stop "finger-frigging" Alice. In this version, Frankie shoots Johnny five times and, in court, tells the judge, "I didn't shoot him in the third degree. I shot him in his big fat ass."

There has never been a recorded version of this spoken-word story, but here are a couple of the verses that will give you a taste of how it appeared in print. The first is when Frankie takes a break from servicing her customer to hand over her cash to Johnny:

Frankie hung a sign on her door,
"No more fish for sale,"
Then she went looking for Johnny,
To give him all her kale,
He was a-doin' her wrong,
God damn his soul!

And then there is what happens when she discovers the awful truth about Johnny's cheating:

Frankie ran back to the crib-joint,
Took the oilcloth off the bed,
Took out a bindle of coke,
And snuffed it right up in her head,
God damn his soul,
He was a-doin' her wrong!

There are several variations of the lyrics, adding things like having Frankie shoot Johnny in the groin or firing the bullet directly "up his hole."

In one version, she brings his penis back from the cemetery, explaining that it's "the best part of the man who done her wrong."

As brutal as the spoken-word version was, it's probably much closer to the truth. We know from the newspapers of the time that cocaine was a popular drug in brothels of the 1890s, so it made sense to imagine Frankie using the stuff. Street-level prostitution was a violent and squalid profession – then and now – so it's hard to accuse the spoken-word version of being unnecessarily lurid when it comes to that. It isn't pretty – but Frankie's real life definitely wasn't either.

HOPING TO ESCAPE FROM HER NEW NOTORIETY IN St. Louis, Frankie fled the city and went west in 1900. She moved first to Nebraska, then Oregon, but the song seemed to follow her everywhere she went.

She eventually settled in Portland, opened a little shoeshine parlor there, and spent her days playing solitaire in the front window when business was slow. The ballad never went away – Mississippi John Hurt, Riley Puckett, and Jimmie Rodgers all recorded it in 1928 and 1929, and the first film adaptation was released in 1930 – and at least for a little while, Frankie was left alone.

But that changed in 1933. That year, Paramount Pictures released a film called *She Done Him Wrong*, which was the first starring vehicle for Mae West and kicked off the career of Cary Grant. Based on West's play *Diamond Lil*, it contains many of her best lines, as well as her rendition of "Frankie and Johnny." Advertisements for the movie made it clear that it owed a debt to the popular ballad – "Frankie and Johnny were sweethearts," the ads read, "He was her man, but She Done Him Wrong." West's character in the film is a sex-bomb singer named Lady Lou, and she underlines the connection to the ballad in dialogue. "Some guy done her wrong," she says of another woman in the saloon where she works. "The story's so old it should've been set to music a long time ago."

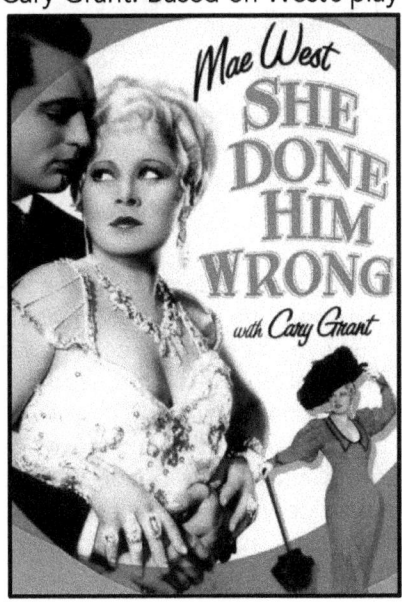

Prompted by the release of the film, a reporter tracked down Frankie in Portland, where he found a "gray-haired woman" of quiet disposition who just wanted to be left alone. He wrote: "She refused to discuss her past. The shining of shoes and the dealing of solitaire keeps her busy."

When the movie began showing in Portland theaters, Frankie found strangers gathered outside her home, day and night. She told another reporter, "I'm so tired of it all. I don't even answer anymore. What I want is peace – an opportunity to live like a normal human being. I know that I'm black, but even so, I have my rights. If people had left me alone, I'd have forgotten this thing a long time ago."

By the time the Mae West film came out, Frankie Baker had been avoiding publicity about the murder for decades.

Adding to her irritation was her growing resentment about the way that everyone seemed to be profiting from her story but her. She had already convinced herself that people like John Huston must be making a fortune thanks to her, and now, there was a movie studio capitalizing on the case, too. She complained to one newspaper reporter, "All these writing fellows and such have been writing about me for years. One man made $25,000 on a book about "Frankie and Johnny," and I never got a quarter from him writing me up that way. Not five cents! Here I am sick and almost broke and they're making money writing my life! I'm sore. They've got to pay me from now on."

Frankie sued both Paramount Pictures and Mae West herself, asking for $100,000 in damages. Mae West allegedly just chuckled when she was told about the lawsuit. "What's she going to do?" Mae supposedly asked, "Sue everybody in the country who sings the song 'Frankie and Johnny?'" The legal counsel for the studio, Louis Phillips, added that the lawsuit was "ridiculous."

To Frankie, though, it was no laughing matter. She argued that the song's account of her life – and, by extension, the movie, too – was defamatory and was filled with factual errors. The shooting happened at home, she said, not in a saloon, as the song often claimed. Allen was a "conceited piano player," not a gambler. Her gun was of much smaller caliber than the one described, and she'd only fired it once, not three times like the song claimed. Most important of all, she had killed Allen because he was attacking her with a knife, not in a fit of sexual jealousy, like it was in the song. She reminded everyone – again – that the actual verdict in the case had been justifiable homicide.

Frankie's lawyer stated that West's movie portrayed his client as a "woman of easy virtue, as the consort of gamblers, and notorious criminals, and as a murderess." It had brought her "public scandal, infamy, shame, and disgrace," he added, making Frankie an object of "hatred, ridicule, shame, and contempt." But despite these claims, the court was not convinced that she deserved any compensation.

Frankie lost the case, but she wasn't done.

In 1936, she sued Republic Pictures for its film *Frankie and Johnny*, which starred Helen Morgan in another loose adaptation of the story from the song. Just as she did when Mae West's movie came out, Frankie alleged that the new film presented a false and humiliating account of her life. This time, she sued the studio, Helen Morgan, two of the film's other actors, its director, its screenwriter, and two of Republic's distribution companies. She also doubled her demand to $200,000, which is well over $4 million in today's dollars.

Frankie's attorneys, the black law firm of McLemore and Witherspoon, filed the lawsuit in April 1938. The studio stalled for as long as it could, but finally, in August 1941, Frankie's case went before a jury in St. Louis Circuit Court. This gave Frankie herself a chance to once again provide a first-hand account of what happened on the night of the shooting.

Republic fought the case by hiring a string of academics to testify that the ballad "Frankie and Johnny" predated 1899 and, therefore, couldn't have been based on Allen's killing. Their evidence for this was flimsy at best, relying mainly on when the term "crib-man" first came into use. One of Republic's witnesses was musicologist Sigmund Spaeth, whose testimony contradicted his contribution to a 1927 book called American Mountain Songs. In the book, which he edited, he noted that the ballad about "Frankie Baker" was a "St. Louis classic." Even so, he backed the studio in court, and once again, Frankie lost her case.

And honestly, that's not all that surprising. Her chances at victory had always been pretty slim, and watching the two movies now, it's hard to understand how she'd ever thought she could make a case. Frankie – or Lady Lou in Mae West's film – is presented as a sympathetic character in both films who never actually kills anyone herself. The worst you can say about Lou is that she sends a man to his death, but he's such a terrible character that you can't help but feel like he deserved it. The Helen Morgan movie sticks closer to the real story but makes Frankie a saintly figure who is saved from pulling the trigger by another character who does it first.

In truth, the damage that Frankie suffered from the two films wasn't from the plots but from the fact that they brought the song back into popular culture and made it even more famous than it had already been. *She Done Him Wrong* was a huge hit, raking in over $2 million for Paramount, which in 1933 meant that it was seen by a massive audience. That was what had generated a new surge in curiosity about Frankie, but it wasn't enough to win her any money.

Frankie lost her shoe-shine parlor in the 1940s when city officials in Portland condemned and demolished the building in which it was located. By 1950, she had turned 74 and was on welfare. She moved into the Multnomah County Home, unable to care for herself. She was still perfectly lucid about killing Allen but was confused about every other aspect of her life. Officials at the home reported that she was frightened by other residents and imagined they wanted to attack her. In May 1950, a judge ruled that Frankie was a danger to herself and others, declared her insane, and sent her to the state mental hospital in Pendleton, where she died 18 months later.

Even in death, she couldn't escape the ballad. One headline announced, "Frankie of song fame dies at Pendleton."

The real-life Frankie was gone, but her fictional alter-ego lived on. A 1962 thesis found no fewer than 291 versions of the song. Since then, there have been two more "Frankie and Johnny" movies – one with Elvis Presley in 1966 and the other with Al Pacino and Michelle Pfeiffer in 1991. Though both were happy to milk the song's title, neither bothered with much of the story that went along with it. Elvis' film puts Frankie and Johnny on a Mississippi riverboat and lets them live happily ever after when the credits roll. The Pacino movie offers a couple of knowing nods to the song but crafts its plot from scratch. One day, there may be a "Frankie and Johnny" movie with African American actors in the title roles, but it hasn't happened so far.

Songwriters have not been shy about using artistic license either. Sam Cooke's 1963 version had Frankie give her lover a sports car and some "Ivy League clothes." Jimmy Anderson's 1969 blues version ends with Frankie getting drunk in the bar where she found Johnny and then merely dumps him instead of shooting him. Bob Dylan included the song on a

1962 album and couldn't resist adding details about Frankie on the gallows.

Although you can't measure the success of the song by it, if it's accuracy you want, then you can't beat Mississippi John Hurt's 1928 version. Recorded relatively soon after the murder, it gets just about everything right. All the characters are given their real names, the fight in the street described by the neighbor is sketched out, and Frankie walks out of court as a free woman.

Even though Frankie, in his version, shoots Allen three or four times and has her going to a funeral the real Frankie never attended, these are minor offenses when compared to the many liberties taken with the story elsewhere.

5. "THE BALLAD OF BEAUTIFUL NELL CROPSEY"

ON A CHILLY NIGHT IN 1901, A YOUNG WOMAN NAMED Nell Cropsey vanished from her family's home in North Carolina. After a search that lasted more than a month, Nell's body was discovered floating in a nearby river. She had been brutally murdered – but the identity of her killer remained a mystery.

The boyfriend with whom she'd recently split spent more than a dozen years in prison, proclaiming his innocence, before being pardoned by the governor. Some believed he'd been guilty, but others argued he didn't do it, but we'll never know for sure. He committed suicide soon after being released from prison.

This is a case filled with mystery and many unanswered questions, which is perhaps why Nell's ghost still haunts her family home today – and why so many songs have been written about her story.

The excitement over her disappearance was so great that at least two songs were written between the time she vanished and when her body was found more than a month later.

At least one song written about Nell was written from the viewpoint of the man accused of her murder. However, the writer wasn't swayed by his claims of innocence since it's a confessional ballad, warning other men about the influence of the Devil – which was always a woman wearing a skirt.

NELL MAUD CROPSEY WAS BORN ON JULY 17, 1882. Her parents, William and his wife, Mary Louise, lived in Brooklyn, New York, but in 1898, they left the city for the quieter southern community of Elizabeth City, North Carolina.

William had been corresponding with a man named John Bartlett Fearing for some time, and Fearing encouraged the family to make the move. He had substantial land around his mansion on Riverside Drive in Elizabeth City and offered to rent comfortable quarters in his home for the Cropseys until they could buy or rent their own.

After their arrival, William began hauling crops for farmers down to the busy riverport and later turned to potato farming. The family settled into their new home, and the four older daughters – Lou, Lettie, Olive, and Nell – enjoyed some appeal as newcomers and began to attract a few suitors and admirers.

Nell Cropsey

Olive began a relationship with a man named Roy Crawford while Nell was courted by Jim Wilcox, the local sheriff's son – but rumors claimed she was actually in love with another man. The stories claimed that Nell was having an affair with John Fearing, the man her family rented from, who was nearly 20 years older than Nell. Fearing had a reputation as a notorious lothario, recklessly chasing girls and women in town. His wife knew about his antics, but divorce was unthinkable at that time in the small town of Elizabeth City, so she joined the legion of other suffering wives who lived through their betrayals with steely silence.

For Nell, Jim was useful for providing steady social engagements and covering up the truth about her secret affair – if there was an affair, of course. It wasn't long before townspeople got used to seeing Jim accompany Nell to shows, events, and carriage rides around town. Jim was immensely loyal to Nell despite her often difficult personality. In time, he began to realize just how one-sided their romance was, but by then, it was too late because he'd fallen madly in love.

Two years passed, and Jim remained a regular caller at the plantation house owned by John Fearing, where Nell and the other Cropseys were still staying.

Soon after that, however, William Cropsey obtained a home for his family called "Seven Pines," located a short distance away from the Fearing mansion on Riverside Avenue. Built in 1891, it was one of the most distinctive homes in the city. It was an eclectic Queen Anne-style home with an impressive wraparound porch, a three-story square tower, and a sharp pyramidal roof.

Soon, Jim became a regular caller there, as well. He continued to offer Nell his time and money, but she remained lukewarm toward his affections. Even her sister, Olive, who didn't like Jim, admitted he had been generous to her, giving her a silver dish at Christmas, a beautiful pin the next, and a fine gold ring on her birthday.

Jim Wilcox – the young man who pursued Nell for years and who would eventually be accused of her murder.

Nell spent only pennies in return. She eventually gifted him a photograph of herself and an umbrella.

But Jim didn't seem to notice. He came to Seven Pines at least three nights each week, escorted Nell to events and performances, and took her riding, sailing, and dancing. They frequented the new soda shop that opened in 1901. They enjoyed the circuses and fairs that came to town and often visited Munden's Roller Skating Rink because Nell loved to skate.

Around the time the chilly winds of autumn began to blow, Jim's passion for Nell started to cool. He finally realized their relationship had no future and that he had been taken for granted since it began. Nell's iciness toward him had finally driven him to despair, but it seemed impossible for him to think he was losing her.

At the beginning of October 1901, Nell's cousin, Carrie, visited the family from New York. She and Nell had an especially close relationship. She would later recall walking downtown with Nell and running into Jim. He hurried over to greet them, and Carrie shook his hand, but Nell rudely turned her back on him and studied the display in a department store window. Despite this, Jim continued to come to Seven Pines to see Nell, unable to let her go. And it worked – kind of. Nell agreed to go with Jim when he bought circus tickets for himself, Nell, and Carrie later that month.

Nell's kindness toward him lasted for about two weeks after the circus performance, but his visits to her home became a test of patience and nerves for the lovesick young man. Nell began to ridicule and scorn him routinely. She spent entire evenings not speaking directly to him and didn't bother walking him to the door after his visits. She also openly flirted with other men.

Jim nursed his hurt feelings by paying attention to Carrie Cropsey, taking her and one of Nell's sisters sailing and for evening meals at local restaurants. Unknown to him, Nell had been planning to return to New York with Carrie on November 3 for the Thanksgiving holiday and perhaps to stay longer.

On Tuesday, November 19, Carrie accepted an invitation from Jim to go to the roller skating rink. Jim arrived at Seven Pines and rang the bell, and Nell, angry and perhaps a little jealous, refused to answer it. Carrie went to the door and welcomed Jim inside. The two of them sat down in the parlor with Olive and Nell. A few strained pleasantries were passed between them before Carrie got her hat and coat and suggested they leave.

After reaching the rink, they skated for an hour or so and then started to walk home. Jim bought a bag of apples from a grocer's stand on Poindexter Street, and Carrie ate one as they walked along.

Carrie turned to Jim and asked, "Why is it that Nell dislikes you so much?"

Jim shrugged sadly. "You tell me, and I'll tell you."

"You've had a quarrel, haven't you?"

"No, not a quarrel – she just doesn't care enough about me to go to the door with me, so I'm going to drop her."

"You mean she will drop you?" Carrie replied.

Jim sighed. "That's about the size of it."

When they returned to the house, Nell and Olive were in the sitting room, and without speaking to Jim, Nell said, "I certainly would enjoy a good apple tonight."

Carrie offered apples from the bag that she and Jim brought back, and Nell made a big show of shaking her head and refusing the fruit. Stinging again, Jim put on his hat around 11:00 P.M. and left for the night.

As soon as the front door closed behind him, Nell took an apple and started eating it. "This is a good joke on Jim," she said.

Unknown to the young women, Jim was still on the porch and could hear them laughing. He also heard it when Carrie said, "Nell, I had to laugh at you when you refused the apple because I know you wanted it so bad."

Jim was wounded again. He had believed that Carrie was his one ally in the Cropsey family, but he realized he was wrong. What he heard next just made him feel worse.

"Nell, you ought to have seen us going to the rink," Carrie laughed. "We certainly did look funny. I am so tall and Jim so short. I felt like an elephant going in there with that little thing."

As the girls squealed with laughter, Jim walked away. He didn't need to listen to the rest.

The following day, though, Jim saw Carrie and Nell's sister, Lettie, harnessing a buggy for a ride into town. He left work and climbed onto the back of the vehicle as the women passed by.

"You are a nice girl," he said coldly.

Carrie was startled. "What's the matter, Jim?" she asked.

"Listeners never hear any good of themselves," he replied. "When I went out last night, my cigarette went out, and I stopped to light it and heard what you said."

"I'm sorry if I hurt your feelings."

Jim shrugged and quietly said, "Oh, Jimmie doesn't care."

Lettie then asked Jim, "Why didn't you come and harness the horse for us?"

Jim sighed as he sadly told her, "I have been a lackey long enough."

The three of them returned to Seven Pines around 5:30. Jim stayed for a half-hour. He struck up a conversation with Olive, but he and Nell ignored each other.

Enough was enough, he thought.

THAT EVENING, WEDNESDAY, NOVEMBER 20, JIM returned to Seven Pines around 8:00 P.M. It was a cold night marked by bright moonlight and a chilling wind. Carrie welcomed him at the door, knowing he was suffering from a broken heart.

Jim still loved Nell, but brutal truths had peeled away the veneer of their relationship. Nell wounded him at every opportunity, belittling him, ignoring him, and taking advantage of him. He had heard whispers about her affair with John Fearing, but he had dismissed them, choosing to

Seven Pines – the home of the Cropsey family

believe the stories were nothing but neighborhood gossip. However, it was time to end things, he thought, once and for all.

In hindsight, we must wonder what Jim could have ever seen in Nell in the first place if she treated him as poorly as he would later claim. He had allowed her to behave miserably with him for more than three years, and he simply accepted it as the cost of being in love with her.

Or so he said. Or so he believed.

But what if Jim was wrong? What if Nell never considered them anything other than friends? Perhaps she really was in love with John Fearing, as the rumors claimed, and used Jim as a cover for her relationship – or maybe she never considered Jim as a romantic partner at all. Could Jim have taken the whole thing more seriously than Nell ever did? Perhaps he imagined some great love between them that was never there.

If that's true, then the tragedy of Nell Cropsey soon took a horrific turn.

Jim greeted Carrie when she opened the door. He carried the small umbrella that Nell had once given him as a gift, and he hung it from the hat rack in the front hallway. Jim then found several of the Cropseys and another guest, Olive's boyfriend, Roy Crawford, in the dining room after the evening meal. Jim sat down in a chair near the door from the dining room to the hallway. Nell was sewing at a nearby table but ignored him.

The clock ticked, and one by one, members of the family retired for the evening, leaving Jim, Roy, Carrie, Olive, and Nell in the room. Jim was quiet throughout the evening, occasionally taking his watch from his pocket and checking the time.

Jim finally spoke up and asked if there was water from the pump in the kitchen. Olive rose to get a glass for him, but Jim stopped her with a blunt comment, "I don't want your glass – you might poison it."

Carrie said that Jim then began to smile as if what he said had been a joke. If so, it wasn't a funny one. "What are you smiling about?" she asked him.

Jim looked perplexed. "Was I smiling?" he asked. "I didn't know it."

A little later, Carrie recalled that someone mentioned the subject of suicide by drowning. It might have been something from the newspaper, she admitted later. Jim said that he almost died in the river one time but remembered it as an almost pleasant sensation. "I would not mind drowning," he stated.

Nell barked out a short laugh. "Drowning is one thing I would never want to do because my hair could come out straight. I would look a fright. If I die by my own hand, I want to freeze to death."

Carrie, unsettled by the morbid conversation, excused herself at about 10:30. She climbed the stairs to her bedroom above the sitting room and recalled later that she paced around for 10-15 minutes, troubled by the talk of death. She remembered looking out the window and seeing a buggy passing by the house in the moonlight, then she blew out the lamp and went to bed.

Downstairs, a strained, awkward conversation continued for another half hour. Shortly after 11:00, Jim pulled out his watch and looked at it. He stood up, suddenly deciding to leave. The others also stood, likely relieved that the night could be over.

Before Jim left, though, he turned to Nell with his hat in his hand. "Nell, can I see you out here for a minute?" he asked. It was the first thing he'd said directly to her all evening.

Nell looked at Olive but said nothing and joined Jim in the hallway. Olive walked over and closed the hall door, then returned to the dining room with Roy.

Jim later said that he walked out onto the front porch with Nell, who was wrapped only in a sweater. She was dressed much too lightly for the cold temperatures and icy wind, but she walked out with him anyway.

Outside, Jim claimed that he ended their relationship by returning Nell's umbrella and photograph. He told her that he would not be coming back again. According to Jim, she was unprepared for his rejection and began to cry. He told her to go back inside, or she would catch her death in the bitter cold. He then walked away, leaving Nell crying on the porch.

Was his story true? We'll never know, but I feel that it's just as likely that Nell didn't cry when Jim left that night. I think it's very possible she was relieved. She might have thought that Jim wouldn't bother her anymore and she'd be free from the lovesick man for good.

But we'll never know if it happened the way Jim said or how I imagine it did – because Nell Cropsey was never seen alive again.

A HALF-HOUR PASSED BETWEEN THE TIME THAT NELL walked out into the hallway with Jim and when Roy Crawford left the Cropsey house. He saw no one outside, so he assumed that Jim had walked home, and Nell had gone upstairs. Olive assumed the same. She later said she was slightly irritated to see that Nell had gone upstairs to bed and left her to close the house by herself.

When Olive went to the room that she shared with her sister, she got dressed in the dark, not wanting to wake Nell up. She reached over to Nell's side of the bed and was surprised to find that she wasn't there. She assumed that Nell was still with Jim and went to sleep.

Around midnight, the family dog suddenly began barking loudly. The entire household was awakened, and they went out onto the front porch to see the cause of the disturbance. There was no one there, but at that point, Olive realized that Nell had never come to bed. Her sister was missing.

Mrs. Cropsey was terrified, and her husband tried to calm her by going out to search the neighborhood. Along with Nell's brother, Will Jr., William took a lantern and searched the property and along the nearby river. Finding nothing, they headed straight for the Wilcox house a short distance away. William, not knowing the state of the relationship between Nell and Jim, thought it might be possible the couple had eloped.

He knocked on their door around 1:30 A.M., and Tom and Mattie Wilcox, Jim's parents, discovered the cause of the early morning intrusion. Mattie roused Jim from sleep, and he told his mother that he had left Nell at home. The last time he'd seen her, Jim said, she had been standing on the front porch. That was all he had to say. He turned over and went back to sleep. Mattie passed this along to William and her husband, the former sheriff.

William and Henry then hurried off to the home of Crawford Dawson, the current police chief. He promised to get dressed to investigate the matter and sent the Cropseys back to Seven Pines.

Crawford did as he promised. Along with one of his officers, he went to the Wilcox home, and they, along with Tom Wilcox, woke Jim from his sleep again. He told Jim that he wanted him to go to the Cropsey home with him.

Jim agreed and got dressed. As they walked over to Seven Pines, Dawson pressed him for answers.

"What do you think of this case?" he asked Jim.

"I don't know what to think."

"When was the last time you saw Miss Cropsey, and where was she?"

"I left her standing on the front porch."

"Did she seem to be in any trouble?"

"Well, yes, I left her crying."

"What was she crying about?"

"I gave her back her picture, and she said, 'I know what that means.' She began to cry, and I turned and left her. I came home."

Dawson frowned. He asked Jim, "Have you had any quarrels – any lovers' quarrels or anything like that."

Jim let out a short barking laugh. "Well, no. Nothing more than she laughed in my face, and I told her the laugh would haunt her in the afterlife."

Jim may have then realized that this statement didn't sound the way that he likely wished it would have and quickly explained the discussion they'd had recently about suicide and drowning.

And that didn't sound much better.

As they walked, they passed a bridge, and Jim suddenly remembered that he had stopped at this spot earlier that night to chat with an acquaintance, Leonard Owens. He had run into him just after leaving the Cropsey house.

They arrived at Seven Pines just after 3:00 A.M., and Jim seemed nervous when the family confronted him with unfriendly glares on their faces. Nell's mother, Mary, was the first to speak up. She gripped Jim's arm tightly. "Jim, for my sake and your mother's sake, tell me where Nell is!" she begged him.

Jim seemed stunned by the question. "Mrs. Cropsey, I don't know," he answered. "I will swear and kiss a Bible, I don't know."

Despite more tearful pleas from Mary and Olive, Jim maintained that he knew nothing about Nell's whereabouts.

No one believed that Nell ran away. She had been excited about her upcoming trip to New York. None of her belongings were missing. Her clothing and suitcases were still in the closet.

By morning, with no further clues, Chief Dawson went to the Wilcox house and arrested Jim on general suspicion in the disappearance. However, Mayor Tully Wilson ordered his release, saying that Dawson lacked credible evidence to justify holding him.

Roy Crawford was questioned, as was Leonard Owens, the friend that Jim met on the roadway. Roy claimed to know nothing, and Leonard confirmed the meeting at the time that Jim said it occurred.

Oddly, based on the time that Jim left the house and met with Leonard by the bridge, Roy Crawford should have passed them on his way home since he left shortly after Jim did.

But he didn't.

A MASSIVE HUNT FOR NELL CROPSEY BEGAN. LAW enforcement officers, volunteers, and trained bloodhounds combed the area, searching the forests and swamps. There was no sign of the missing girl.

Jim's parents asked Deputy Sheriff Charles Reid to go with their son to Seven Pines and try to smooth things over with the Cropsey family. Mattie suggested that Jim could "touch the hearts of the Cropseys" by showing concern for Nell.

On the way to the Cropsey home, Deputy Reid suggested that Jim tell everything he knows about Nell, at least for the sake of her distraught family and his own mother. But Jim insisted that he'd told all that he could tell, and his second visit to Seven Pines after the disappearance also didn't go well.

Mary questioned him again. "I don't know where she is," Jim insisted.

"You say you left her crying?"

"Yes."

"Had you ever seen her crying before?"

"I don't know what Nell was crying about unless she became upset when I told her that I was going to quit her."

Mary sobbed, mostly because Jim seemed so indifferent to Nell's disappearance. It didn't help that Olive spoke up and said that she doubted Nell would cry because she'd already lost interest in Jim if she had any in the first place. Carrie agreed, and Jim left.

Mary and Olive spoke with reporters and friends about the case and about Jim's apparent lack of concern about Nell's disappearance. Rumors surfaced that painted an ugly picture of the relationship between Nell and Jim Wilcox. Friends told the police about fights they'd had and Jim's unhappiness with Nell in recent months.

But rumors and gossip weren't enough to arrest Jim – and they certainly didn't help find the missing young woman.

Weeks passed with still no trace of Nell. The river was dragged, but nothing was found. Some believed that Nell had drowned herself in the river in a fit of sorrow over the end of her relationship with Jim. Of course, they didn't know how little interest Nell had in that relationship.

Others claimed that Nell fell into the river from a pier at John Fearing's house, where she had gone to meet him for an illicit rendezvous.

Many others believed that Nell was alive and had been kidnapped. Searches were made of empty buildings, warehouses on the river, and – primarily because racism was alive and well – "negro houses" in the southern part of the city.

No matter what they believed about the fate of Nell Cropsey, however, most thought that Jim Wilcox knew more than he was saying. He was now refusing to speak to the police at all. The Cropsey family talked about him to the newspapers, with Mary saying that she "did not fancy Jim so much." Olive said that Jim was "changeable. Sometimes he would hardly speak to her for three or four days, and then he would come back and bring flowers. Nell and Jim had been going together about three years, but I knew they were not engaged. She said she didn't care for him, and I think she didn't care for him, and I think she liked another better."

More time passed, and still no trace of Nell was found. The Cropsey family had begun to fear the worst.

William Cropsey swore out an affidavit against Jim for abduction, and on Tuesday, December 3, Jim was forced to face a preliminary hearing at the crowded county courthouse. It lasted four hours, and in the end, Jim was held on a $1,000 bond for action by a grand jury. He didn't have the money, so he had to wait in jail until a grand jury could be impaneled to hear the case. Meanwhile, he was fired from the Marine Railway Company where he worked, "pending the establishment of his innocence."

After the hearing, William Cropsey spoke to reporters, "Jim Wilcox knows where my daughter is," he claimed. "I do not think that Nell killed herself. I think she was carried away forcibly and that Wilcox knows by whom. The girl had no sweetheart whom I regarded seriously. She had no secret from her sister and mother. There could not have been an elopement. I think she was gagged and carried away in a buggy or a boat. Had she committed suicide, the body would have been found."

The search continued, attracting interest from newspapers all over the country. An expert diver from Norfolk was brought in to search the bottom of the river, but there was no sign of Nell's corpse. A clairvoyant named Madame Snell Newman publicized that she'd had ghastly psychic visions of Nell dying at the bottom of a well. The police, along with two New York reporters, traveled to two old wells in the area but found nothing.

Strange letters and telegrams poured into Chief Dawson's office from people who claimed they'd seen Nell, usually in the company of a man, usually a much older one. These messages came from cities and towns all over Virginia and North Carolina.

Nell's father, William Cropsey, who swore out a warrant against Jim Wilcox and believed the young man knew what had happened to his daughter.

By now, the town was bitterly divided over Jim Wilcox's guilt. Both factions – with William Cropsey on one side and Tom Wilcox on the other – had published letters in the newspapers, blaming Jim or defending him. "Many people appear a damn sight more anxious to convict my son than to find the missing girl," Tom wrote. "They seem to start out with the promise he is guilty, and they are trying to get more evidence against him than to locate Miss Cropsey. Jim and his friends are anxious to find the girl. They have already given up good money to help the search, and they are willing to give more if needed."

More than a month passed before Nell was finally found.

PASQUOTANK RIVER GIVES UP NELL CROPSEY'S BODY

Nell's body was found floating in the Pasquotank River on December 27. The area had been searched several times already so where the body had been during the previous month remains a mystery.

ON DECEMBER 24, WILLIAM CROPSEY RECEIVED ANOTHER strange letter in the mail. It was postmarked from Utica, New York. The anonymous writer suggested that Jim left the house when he said he did on November 20. Around the same time, Nell investigated a barking dog and encountered a man stealing one of the family's pigs. When Nell threatened to call for help, the thief struck her in the head and then took her away in a rowboat.

The letter included a detailed pen and ink drawing of the shoreline in front of the Cropsey house and marked an X where Nell's body could be found in the Pasquotank River. It ended with one sensational line:

Your daughter will appear in front of your house tomorrow.

She didn't, but on December 27, Nell's body, floating face down, was found in the river exactly where the letter writer had predicted.

That spot – along with the rest of the river -- had been searched many times without success, causing many to surmise that the killer had taken the girl's body from a hiding place and dumped it into the river after the mysterious letter was sent.

The news of the discovery spread quickly through town, and it was estimated that at least 2,000 people gathered to watch Nell's body being brought ashore.

She was dressed in a red shirtwaist top and black skirt. Her right shoe was still clinging to the body. Her left shoe was gone. Her hair had fallen and was matted over her face – just as Nell feared would happen if she drowned.

Her body had been found by two fishermen, who had tied her to a stake to wait for the police. They had quickly summoned Dr. Isiah Fearing – John Fearing's cousin – who served as the coroner. He impaneled a six-man coroner's jury to help reach a conclusion about the girl's death.

Dr. Isiah Fearing

An autopsy was hastily held in a small outbuilding behind Seven Pines. The doors were left open for light. A crowd watched as Nell was stripped naked and placed on a crude table. They found that her internal organs were normal and that there was no water in her lungs. There were no broken bones. She had not been raped and, in fact, was a virgin, which cast doubts on the rumors about an alleged affair with John Fearing. The coroner did find a bruise and clotted blood on her left temple. It appeared that she had been struck there, which could have led to her drowning – if she drowned.

Dr. Fearing had a hard time explaining why she had no water in her lungs, and he eventually concluded that the contusion had been her cause of death. It had been caused by her being struck with a "heavy, rounded object." She had been hit hard and was dead before her body was placed in the river.

Of course, most assumed that Jim Wilcox was the killer. He was arrested again and, this time, charged with murder. Death threats poured into the police station, promising that Jim would be lynched for his crime.

On December 28, a mob appeared at Seven Pines, begging William Cropsey to lead them in lynching Jim. He didn't go – but later stated that he regretted not doing so.

A funeral was held for Nell on December 28. More than 1,500 people packed into the Methodist church. She was later buried in the New Utrecht Cemetery in Brooklyn, New York, which had been home to the Cropsey family.

On December 30, a Charlotte newspaper reported that the jail holding "young Wilcox, who was arrested for alleged participation in Miss Cropsey's death, lies only a stone's throw from the church. Wilcox knew the funeral was in progress but showed no emotion and merely inquired if a large crowd had attended. He retains much of the easy manner that has characterized him all through."

The article ended on an ominous note: "Public sentiment is strong against Wilcox."

JIM WAS INDICTED FOR NELL'S MURDER ON MARCH 11, 1902. He waived his right to a preliminary hearing and went straight to trial. The attorneys sparred for more than a week, and then the jury began deliberating on March 21. The judge instructed them not to violate their oaths as impartial jurors by bowing to "frenzied public opinion."

Thirty Years Hard Labor For Jim Wilcox!

Alleged Murderer is to Pay The Penalty.

SUPREME COURT IS OBDURATE

Mysterious Death of Miss Ella Maude Cropsey is to Be Avenged. Many Think A Pardon Will Come Later. Prisoner is Unconcerned.

This had to be said because reports were still circulating in various newspapers about the possibility of mob violence.

The jury returned the following day. Outside the courthouse were knots of seething men, some with ropes, whispering about what might happen if the jury failed to find Jim Wilcox guilty. When the bell rang to signal that the jury had a verdict, several hundred people packed into the courthouse to hear the jury's foreman pronounce the verdict – "guilty of murder in the first degree."

Jim was sentenced to hang on April 25, but before he could go to the gallows, his case was declared a mistrial by the North Carolina Supreme Court. He was tried again for murder in 1903 and was found guilty of second-degree murder this time. He was sentenced to spend the next 30 years in prison.

Jim's time in prison went as well as it could. Several efforts were made to gain his release, but each one failed. In 1910, his mother, Mattie, passed away, and his father, Tom, died in 1915.

In 1918, Jim's case took another turn. A new governor, Thomas Walter Bickett, was elected. Bickett had practiced law in a neighboring county and was very familiar with the Nell Cropsey case. He knew that Jim had served almost 16 years of his sentence without a single blemish. He began investigating the case on his own and even visited Jim in his cell. He soon began to believe that Jim was innocent of Nell's murder. Shortly after the two men spoke, Governor Bickett pardoned him, and he was released from prison. He returned to friends and remaining family members in Elizabeth City, where he was greeted warmly by some and with contempt by others, who refused to believe he was innocent.

After Jim was released from prison, he met with newspaper editor W.O. Saunders, who was planning a book about the Cropsey case. Whatever Jim told him was apparently so shocking that Saunders made immediate plans to start on the proposed book.

But that book was never written.

A short time after the meeting, Jim committed suicide with a shotgun blast to the head. Soon after, Saunders was killed in a car accident. The notes for his book were never found. Whatever Jim Wilcox told Saunders at that meeting will never be known.

And Jim's death was not the only tragedy connected to the case.

Olive Cropsey never married. She struggled with her sister's death for years and eventually became a recluse. She died of natural causes, shut off from society in 1944.

Olive's former suitor, Roy Crawford, fled from North Carolina to Oklahoma. In 1908, he shot himself. Those who knew him said that he had a mental illness toward the end and were not surprised he'd committed suicide.

In 1913, Nell's brother, Will, also killed himself. He drank a bottle of carbolic acid, leaving behind a wife and a five-year-old daughter named Nell.

John Fearing, the alleged secret lover of Nell Cropsey, continued his escapades in town long after Nell's death. He died of natural causes in 1923.

Nell's father, William, gave up farming after his daughter's death and died of natural causes in 1938. He was buried in the local cemetery, steps away from Jim Wilcox's unmarked grave.

Nell's mother, Mary, passed away a decade later in 1948.

The Cropseys all went to their graves without ever knowing the truth behind Nell's death -- a mystery that remains unsolved after all these years.

BUT THE IDENTITY OF NELL'S KILLER IS NOT THE ONLY mystery in this case. We will never know what happened to Nell Cropsey that night in 1901, and perhaps this is the reason why her spirit refuses to rest.

Even at the time of Jim's trial, many tales were going around about communications with Nell's ghost. A spirit medium named Norman Whitehurst claimed that he had a conversation with her during a séance. "Nell spoke to me," Whitehurst announced, "and she said 'Jim Wilcox killed me, but it was my fault – I provoked him to do the deed. He struck me in the heat of passion, struck me harder than he intended, and killed me. Go and do your best to save his life.'"

Unfortunately for Jim, these "communications" did nothing to spare him a trial and 16 years in prison. And did nothing to put an end to other encounters with Nell's restless spirit.

For the past century, those who have lived at Seven Pines have reported strange occurrences. Lights go on and off, doors open and shut, water rushes from the sink even when no one turns the handle, and strange cold gusts of air waft through the house without explanation.

Some reports also include sightings of a pale young woman who has been seen walking through empty rooms, in hallways, and on the front porch. People passing by on the street have seen the same pale figure looking wistfully from an upstairs window. One resident claimed to recognize Nell when she awoke and saw the murdered girl standing at the foot of her bed one night.

Will the enduring mystery of Nell's death ever be solved? It seems unlikely after all these years, which means that the unfortunate young woman is just as unlikely to find the peace that she still seeks.

Her lingering presence reminds us that she never truly received the justice that she deserved, and because she still walks, she is never forgotten.

Her sad story is told over and over, in both word and song, as the tragic tale of Nell Cropsey is recalled. Dead men – or, in this case, a dead young woman – really do tell tales.

AND OFTEN THOSE STORIES ARE TOLD WITH SONG.

The first murder ballads that were written about Nell Cropsey appeared before her body was even found. Although not collected until 1912 by West Virginia folklorist Louis W. Chappell, who was only a boy growing up in North Carolina when the murder occurred. Chappel believed the first two ballads – including one collected by Mrs. L.A. Spencer of Elizabeth City in 1902 – had been composed between when Nell vanished in November and her body was discovered in the river the following month. He believed that both were revised when Nell's corpse was found.

The first ballad, which he referred to as "Nell Cropsey I," appeared in his 1939 book *Folk Songs of Roanoke and the Albemarle*, ended on an ambiguous note:

Days went by, they searched for Nellie,
But their search was all in vain,
And perhaps they thought her living,
And would soon return again.

However, the first two stanzas of the ballad made it clear that the composer was aware that Nell was murdered. Apparently, they had returned to the song after the body was found but never corrected the end of the ballad.

The first stanza states:

On the twentieth of November,
A day you all remember,
'Twas then a handsome girl was murdered,

Of her story I will tell.

The second stanza included a warning to girls "on how you treat a man," of course implying that it was Nell's fault that she'd been murdered. She had driven her man to kill her, which is a reminder of the alleged "spirit communications" from Nell after Jim was arrested.

For they will pretend to love you,
And will kill you if they can.

The second ballad, which Chappell referred to as "Nell Cropsey, II" since it apparently had no title, was rewritten for the Pasquotank River, which was a character in the song. It had changed after Nell's body was found floating in the cold water:

Oh, swift flowing river,
A secret you hold
Way down in the depths
Of the water so cold.

A third Nell Cropsey ballad – I'm not going to bother giving you the numeric name of this one – was also collected by Chappell. It was composed from the viewpoint of Jim Wilcox and was a confessional ballad, purporting to be his confession to the murder. It contained a warning to other young men to avoid the influence of the Devil – and wily women.

In his book, Chappell pointed out that this ballad was actually a variation of the old British ballad that was mentioned in an earlier chapter. The "murdered girl" ballad went by many names, including the "Knoxville Girl" and the "Cruel Miller."

My dear old parents brought me here
Provided for me well,
And in the city of Dixie Belle,
They placed me in the mill.

I went over to her sister's house
Twas eight o'clock that night,
And little did the poor girl think
Against her I had a spite.

I asked her to take a little walk,
A little ways with me,
So we might have a little talk
About our wedding day.

Chappell collected other variations of the ballad, and he compared some of those to another earlier ballad called "Fair Florella," another standard "murdered girl" tune. As we mentioned in the earlier chapter, it was common to update and adapt the older songs and attach them to violent crimes that were widely separated by time and place. It's worth noting that in this context, most of the Nell Cropsey ballads don't mention her by name.

From what I've been able to discover, it appears that Nell Cropsey ballads somehow managed to elude being commercially recorded until the 1970s. Even then, it was recorded in the Outer Banks region by ethnomusicologist Karen G. Helms as a collection of songs from the region. A version of "Nell Cropsey III" with slightly different lyrics was performed by Isabelle Etheridge for an album called *Between the Sound and the Sea: Music of the North Carolina Outer Banks* in 1977. This cut, along with the others on the album which other artists performed, were field recordings by Helms. The ballad was finally given a title – "Nellie Cropsey."

The Red Clay Ramblers

The only other recording about Nell's murder was written and performed by the award-winning group, the Red Clay Ramblers. It was released as "The Ballad of Beautiful Nell Cropsey" in 2009.

The murder of Nell Cropsey – which may or may not remain unsolved – didn't leave much of an impression on the annals of American crime, but the story of her ghost and her tragic ballad have managed to live on.

6. "LOVELY PEARL BRYAN"

WHEN THE HEADLESS CORPSE OF A YOUNG PREGNANT woman was found on John Locke's farm near Fort Thomas, Kentucky, on February 1, 1896, the shock of the discovery was felt far beyond the Ohio River Valley. In fact, for the rest of that winter and most of the spring, the tragedy involving the dead woman unfolded daily in newspapers across the country.

The "murdered girl" turned out to be Pearl Bryan, from the small town of Greencastle, Indiana, and the story of how she had come to Kentucky and met such a gruesome fate seemed incomprehensible to the people of turn-of-the-century America.

But unlike so many killings that inspired murder ballads, the case of Pearl Bryan was quickly solved, and the killers were hanged. There seemed to be no loose ends and no dangling mysteries to be wrapped up – or that's how it seemed.

In truth, though, there are many questions about this story that have been left unanswered, and there seem to be mysteries at every turn, including one very important one – what happened to Pearl's head?

That is a question that has haunted the real-life story of Pearl Bryan, as well as the dozen or so songs that have been written about her cruel demise.

WHEN TWO YOUNG MEN WHO WORKED FOR John Locke stumbled across the body of a headless woman in an orchard at the edge of the road, they immediately informed their employer and the authorities about what they'd found. The body was taken to the Cincinnati morgue, and efforts began to try and discover who she might be, although privately, police officers doubted her identity would ever be known. Because she was found so close to the fort, a missing prostitute or a dance hall girl seemed the most likely candidate for the corpse, with her killer being one of the soldiers stationed at Fort Thomas.

But amazingly – especially for 1896 – the mystery was solved very quickly. L. D. Poock, a local shoe store owner, took an interest in the shoes the victim was wearing and discovered that inside one boot was the imprint of a shoe store in Greencastle, Indiana. He also spotted what he knew to be the manufacturer's lot number. After a little investigation, the shoe factory told him the date of the shipment to Greencastle and that there was only one size that matched that of the victim in the lot.

This sent Campbell County Sheriff Jules Plummer and two Cincinnati police detectives to Greencastle and to the Louis and Hayes shoe store, which checked their records and saw the shoes had been purchased a few months earlier by Pearl Bryan. Late that night, her parents identified Pearl's clothing and learned about their daughter's awful daughter's death.

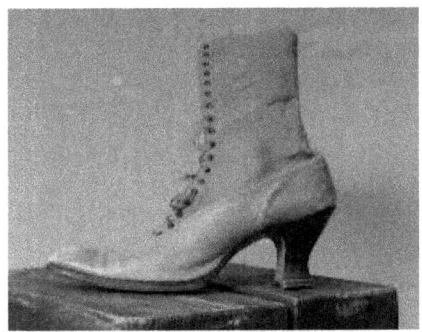

The woman's shoe that led the authorities to the identity of Pearl Bryan.

(Below) Professional photograph of Pearl Bryan taken at a studio in Greencastle, Indiana.

The Bryan home in Greencastle

Although Pearl was easily identified by her shoes, who the young woman really was is just one of the many mysteries in this story that will never be solved.

In the newspapers, she was portrayed as a poor, innocent farm girl, seduced and ruined by an older man. But while she was a farmer's daughter, none of the rest of that was true. Pearl's father was the wealthiest man in Greencastle. She lived in one of the town's finest homes and was no naïve farmer's daughter. The pretty, blond, 22-year-old was a music student at DePauw University. She also worked in her sister Mary's dress shop, making sure they stocked all the latest big city fashions. So, she was undoubtedly not unsophisticated.

When she'd left town in late January 1896, she told her parents she was going to Indianapolis to visit some family friends but went instead to Cincinnati, where she planned to have an abortion.

Pearl's cousin, Will Wood

When it was discovered that Pearl was pregnant when she was killed, her family and many of her friends first assumed that Will Wood, Pearl's second cousin, was the father. Will had known Pearl his whole life, and the two had always been close. Though popular with the boys, Pearl had no regular boyfriend, and Will was always around.

Others, though, believed that Pearl was having a secret romance with Scott Jackson, a slightly older young man who had come to Greencastle from New Jersey a year earlier. Jackson was friends with Will Wood. He lived with his mother next door to the church where Will's father was the pastor.

At the time of Pearl's death, Jackson was studying dentistry in Cincinnati, just a short trip across the Ohio River from the spot where the body was found. Jackson quickly became the prime suspect.

Jackson was arrested outside his rooming house in Cincinnati, and Will was detained for questioning. After initially denying everything, Jackson eventually admitted that Pearl had come to Cincinnati for an abortion that he was supposed to arrange – but only as a favor for his friend, Will, who'd gotten her pregnant. Will, of course, said the opposite – that it was Jackson who was responsible for his cousin's pregnancy.

(Left) Scott Jackson, the slightly older man that Pearl was rumored to have been seeing.

(Right) Jackson's roommate in Cincinnati, Alonzo Walling.

Which of these two was the father of Pearl's child was never wholly established, but Jackson later admitted on the witness stand that he'd had sex with Pearl. He claimed, though, that it hadn't occurred until Christmas of 1895 when he was home from school and already knew Peal was pregnant. Will denied ever sleeping with Pearl, but several witnesses later swore that he'd bragged in detail about his sexual encounters with her.

So, while neither of these men were exactly reputable, there was one more character that had to be added to the story. His name was Alonzo Walling, and he was Jackson's roommate in Cincinnati. He was also arrested after Jackson said he left Pearl in his care and that he was supposed to arrange the abortion. Jackson claimed that Walling had murdered her instead.

Walling, of course, told a different story. He claimed that Jackson told him that he planned to lure Pearl to Cincinnati by telling her he'd pay for her abortion, but then he was going to poison her, cut her body into pieces, and scatter them around in outhouses throughout the city.

An 1896 illustration of George Johnson driving the two men and their victim to the place in the woods where he left them — or so his testimony claimed.

Was this another wild story? Or was it Jackson's actual plan? Who knows? Both men denied being responsible for Pearl's murder and blamed her death on the other one.

Without confessions, the police began building a case against the two men based on testimony from witnesses who had seen them with Pearl during the week before her death. The witnesses included a clerk at a piano store and a Spiritualist medium who said that Jackson accompanied Pearl to her home for a séance. I assume that she was not a very good spirit medium, though, since she didn't warn Pearl that she was about to be married.

In addition, Pearl, Jackson, and Walling were also seen at a saloon in the city by owner Dave Wallingford and his porter, who also saw them get into a cab outside the bar.

The police eventually tracked down the cab driver — an African American man named George Johnson who said he'd been approached by Walling, who offered him $10 to drive Walling, a doctor, and a patient across the bridge into Kentucky.

They were driving away from the saloon when Johnson heard the woman moaning inside his cab. He tried to stop — not wanting to get involved in any trouble -- and tell his passengers to get out, but he said Walling threatened him with a pistol. Johnson drove on, but when they reached their destination, the two men took the woman into some woods, and George quickly fled back to Cincinnati.

To the authorities, the case against the two men seemed rock solid with an unbroken string of eyewitnesses who took them from the saloon to the farm in Kentucky, but as it was soon discovered, it wasn't as solid as it seemed.

JACKSON AND WALLING BOTH ADMITTED BEING at Wallingford's saloon with Pearl but claimed it had been one night earlier than the witnesses claimed. As further proof of that, both the tavern owner and George Johnson, the cab driver, said Scott Jackson was wearing a full beard when they saw him. He had been wearing a beard for at least six months, in fact.

The location in the orchard where Pearl's body was discovered by the farm workers.

But Jackson testified that he had shaved off his beard on the afternoon after he visited the tavern with Pearl and Walling. His barber corroborated this. As suspicious as it seemed that Jackson shaved his beard off on the day that Pearl died – completely changing his appearance -- he couldn't have been seen with a full beard in the saloon that night.

Also, when Pearl's body was found, she was wearing a checked house dress that her mother had made for her sister Jenny, handed down to Pearl when Jenny died. It was not a dress worn outside the house and would surely not have been worn to a saloon by someone as concerned about fashion as Pearl had been.

But it was the cab driver's story that turned out to be the most controversial. The first mystery is why the two would have hired him, essentially paying him to be a witness to the murder they planned to commit. George brought his story to the police two weeks after it occurred, which was plenty of time to study newspaper pictures of the prisoners, but even so, he had a hard time picking them out of a lineup. His reputation as a con artist and attention seeker also cast doubt on his story. Even his employer expressed his belief that he was lying.

And to throw in one more bit of doubt – after he testified at Scott Jackson's trial, George was tried in an unrelated case and convicted of perjury.

However, the district attorney went ahead with the prosecution, and both men were separately put on trial.

Jackson and Walling each testified in their own defense, but neither added anything to what they'd been saying all along – that they didn't

The jail where Jackson and Walling were held before their execution.

know what happened to Pearl after last seeing her three days before her death. Neither jury believed them, and both men were convicted and sentenced to death. Both appealed, but the verdicts were upheld, and a double hanging was scheduled for March 20, 1897.

But before they could be hanged, the press, public, and prosecution wanted the truth from them. They needed a confession to justify the executions, and besides that, they really wanted to know what they'd done with Pearl's head.

After their appeals were lost and the date for their executions drew closer, Jackson and Walling decided their only hope was to tell all and plead with the governor for mercy.

Specifically, Walling could be saved if Jackson told the truth. The public did not doubt Jackson's guilt, but there was a growing belief that Walling's crime had been a lesser one and had only been committed due to Jackson's influence.

Two days before the men were scheduled to hang, they were placed in a room together, given pencils and paper, and were ordered to write their confessions.

The separate statements told basically the same story, starting with Pearl's arrival in Cincinnati for an abortion. Walling said that he contacted May Smith, his girlfriend at the time, and asked for the name of a doctor willing to perform the illegal operation. She sent him to Dr. George Wagner of Bellevue, Kentucky, and arrangements were made to send Pearl to his house.

On January 29, Walling met Pearl in Cincinnati and gave her directions, sending Pearl to see Dr. Wagner by herself. The next day, Jackson and Walling delivered Pearl's suitcase to her in Bellevue. They returned the following day for the operation.

Both men stated there had been complications from the start. Pearl seemed to be in terrible pain, and so the doctor sent Jackson to the drugstore for something to give her some relief. It didn't help. Then the doctor opened her dress, injected her with some kind of clear liquid, and gave her whiskey to drink. Pearl became unconscious after that – and didn't wake up. Dr. Wagner soon announced that she was dead. Jackson and Walling then loaded her body into a wagon and took her to a secluded spot, where Dr. Wagner severed her head to prevent her from being identified. He had taken the head away with him, both men insisted. After that, the pair were driven across the bridge back into the city, and they went their separate ways.

No one was happy with the confessions. Jackson didn't admit guilt; he didn't exonerate Walling, and they'd also implicated a prominent doctor in their story. Obviously, he had nothing to do with any of it, the public insisted.

But not so fast.

When the confessions were printed in the newspaper, Walling's girlfriend, May Smith, came forward and confirmed that she'd sent Walling to Dr. Wagner. The druggist at the store near Wagner's home confirmed he'd filled a prescription for a painkiller on the night in question and added that he'd received telephone messages from Scott Jackson to Maude Wagner – the doctor's daughter – earlier that week.

The confessions were unpopular, but they were becoming more credible.

It also couldn't be denied that there had been rumors of the Wagner family's involvement in Pearl's death even before Jackson's trial. His attorneys subpoenaed Anna, Nellie, and Maude Wagner, the wife and two daughters of Dr. Wagner, but they were never called to testify. Dr. Wagner himself could not be subpoenaed because shortly after Pearl's body was found, he was committed to the Eastern Kentucky Asylum for the Insane.

These new additions to the story were sensational – but they also had some flaws.

May Smith was already a familiar figure in the case. Early on, she told the press that she had letters from Scott Jackson in which he admitted his guilt. The next day, though, she recanted, claiming she was drunk when she told the story. May probably had some knowledge of this mess but was considered too unreliable to testify for either the defense or the prosecution.

The druggist had already testified at Jackson's trial – he was one of several witnesses who could put Jackson, Walling, and Pearl together in Kentucky, but, during the trial, he'd made no mention of the prescription or the telephone messages when he was on the stand. It was also later discovered that he and Dr. Wagner had a longstanding feud.

The gallows on which Jackson and Walling were finally hanged.

The Wagners were outraged by the accusations, and they produced telegrams that proved that Dr. Wagner had been at his father-in-law's home many miles away on the night of Pearl's death. The doctor was so angry that he was pronounced cured of his insanity so he could go home and address the situation.

The confessions were sent to the governor, but he wasn't impressed. He saw no reason to overturn the death sentences of Jackson and Walling, and the hangings took place on March 20, just as they'd been scheduled.

The executions of Scott Jackson and Alonzo Walling essentially closed the book on the Pearl Bryan case, but I'm not convinced the story is really finished. Jackson and Walling were certainly not innocent of Pearl's death, but the evidence used to convict them was questionable at best.

Worse, despite the best efforts of the police and various search parties, Pearl's head was never found. Some legends even claim that Jackson and Walling were both offered life sentences instead of execution if they revealed the location of Pearl's head.

Both men refused.

Pearl's father waited for weeks before he allowed his daughter's remains to be buried without her missing head, but he eventually reconciled himself to the idea that it would never be found. Her coffin was removed from a temporary vault and was taken to her final resting place.

Pearl's sad and tragic journey had finally come to an end.

IF THERE WERE EVER A GHOST WHO WAS DOOMED to spend eternity in search of something, it would be the spirit of Pearl Bryan. And if the stories are to be believed, that's exactly what she continues to do well over a century after her death.

Just a short distance away from the orchard where Pearl was discovered was an abandoned slaughterhouse that had been built in the 1850s. For years, it was one of the largest in the region, but by the time of Pearl's death, it was empty and had been closed for several years. And while rumors spread that her missing head might have been tossed into a well on the property, it was never recovered – or even searched.

A photograph sold to tourists who came looking for the place where Pearl's body was found.

Why? The stories say that locals were too afraid of her ghost. It was said that Pearl's restless and unhappy spirit haunted the old building and the farm around it for many years, even after the structure was torn down in the 1920s.

The stories about the haunting continue to be told even today, and just as the ghostly tales about Pearl Bryan have managed to survive, so have the murder ballads that were created to tell her story.

THE BALLADS OF PEARL BRYAN HAVE NEVER BEEN AS widely recorded as some of the other stories in this book, and there was only a dozen or so versions collected or recorded.

The early versions of the ballad started circulating around 1913, when interest in her story was still high, and visitors were still going out to John Locke's orchard to see the murder scene for themselves and handing over a dime to see his gruesome photographs.

The initial versions of the song were adapted from an older tune called "The Jealous Lover," which inserted Pearl's name into the song. For example, the first verse went:

Down deep in a lonely valley,
Where the violets fade and bloom
There lies my own Pearl Bryan,
So silent in the tomb.

Other versions followed over the next few years, eventually becoming a ballad all its own. None of them raised any doubts about the fact that Jackson and Walling were guilty. They also served as a warning to the young women who listened to the song. This is one of the last verses in the original "Lovely Pearl Bryan" ballad:

Now all young girls take warning,
For all men are unjust,
It may be your truest lover,
You know not whom to trust.

Pearl Bryan died away from home,
On a dark and lonely spot,
My god, believe me girls,
Don't let this be your lot.

Other versions of the ballad followed, and most of them changed the facts in the story on a whim. Some have Pearl in love with Jackson, some with Walling, and others with Will Wood. One version even changed the names of the two villains to Jack and Walter.

One thing they all seemed to have in common was a verse or two that pleaded for the location of poor Pearl's missing head:

Next morning the people were excited,
They looked around and said,
'Here lays a murdered woman,
But where, oh where is her head?'

In came Pearlie's sister,
Fell down on her knees,
Pleading to Jackson,
'Give me sister's head, oh please!'

Jackson was so stubborn,
This is what he said,

*'When you meet your sister in heaven,
There will be no missing head!'*

In 1926, Pearl's ballad was recorded for the first time by folk singer Vernon Dalhart, who used the name Jep Fuller when he cut the record. Dalhart stuck close to the facts of the case, and his version became easily recognizable in the future because it dates the murder to "January 31," not "late in January," as other versions did.

A year later, the earlier version of the song was recorded by Charlie Poole and the North Carolina Ramblers. It drew from the old "Jealous Lover" song but tailored the lyrics to the way that Pearl was killed.

Charlie Poole and the North Carolina Ramblers released one of the first recorded versions of Pearl Bryan's ballad.

The first sheet music published for a Pearl Bryan ballad was printed in 1935. The arrangement was credited to Nick Manoloff, who made no claim to the lyrics. It's believed the lines were written by a folk artist named Vernon Dalhart, who may have been the composer of the version that served as a warning to young women.

In 1944, Doc Hopkins, then a popular radio performer in Kentucky, recorded his own version of the ballad. He mainly drew from Vernon Dalhart's lyrics but added a verse about the discovery of Pearl's corpse:

*It was in the month of January,
The people for miles around said,
'We've found this poor girl's body,
But we cannot find her head.'*

Hopkins also tweaked the final warning verse, using it to stress how unique Pearl's murder had been:

Now all young girls take warning,

Before it is too late,
From the worst crime ever committed,
In our old Kentucky state.

Bruce Buckley, a graduate student at Indiana University, included "Pearl Bryan" on his 1954 album *Ohio River Ballads*. Like Doc Hopkins, he used many of the Vernon Dalhart verses but couldn't resist adding a few macabre additions of his own. He included lyrics about Pearl's head being carried away in her own bag and then has Jackson and Walling practically dancing around her corpse in joy. Pear's parents couldn't have yet suspected their daughter's fate, he sings, but:

How sad it would have been to them,
To have heard Pearl's lonely voice,
At midnight in that lonely spot,
Where those two boys rejoiced.

Buckley also brought Pearl's sister into the story, getting down on her knees to beg for the location of Pearl's head. But when the men refused to answer, she delivered the last two lines in contempt:

Scott Jackson set a stubborn jaw,
Not a word would he have said,
'I'll meet my sister in Heaven,
Where they'll find her missing head.'

The most famous version of "Pearl Bryan" was recorded by the Phipps Family in 1965. It contained a chorus that was sung from the point of view of Pearl's mother:

The Phipps Family

Please tell me where's her head,
Please tell me where's her head,
Pearl Bryan was dead,
Can't find her head,
Walling and Jackson are hung.

It delights in putting the decapitation front and center:

The message brought back to her home,
    That poor Pearl Bryan was dead,
        Killed by Walling and Jackson,
            And they took away her head.

The Crooked Jades, caretakers of Pearl Bryan's ballad today.

The Phipps Family record inspired the Crooked Jades, a San Francisco bluegrass band, to tackle Pearl's ballad for their album *Seven Sisters: A Kentucky Portrait* in 2001.

Not only were they the first band to record the song in at least 50 years, but they seem to be the modern caretakers of the ballad today.

7. "MURDER OF THE LAWSON FAMILY"

THIS IS A STORY ABOUT A FAMILY – A FAMILY WHO NOT only ruined Christmas for many people but about whom there have probably been more versions of the murder ballad written them than any other family in the history of American tragedies.

And what a family it was – a farmer, his long-suffering wife, and his seven children. All those children had been looking forward to the holiday, but for most of them, they wouldn't live beyond Christmas Day of 1929. And to make matters worse for those children, their killer was their own father, who would also die before the sun went down that day.

The murder of the Lawson family shocked the residents of nearby Germanton, North Carolina, the people of the state, and the entire nation.

Why did it happen?

No one knows. It's likely this unknowing that spawned dozens of theories and rumors in the aftermath of the massacre and helped to inspire so many different versions of the murder ballad that went on to commemorate that terrible event for generations to come.

CHARLIE LAWSON WAS A SIMPLE MAN WITH SIMPLE needs. He owned a thriving tobacco farm outside of Germanton, and even as the country was slipping into the throes of the Great Depression, life was good for the Lawson family. Charlie was a hard-working father and husband. He kept his family fed, made sure his debts were paid, and kept a roof over the heads of his wife and children. Everything seemed right in the world for Charlie Lawson and his family, but as they say, looks can often be deceiving.

The Lawson family home near Germanton, North Carolina in 1929.

Soon after Charlie had bought his tobacco farm two years earlier, he became convinced that people in town were talking about him. They envied his business, his farms, and his fields. They gossiped about his family, his children, and his pretty wife. He knew they were talking about him because the voices told him so.

The voices. At first, they were just whispers, but soon the voices became so loud they couldn't be ignored. Charlie answered the voices quietly, under his breath. At first, his wife, Fannie, thought he was praying to himself or perhaps reciting Bible verses while working the fields. But then he started talking to himself at home, too.

Something, she thought, was not right with her husband. He'd had some "nervous troubles" for the past year, but things were stranger now.

The quiet, unassuming man had become more outgoing, especially with the children. He laughed and told jokes, which he never did. She might have been happy with those changes in her husband if they hadn't been so abrupt – and if Charlie had not been spending an inordinate amount of time with their 17-year-old daughter, Marie.

Something terrible was going to happen.

Charlie Lawson

CHARLES DAVIS LAWSON WAS BORN ON MAY 10, 1886, in Stokes County, North Carolina. He grew up on a tobacco farm. His father worked the land and as a boy, Charlie, along with his younger brothers, worked it, too. In 1911, Charlie married Fannie Manring, and as was common then, they started having children immediately. Their daughter Marie was born in 1912. She was quickly followed by James Arthur – who would grow into the nickname of "Buck" – in 1913, followed by William in 1914. Another daughter, Carrie, arrived in 1917.

Charlie's brothers, Marion and Elijah, decided to start their own farms and moved a short distance from their father's farm, settling near Germanton. In 1918, Charlie decided to follow them, packed up the family, and moved to the same small community. He found a farm to work as a sharecropper, but his dream was to own land.

Sharecropping could be a hard way of life. Charlie was essentially a tenant who worked the land and had to pay a share of the crop that he raised to the property owner. He was responsible for the cost of planting, seed, harvesting, and labor. After selling the crop, the landowner took his share of the profits as rent, and the farmer kept the rest. Depending on the season and how well the crop did, a sharecropper could make a little or make next to nothing. It was almost impossible to feed a family as a sharecropper, which was why Charlie wanted to own his own land someday. It was his dream, and he was determined to succeed.

More children followed. Although Charlie and Fannie lost their son, William, to pneumonia in November 1920, Maybell was born in May 1922, James in April 1925, and Raymond in February 1927.

After years of scrimping and saving every penny, Charlie bought a house and barn on Brook Cove Road – and the 128 acres that went with it -- just two months after Raymond was born. He borrowed $3,200 from the Wachovia Bank for the purchase, making a deal that set his mortgage payments at $500 a year. The farm was just outside Germanton and close to the Lawson and Manring families. It was important to Charlie and

Fannie to be near their families so their children could grow up with cousins and other children. That sentiment became even more significant in 1929 when another daughter, Mary Lou, was born.

The family began to make their primitive but sturdy cabin into a comfortable home. Soon, Charlie's tobacco crop was doing well enough that he started thinking about replacing the cabin with a modern home. He was respected by his neighbors, who all described him as a hard-working, sober, and honest man. He was strict with his wife and children -- often to the point of brutality – because Charlie had a bad temper. He quickly punished the children with a switch, an open hand, or his fists. Fannie was not exempt from his punishments. Neighbors saw it, as did family and friends, but in the 1920s, such behavior was rarely seen as abuse. It was far too common and either ignored or never talked about. Most believed it was no one's business what a man did in his own home.

In the summer of 1928, an incident occurred that likely affected the rest of Charlie's life – and led to the start of the whispers that turned to voices in his head.

He was digging a trench to drain water out of the basement of his tobacco pack house and using a mattock to do it – that wooden-handled digging tool favored by "Tom Dooley."

Tom Manring, Charlie's brother-in-law, later recalled that Charlie had marked off an area to be dug, which was next to a wire fence. He was concentrating on where he needed to dig and forgot about the fence. The mattock stuck on a strand of wire and sprang back, swinging up and hitting Charlie in the head.

The injury left Charlie with a nasty cut on his scalp and two spectacular black eyes. He didn't seem severely injured at the time, but several weeks later, he started seeing the local doctor for the "misery in his head." He began to suffer from blinding headaches and had trouble sleeping. Fannie often found him sitting in bed, rubbing his hands together and muttering. He would frequently sit calmly at night and then suddenly jump up and run around the house to be sure his guns were loaded – which was unnerving, to say the least.

The Lawsons' family doctor, Chester Helsabeck, later confirmed that Charlie suffered from "some sort of nervous trouble." The exact definition of what he considered "nervous trouble" will never be known. Local doctors in the small towns of North Carolina in the 1920s were not known for their psychiatric expertise.

Soon, Fannie wasn't the only one who noticed his odd behavior. Friends, neighbors, and relatives saw him walk away in the middle of a conversation or wander around the house at night. One night, Fannie woke up to find the bed next to her empty. She went outside and found Charlie kneeling alone in the middle of a harvested cornfield, where he seemed to be alternating between fervent prayer and periods of uncontrollable weeping. It was only after she convinced him to stand up and come back into the house that she realized he had brought his shotgun with him.

Charlie had always had a bad temper, which he took out on his wife and children, but his fits of rage grew worse after his injury. Buck was the only one of the boys old enough to help with the heavy work on the farm, but Charlie often found fault with the job that he did and would beat him with a wooden switch. Buck endured this until May 1929. By then, he was 16 years old, strong, and an inch taller than his father. Charlie confronted him and told him to stand still for a beating, and Buck refused.

"You'll never be man enough to whip me again," he told his father, took the switch from his hands, and snapped it in two. Charlie just looked at him and backed away.

Buck was now determined that Charlie would never beat him or any other family member again. He started sleeping in his clothes, ready to defend the rest of the family in case Charlie had one of his violent fits in the middle of the night. He was strong enough to control Charlie, who had no choice but to accept that this son was bigger and stronger than him. Buck had become the family's protector, a responsibility that wore on him and haunted his sleep.

THE SUMMER OF 1929 TURNED INTO FALL. ASIDE from Charlie's occasional outbursts of temper – now muted by the watchful eye of Buck – the Lawson family went on with their lives as they always had. They tended the fields, worked the garden, and cared for their livestock. The older children attended school and cared for the little ones, and overall, their lives were happy ones.

Autumn came and went with relative calm. Buck stayed vigilant, and Charlie managed to hold his temper. Winter arrived, and the days got colder. The farm chores changed, and the children spent more time indoors. Then, a little less than two weeks before Christmas, Charlie announced that he had a surprise for the family, but he had to take them to town for it. He was happy, almost giddy around the children, which was completely unlike him.

Fannie saw it, and she began to worry again.

The Lawson family photograph, taken shortly before the Christmas 1929 murders.

Any trip to town was exciting for farm children, but with the promise of a surprise, the littlest ones could hardly contain themselves. They piled into the truck and rode into Germanton, where Charlie sent them on a shopping trip. He told them to pick out new sets of Sunday clothes, whatever they wanted, no matter the cost. Many of the children had never had new clothes before. Hand-me-downs were common with so many children in the family, each outgrowing clothing that could be passed on to the next, so this was a special event.

After they had picked out new clothes and changed into them, Charlie revealed the rest of his surprise – they were going to visit the town's photographer for their first family photograph. They excitedly lined up for the portrait and then waited patiently for the photo to be taken and for the plates to develop.

It must have been a happy occasion, yet the existing photograph shows a family that seems haunted by the world's cares. Buck, a boy of only 16, yet looking like a powerful young man in his 20s, seems already worn down by the weight of protecting his family. None of the children, save for a slight smile on Carrie's face, seem glad to be posing for the portrait. The eyes of Fannie, who is holding Mary Lou, the baby at four months old, are filled with suspicion, while Marie, a beautiful young woman who had a boyfriend and was likely planning to move away from her family's home soon, seems stunned. If some versions of the Lawson family story are to be believed, Marie may have been hiding a secret from her family – a secret that some say led to her death.

But it's the eyes of Charlie Lawson that are the most captivating in this family portrait. He is looking at something just off to the right of the camera. Was it the photographer or someone else in the room? Perhaps someone was talking to him in a voice that no one else could hear.

We'll never know, of course, but in hindsight, there is one thing that we can say about Charlie Lawson's eyes – they are the eyes of a madman.

As Christmas approached, the children grew more excited. They knew they couldn't expect many presents, especially since they had already received new clothes, but Christmas Day was always special. There would be lots of food, and Christmas was traditionally a time for special dishes that were enjoyed only once a year. Family and friends would spend the day visiting back and forth, and Christmas supper would be shared with the Manrings, Fannie's parents, and family.

As often happens in much of the country, but not usually in North Carolina, it snowed on Christmas Eve. By Christmas morning, there was a six-inch blanket of snow outside. The day started with a hearty breakfast shared with Charlie's nephew, Sanders, who had stayed the night.

At the same time, another Lawson family was also having breakfast a few miles away. It would be one they would never forget. John, one of Charlie's brothers, had a premonition that something terrible would happen. He was not a superstitious man, but he just knew that something was wrong. The feeling was so strong that he started to cry and had to leave the table. He tried to convince himself that he was being foolish, but he couldn't shake the dread that had overcome him.

He would soon receive news that proved his premonition was correct.

AFTER BREAKFAST AT THE HOME OF THE OTHER Lawsons, Charlie, Buck, and Sanders joined a group of other farmers for a friendly shooting competition. They set up bottles and cans to bang away at, all the while pointing out the fresh rabbit tracks that could be seen in the snow. Several men mentioned trying to bag one for the stewpot later in the morning.

Inside the house, Fannie and Marie – listening to the sounds of shots ringing out in the woods – prepared the family's festive evening meal. Marie made a cake for the occasion, coating it with white frosting and dotting the entire surface with raisins as decoration. She placed it in the center of the table – hopefully out of reach of little brothers' probing fingers – and then turned her thoughts to the date she had that evening. She and her boyfriend, Charlie Hampton, planned to attend the Christmas play at Palmyra Church in Germanton. Marie wanted to look her best. She put out a bowl of water to wash her hair and placed her curlers in front of the fire to warm them up.

Fannie kept busy, dividing her time between the stove and the needs of little Mary Lou, playing in her crib. She darted back and forth, with a wooden spoon in hand, stirring and preparing.

Outside, Charlie, Buck, and the others continued the shooting match, joshing and teasing each other after every hit or miss. Charlie was still in good spirits – almost manic, the other men recalled.

Cooking smells began drifting out of the house around 11:30, which started everyone thinking about lunch. One by one, the men drifted off toward their farms, and the hefty meals awaited them at home. Soon, only Charlie, Buck, and Sanders remained.

Charlie reminded the two boys about his plans to go rabbit hunting in the afternoon and suggested they walk into Germanton to buy some more shells. It was doubtful that any of the local stores would be open, but Charlie assured them they could find someone who would open long enough for them to buy a box of shells. He really had a taste for rabbit, he grinned at them, but he needed more shells if he planned to shoot some.

Buck and Sanders readily agreed. It was a nice walk into town, following the railroad tracks. They could go and be back in plenty of time to eat. With a wave, they started toward town.

Charlie watched them go. His shotgun was resting on his shoulder, and his hand was buried in the deep pocket of his winter coat. It was loaded with shotgun shells. They rattled together as they moved through his fingers. He had lied to his son. He had plenty of shells – more than enough for what he planned to do next.

For what the voices told him that he needed to do next.

About an hour after Buck and Sanders left, Fannie glanced at the clock on the mantle. She saw that it was almost 1:00 P.M. She had arranged for Carrie and Maybell to visit their Uncle Elijah's family for Christmas lunch, so she called the girls over, buttoned them into their winter coats, and sent them out the door. It was a short walk to Elijah's house.

Marie was still busy with her hair. James and Raymond happily played on the floor in front of the fireplace, and Mary Lou was content in her crib.

Fannie finally relaxed for the first time that day. The cooking and dishes were done, and the house was in order. She could rest a bit before she had to get things ready for supper.

The barn where Charlie waited for his daughters as they walked to their uncle's house on Christmas Day.

Carrie and Maybell's trip to their uncle's house took them along the old stagecoach road that ran the length of the Lawsons' farm. Trudging through the snow, they passed the family's wood pile and the tobacco pack house that Charlie had been draining when he was struck in the skull by the mattock. The girls followed the curve of the road toward the first of Charlie's two barns. The barn stood only a few hundred yards from the house, and – like all the farm's other large buildings – it faced directly toward the stage road. As they rounded the road's sharp curve, the girls could see the barn looming ahead of them.

They had no idea that their father was waiting for them there with the shrill voices echoing in his head.

Charlie was standing out of sight behind the northwest corner of the barn with a 12-gauge, double-barreled shotgun and a 25-20 rifle. Hearing his daughters' excited laughter as they approached, he pressed himself against the barn's wooden wall, ensuring he could not be seen. He gripped the shotgun tightly in his hands and waited for the girls to pass by. As soon as they had, he carefully aimed at Carrie's back and pulled the trigger. As she started to fall, he fired the second barrel at Maybell. A cloud of red mist spread over the snow as she fell to the ground.

Charlie snatched the rifle and walked over to the girls. Maybell was perfectly still, but he could see that Carrie was still breathing. He fired a single rifle bullet into her head. Then he took a piece of scrap wood from outside the barn and bludgeoned the two little girls' heads until they were nothing more than bloody, unrecognizable masses.

He stood there for a moment, the board dripping gore onto the snow, and looked down at his daughters. The voices shouted at him. Then, he tossed the plank aside and picked up each girl in turn, carried them into the barn, and laid them on the floor side-by-side. He put a stone under each of their heads as a pillow, crossed their arms on their chests, and drew their eyelids closed. He looked lovingly back at the two dead girls as he latched the barn door shut and started walking toward the house.

As he walked, he loaded two more shells into the shotgun.

When he approached the cabin, he saw Fannie outside. She had gone out into the yard to gather more firewood for the stove. She turned toward Charlie as she started back to the house, and he raised the shotgun and fired directly into Fannie's chest. The wood in her arms flew into the air, and she fell dead before she hit the ground. Charlie dragged her to the house and dropped her on the front porch. Her skull knocked hollowly when her head struck the boards.

In the house, Marie heard the shotgun roar and looked out to see her father dragging her mother toward the house. Fannie was covered in blood. Marie began to scream. The front door banged open, and Charlie fired the second barrel. The load slammed into her chest. Pellets pierced her heart and shattered the mantle clock behind her. Both died at the same time.

The two youngest boys -- James, 4, and Raymond, 2 – had been quietly playing on the floor when Charlie burst through the door. After the door slammed open, the thundering blast of the shotgun, and Marie falling to the floor, the boys began to scream. They ran to hide, but not before Charlie saw them.

He went after James first. The little boy ran to his bed and crawled underneath, getting as close to the far wall as he could. But Charlie reached under the bed, pulled James out, and slammed the butt of the shotgun into his head until his skull shattered.

While James' screams were filling the house, Raymond had frantically scrambled behind the stove, trying to wedge himself into the corner. Charlie first tried to pry him out with the shotgun, using the barrel to try and lever the stove far enough from the wall to get at the boy. As the left barrel began to bend out of shape, Charlie gave up and started clawing for his son, ignoring the heat from the stove, which scorched his skin. He snagged Raymond's shirt and jerked the boy from his hiding place. As Raymond tumbled onto the floor, Charlie slammed the butt of the ruined shotgun into his face, fracturing his skull, just as he had done to James.

Only one child remained alive in the house – baby Mary Lou. She was lying in her crib, screaming at the sounds of terror around her. Thankfully, she was too young to understand what was happening. Charlie raised the shotgun and crushed her tiny skull with the butt of the weapon. He

The scene inside the Lawson home after the murders. Pools of blood can be seen on the floor just inside the door.

slammed it down on her head over and over again. She was now reunited with her mother, brothers, and sisters in death.

Frantic and soaked with blood, Charlie went to work preparing the bodies to be found. The voices warned him that family members could start arriving at any time for a Christmas visit – he had no time to spare.

He dragged Fannie inside, closed the door, and satisfied himself that his entire family was dead. He laid Fannie out on the floor and placed Mary Lou in her arms. He then laid Marie, James, and Raymond alongside their mother. Charlie climbed the narrow staircase to the house's attic room, where the children had slept. He collected four pillows, brought them downstairs with him, and gently placed one beneath each of their heads. Just as he had with Carrie and Maybell, he closed their eyes and crossed their arms on their chests in a position of quiet repose.

Charlie sat down for a moment on the bed that he had shared with Fannie in the house's main room and looked at what he had done. He believed at that moment that he had saved the souls of his family. He truly believed that his wife and children – lying on the floor in spreading pools of blood – would rest in peace.

"Almost done," he sighed to the voices. "Almost done."

ONE OF CHARLIE'S BROTHERS, ELIJAH, AND HIS two sons, Claude and Carroll, had spent their Christmas morning hunting rabbits south of the Lawson farm. Claude had killed a rabbit, which now hung proudly from his belt. By 2:00 P.M., all their ammunition was gone, and they started for home. Since their route across the railroad tracks would take them close to Charlie and Fannie's house, Elijah suggested they stop there and wish the family a merry Christmas. When they got within sight of the house, Claude ran excitedly ahead and bounded onto the porch, ready to greet everyone with a loud holiday greeting.

He threw open the door with a shout on his lips, but the words froze before he could speak. What he saw inside the house was more than his young mind could comprehend. Years later, he would remember nothing in that room except for one thing – blood. He stepped back from the door with no recollection of leaving it open or slamming it to try and make it all go away.

Elijah's view of the carnage was through the front window. He saw the blood, and now he noticed the drag marks on the porch. Something was terribly wrong at Charlie's house. It was obvious that everyone was dead, and they had not been dead for long. The blood that was pooled on the floor was still wet, and it was dripping between the floorboards.

Elijah's first thought was that an intruder had entered the cabin and, for some unknown reason, had murdered the family. But where was Charlie? Realizing that they had walked into something horrible – and with no ammunition to defend themselves if the killer was still around – Elijah and his boys ran for their lives.

Thrashing through the snow, they reached the top of the hill overlooking the Miller farm, which was closest to Charlie's house. Elijah yelled down to Mr. Miller, telling him to call the sheriff and alert the neighbors – "Someone has killed Charlie's whole family!"

Word spread, voices carried the news, and the telephone lines buzzed with panic. Soon, farmers from all around were grabbing their shotguns and converging on the Lawson farm. They wanted to see what had happened and what they could do to help. Dr. Helsabeck was summoned from town, and Sheriff John Taylor followed him.

The first arrivals saw the bloodstained snow outside the house. Someone had obviously been shot there. But it was the bodies they found inside that stunned the men. One newspaper account reported, "The bodies of Marie and James were lying with their heads near the bureau. Raymond's body, in a pool of blood, was to the right, the mother's body at the foot of the cradle. There was a big puddle of blood in front of the fireplace, and in this blood were several combs similar to those used by women to hold their hair."

Photographs that were taken of the blood-spattered room tell their own story. Even with the bodies removed from the frame, the house was horrifying. A dark semi-circle of blood covered the floorboards around the fireplace like a ragged and torn rug. Marie and stained pillows were propped against the bureau. The black-and-white photographs showed a black spray of gore at the head of Mary Lou's crib. There was another grim stain on the bed next to the fireplace, left there when Charlie sat down to contemplate the horror he had unleashed.

One eyewitness later recalled, "There was blood all over the place. I mean blood everywhere! I haven't forgotten a bit of it."

As the news of the murders spread throughout the county, more and more people arrived. Worried men left home with instructions for their wives and children to prop chairs under the doorknobs – few people in the area had locks on their doors – and to let no one inside until they returned home. There was, they believed, a deranged killer on the loose.

At this point, Charlie, Buck, Carrie, and Maybell were still missing. Sheriff Taylor began organizing men into a search party to find them. First, though, they had to ensure the killer was not hiding in the house's attic. It was the one place where no one had looked. The only access to the attic was through a narrow, enclosed staircase, making anyone climbing those stairs an easy victim for a killer waiting above. Deputy Robert Walker and a local doctor named Bynum carefully climbed those stairs with guns in hand but found nothing in the attic except a few bloody footprints. Searching the house downstairs, others in the search party discovered Charlie's rifle but saw that both his shotguns were missing.

A neighbor named Steven Hampton found the bodies of Carrie and Maybell in the barn. He first discovered blood and drag marks in the snow and followed the trail into the building. As the men looked around the barn, they found a trampled spot in the snow where their killer had waited in ambush for the two girls, along with a discarded plank of wood with one end soaked in fresh blood. A little blue hat that had belonged to Carrie, now crushed and blood-soaked, was found near her body on the floor of the barn.

It wasn't long before word finally reached the farm that Buck was in town with his cousin, which meant that only Charlie was missing. Had he been killed, too?

Someone in the search party spotted tracks in the snow leading away from the tobacco barn where Carrie and Maybell had been found. They veered off toward the trees and the creek beyond. The footprints were those of a full-grown man; from the length of his stride, he had apparently been running. Cautiously, the men followed the tracks into the first thicket of trees, across an open field, and into the woods again. It was there, just after 4:00 P.M., that they found Charlie Lawson's body. He was slumped against a tree a few hundred yards away from the house and barn.

The scene around him was a strange one. Charlie had evidently been in the woods for some time, walking around and around a single tree. He had circled the tree so many times that the snow had melted from the path he had walked. He eventually sat down on the ground at the tree's base, put his single-barreled shotgun to his chest, and pulled the trigger. He had a gaping wound in his body, and the gun had fallen on the ground beside him.

Four men picked up Charlie's body, each taking a limb, and hauled him back to the farm. His suicide confirmed what the lawmen and Charlie's neighbors had started to suspect – that Charlie had finally snapped and murdered his entire family. The coroner's jury, which Dr. Helsabeck convened, agreed. Sheriff Taylor searched the dead man's pockets and found several bills of sale recently struck with tobacco buyers in the area. Two of them had Charlie's penciled handwriting on the back. One note cryptically read, "Trouble will cause." The other began, "Blame no-one but..." Everyone assumed the missing word was "me," but no one could say for sure. He never finished writing it.

A few believed that Charlie had started to explain his actions that day and then decided against it. Perhaps, in the end, he decided to leave it a mystery. No one will ever know what was going on in Charlie's head when he decided to slaughter his family. When his body was found, he had $58 in his pocket, and the tobacco paperwork showed that his farm was doing quite well. Whatever problems had led to Charlie's breakdown, money trouble was not among them.

Why did Charlie spare Buck from the murder spree, intentionally sending his son away that day? Was it because he loved him more? Or did he want his son to suffer as the family's only surviving member? This seems to be the most likely scenario – a bit of petty revenge against the boy who stood up to him. He knew that Buck would have to live with his failure to protect his family for the rest of his life. Buck would have died to protect his mother, brothers, and sisters, and Charlie knew it. He was the only obstacle in Charlie's twisted plan. He sent Buck off to town, and the boy went willingly, never realizing that he would never see his family alive again.

Charlie Hampton, Marie's boyfriend, found Buck on the snowy streets of Germanton after he learned of the murders. He had to break the news that his entire family had been dead. Buck was brought straight back to the farm, where his uncles and their families tried to comfort him as best they could. "I don't know why he did it," Buck wept to one of the reporters on the scene. "I guess it's just like they say – he must've suddenly gone crazy."

There were no formal crime scene arrangements in those days and no official police clean-up crew either, so it was left to Charlie's relatives and neighbors to help Sheriff Taylor deal with the aftermath of the massacre. Women from nearby farms brought their bedsheets to give the bodies a decent covering. Volunteers dug the Lawson grave at Browder's Cemetery, excavating a trench that would hold eight caskets. Mary Lou would be buried in her mother's arms.

The snow of the past few days had made the steep road leading up to the Lawson house impassable for most cars, so all the bodies had to be carried down to the waiting hearses by hand. Boley Tuttle, a local hardware store owner, took Mary Lou's battered little body in his arms and carried her gently down the hill. Years later, he recalled, "It was just awful. I barely made it to the hearse."

The bodies were taken to Madison, about 13 miles to the east, where an embalming firm – run by T. Butler Knight – and Yelton's Funeral Parlor were waiting to care for them. Dr. Helsabeck was waiting there, as well. He worked through the night to complete his formal examination of the corpses.

Sheriff Taylor's brother, a newly qualified pathologist at Johns Hopkins Hospital in Baltimore, was visiting his family for Christmas by a remarkable stroke of luck. Dr. James Taylor volunteered to assist Dr. Helsabeck with the autopsies. The examinations, combined with what Dr. Helsabeck had seen at the farm, allowed the two men to determine the causes of death in each case – and to piece together each step of the massacre.

They never knew, of course, about the voices in Charlie's head. Only Fannie knew they existed, and she only told a few people. But it was clear to everyone that Charlie Lawson had gone insane.

ON THE MORNING AFTER THE MURDERS, THE massacre at the Lawson farm made front-page news in at least 19 different states. Wire services, like the Associated Press, sent the story out from New York to

California. Radio broadcasts and local gossip spread the story even further.

By December 27, newspapers were illustrating their stories with a copy of the family portrait Charlie had so thoughtfully provided a few days before things went terribly wrong. On the same front page, they also carried a crime scene photograph that showed the family's living room painted with blood.

The newspaper and radio coverage brought scores of curiosity-seekers to the scene. Everyone wanted a piece of history. There was so much dried blood in the house that one of the volunteers who helped clean up the crime scene had to scoop it up with a coal shovel. He dumped it into an old tin wash tub, and a neighbor helped him carry it outside. They dug a shallow grave out of decency and poured the blood into the ground before covering it. While they were doing it, he later recalled, a visitor was busy funneling Fannie's blood from the house's porch into a little souvenir jar.

The morbid visitors looted the cabin. Even the tree that Charlie leaned against as he took his own life was stripped bare within a few hours of the discovery of his body. The crowds wanted something to take with them – something to say that they had been at the scene of the tragedy. They took Charlie's guns, the bricks from the house that was later demolished, and even the raisins from the cake Marie had baked a few hours before her death.

The crowds also turned the funeral into a nightmare.

There would be no formal church service. There were to be just a few words from two pastors at Browder's cemetery and burial in the mass grave that had been dug there by neighbors. The ceremony was scheduled to start at noon on December 27.

Six hearses were loaded with bodies at Yelton's in Madison that morning. The funeral parlor had been hard-pressed to handle so many bodies at once, so even though the family had wanted white coffins for everyone, a light gray one had to be substituted in Charlie's case. Someone scrounged up a piano stool and a small table to supplement Yelton's five coffin stands for the viewing at the cemetery. Lacking enough hearses, they transported little Raymond's casket in a private car.

Rows of men – with only a few women in the crowd – lined the sidewalks to watch the hearses pull away. Hundreds of tourists were waiting at the cemetery to watch them arrive. Automobiles had crowded the highway coming into town and were parked several miles up the road. People walked through mud, water, and wet grass to be close to the show.

Father And Seven Of Family He Slew To Lie Side By Side

Charles D. Lawson Brutally Murdered Nearest Kin in Fit of Insanity on Christmas Day.

Special to The Charlotte Observer

WALNUT COVE, Dec. 26.—Preparations were being made today for the mass funeral tomorrow of Charles D. Lawson, well known Stokes county farmer who went suddenly insane Wednesday afternoon, and his wife and six children who were slain by him before he took his own life. The only member of the family left alive is a son, Arthur, 19, who was visiting his uncle in Germantown at the time of the tragedy.

News of the murders was printed in papers all over the country, noting the fact that the bodies of the family would all be laid to rest side-by-side.

They soon filled the surrounding woods, too. Reporters circulated through the crowd and found onlookers who had traveled more than 100 miles to view the funeral. The newspapers agreed that at least 5,000 people turned up at Browder's that day. Some watched in silence, and some came and went, taking the opportunity to visit the Lawson house while in the area.

The quarter-mile dirt road leading from the highway to the cemetery was too wet for cars, and soon the highway was also impassable. It had not been designed for so much traffic, and the melting snow soaked the ground. Dozens of cars became stuck and had to be pushed out. The traffic and muddy conditions caused the hearses from Madison to arrive more than an hour late.

The vehicles got as close to the cemetery as they could, and then the pallbearers – friends of Charlie's from better days -- had to shoulder the caskets the rest of the way. Sheriff Taylor, who had already recruited some men to keep an area next to the grave free of spectators, pushed open a path through the crowd for the pallbearers to use. The seven coffins were laid out in a line, starting with Charlie's full-size casket and tapering down to Raymond's tiny one at the other end of the row. Charlie had been a member of the Primitive Baptist Church, whose elders Watt Tuttle and

Boss Brown conducted the service at the graveside. "Why this thing has occurred," Brown said, "I do not know."

The coffins were then opened so anyone who wished to do so could say one last goodbye. Seeing the battered faces of the family was too much for Buck. He collapsed in grief and had to be helped to recover so the viewing could continue. His distress was made worse by what would haunt him for the rest of his life – if he had not fallen for Charlie's ruse in sending him to Germanton, he might have been able to stop his father before the killing ever started.

As friends consoled the heartbroken boy, a line formed on each side of the coffins, and people started slowly filing past. It took more than three hours for everyone present to get a look.

As the afternoon light faded, the coffins were sealed once more and were lowered into their shared grave. For the mourners – and the ghouls – gathered at the graveside, it was time to go home.

BUCK, HIS UNCLES, COUSINS, AND RELATIVES WERE NOT the only ones haunted by the murders – the entire community was confused, angry, saddened, and stunned by the tragedy. The mystery of why Charlie had done it hung over them like a dark, angry cloud. It was a topic of conversation at every dinner table, over coffee at the local diner, and across every neighborhood fence. People wanted to know – they needed to know – why he had committed such a horrible act. Rumors spread. Stories were concocted. Everyone had an idea, but no one had any real answers.

Most believed that Charlie's head injury was at the root of the murders – he had been driven insane by the blow to the head. Others thought that since the murders coincided with the start of the Great Depression, some leaped to the conclusion that Charlie's farm had gone bust, but that wasn't true.

The craziest theories were, of course, the ones people talked about the most – namely, that Charlie hadn't killed anyone and his suicide was staged to make him look guilty. They couldn't believe that someone they'd known all their lives could go crazy and kill his entire family.

Others theorized that Charlie might have witnessed some organized crime activity, perhaps a mob murder. He and his family must have been killed in retaliation, they claimed. But since Stokes County wasn't exactly a hotbed for gangsters, this theory didn't hold water either.

The discussion about Charlie's motives went on for years. Then, six decades after the massacre, the rumors turned even more sinister. Stella

Boles, born in 1915, was Marion Lawson's daughter, and she'd had a front-row seat for everything that went on in the family before and after the murders. She confirmed some dark Stokes County rumors by telling the story of a meeting of Lawson women that took place on December 27, 1929, when she was 14 years old. Ida and Nina Lawson, who had each married one of Charlie's brothers, were among the group. Years later, Stella questioned her Aunt Nina about what was said that day.

Nina told her that Fannie had discovered that Marie, Charlie's daughter, was pregnant, and to make matters worse, Charlie himself was the father of the baby. Charlie had warned his daughter that if she told her mother or anyone else about the baby, "there would be some killing done." Fannie had discovered the incest in her family just before Christmas and had confided in Ida and Nina. She agonized over what she should do. Even years after the fact, Nina insisted that Stella keep the information to herself, so Stella did not reveal the secret until 1990.

A few years later, Stella's story was confirmed by Ella May Johnson, who had been Marie's best friend. Ella May said that Marie had slept over at the Johnsons' house a week or two before Christmas 1929 and confided that she was pregnant by her father. Soon, others grudgingly admitted that they had heard the rumor.

It's certainly possible that the shame over such a horrible misdeed could have helped to spark Charlie's killing spree, and I'm also sure that a family of that era would have guarded such a secret very closely. Hill Hampton, Charlie's closest friend and neighbor, later admitted that he knew of serious problems going on within the family. He knew the nature of the problem, but it was personal, and it was not his place to reveal it.

Hill Hampton was as shocked as anyone would be to learn such a thing – then or now. He likely felt it hard to believe that someone with Charlie's religious convictions would do what he was accused of, but he didn't know that Charlie was no longer himself by this time. The voices had started long before he raped his daughter – they likely told him to do it – and Charlie may not have even been in control of his actions by then.

What if the voices told Charlie that his only way out was to destroy all the evidence and the witnesses to his misdeed?

And Charlie did it. The unending voices in his head wouldn't stop until he was finished.

In the end, the only thing that we really know about what was going on in the mind of Charlie Lawson is that we will never know. It was then – and remains – an unsolvable mystery.

WITH THE FUNERAL BEHIND THEM, CHARLIE'S BROTHER, Marion, started worrying about financial matters. Buck was the next in line to inherit the farm, but that was a mixed blessing since that also put him in line to inherit Charlie's mortgage payments. Buck was only 16, so he could hardly be expected to run the place, so this meant that another source of income needed to be found.

Marion remembered the huge crowds that had come to town to watch the funeral. There were still at least 90 carloads of strangers showing up at the Lawson house every single day to look around. There was no indication that interest in the murders would fade away anytime soon.

Most of the family's property was still in the house, just as they had left it. Though relatives tried to watch over the place, many things had already been stolen. They had their own farms to operate, though, and couldn't be on hand all the time. The neighbors weren't much help. Most of them took exception to the "ghouls," and several fights had started when sightseers were run off the property. The most serious involved a man who needed three stitches in his arm after being slashed by a neighbor's knife one night. He had been peering into the window of the Lawson house. Clearly, a long-term solution was needed.

After consulting some friends, Marion came up with a decision. Along with his sons and a few other relatives, they went out one morning and started planting posts in a circle around the house and tobacco barn. They strung a heavy chicken wire between the posts, effectively fencing off the murder scene. Some neighbors believed that Marion was trying to keep the curiosity-seekers away, but he had a much different idea.

Taking advantage of the rabid interest in the killings, he decided to charge visitors 25 cents each to take a guided tour of the property. The cash raised would go to Buck to help him make ends meet, make the mortgage payments, and, hopefully, ensure that the farm stayed in the Lawson family. Buck agreed to the scheme, even though Fannie's family was appalled by the idea, as were Charlie's other brothers. They tried to talk Marion out of it, but he refused to listen.

The new "attraction" was opened on January 15, 1930, and the steep admission price failed to deter visitors – sometimes, as many as 100 people showed up every day. Marion recruited friends and family to staff the cabin tours. He supplemented the income from admissions by offering refreshments and a pack of five souvenir photographs that visitors could buy before they left.

Members of the Lawson family took advantage of the notoriety of the murders, opening the house for tours and selling the rights to the story to be printed in books.

Fannie's family, the Manrings, made one more attempt to get through to Marion about the tastelessness of the tours. They met with him and begged him to stop, but Marion was unmoved. He told them people would come to see the place anyway, so someone should benefit from the attention. The tours continued.

Locals – especially people in Germanton – complained, too. They said that the tours were shameful, and that Marion was embarrassing them all. A committee approached him and asked him to stop. Again, Marion refused.

Interest in the murders dropped a little after the first few months but remained steady for a surprisingly long time. By then, several murder ballads had been written that told the story of the Lawson massacre, which helped keep bringing tourists to the door.

We'll come back to those in a moment.

The site had become a legitimate attraction to the people who came to see it, like an alligator farm or an amusement park. They paid their admission and could walk right in and see the bloodstains on the floors and walls without having to sneak in after dark. So, they kept coming – for a long time.

After several months, the locals stopped complaining. There hadn't been any real trouble, and while they still considered it to be bad taste, the tourists who showed up also stopped in town to buy gas, eat in the diners, shop in the stores, and stay at the new hotel. Soon, Germanton was thriving during a time when most of America was suffering from the Depression – all thanks to Charlie Lawson.

In time, interest in the Lawson farm started to fall off, but the 1930s saw a rise in popularity in traveling carnivals and sideshows, so the Lawson murders were taken on the road. Parts of the murder scene were sold off to a sideshow promoter, who took the artifacts on tour. Whatever the family wouldn't sell, he simply duplicated and passed them off as the real thing – like Charlie's guns and Marie's raisin cake.

The Lawson family sideshow toured the country for years, appearing along with Bonnie and Clyde's blood-spattered and bullet-ridden "death car," a mummy that purported to be the "real" John Wilkes Booth, and other morbid attractions. Years passed, and sideshows vanished, along with their attractions. No one knows what happened to the artifacts from the Lawson house – they disappeared many years ago.

THE LAWSON FARM ATTRACTION CLOSED, AND THE sideshow disappeared to likely gather dust in a barn somewhere, but stories of the Lawsons lived on. The subject of the tales now turned from murder to ghosts. People started claiming that some family members did not rest in peace.

Rumors spread of eerie happenings that were occurring in the Lawson house after dark, long after the tour guides had gone home and the doors had been locked behind them. Articles appeared in newspapers that freely stated that the house was haunted. A new batch of curiosity-seekers began parking on the road at night, watching the house, unsure of what they might see. Would it be the mysterious lights people spoke of dancing about in the darkness? Or would they hear the reported moans and cries that others had reported echoing in the stillness of the night?

The local chapter of a fraternal order that Charlie once belonged to – the Junior Order of United American Mechanics – began using their most infamous member as part of their initiation ceremony. After the stories of the haunting began to circulate, new members were told to go out to the Browder cemetery and take a rock from the Lawson grave. After that, he had to go to the abandoned Lawson house and walk around the property with only a lantern to light the way. If the prospective member was brave enough to pass the initiation, he was considered worthy of becoming a "Junior."

Decades passed, and the house fell into decay. Children and adults wandered the property, exploring and sometimes looking for ghosts. Many who ventured onto Charlie's old farm claimed to leave the place with a feeling of deep sadness. Many inexplicably burst into tears. Photographs taken there were often found to be blank when developed. Batteries failed in the flashlights that were used for nocturnal explorations.

By 1980, the Lawson house was gone. Some of the wood was salvaged for a small bridge that was built a few miles away, but aside from that, it had vanished. The sites of the house and tobacco barn were plowed under. There is nothing left to see today.

But, even so, it is said that the ghosts remain. Owners of the land next door have told chilling tales in recent years about the spirits of a little boy and girl who began showing up on her doorstep soon after moving into her home.

Over the next few weeks, the children kept coming back. After seeing them several more times, she started investigating and spoke with a local historian – which is how she first heard about the Lawson murders on the neighboring farm.

During the discussions, the owner was shown the Lawson family portrait, taken shortly before the family was killed. She immediately recognized her two visitors in the photograph – Maybell and James Lawson. There was no doubt about it, she told the historian. The mystery was solved, but the sightings continued. In fact, they still go on today.

According to local recollection, the Lawson children often crossed the field where a bed and breakfast now stands so that they could play with the neighbor children. They continue to make this journey, even after death. Their lives violently ended, but perhaps they have finally found some peace.

There is also a lingering haunting in the nearby town of Madison. Long before it was the dry goods store that it is today, it was the local undertaker's parlor, and it was here that the bodies of the Lawson family were prepared for burial. The owners believe that Charlie's ghost haunts the place. Footsteps have frequently been heard in the empty back room, and the owners – and customers – have glimpsed Charlie as he wanders about the place.

There are also said to be ghosts that linger at the Browder Family Cemetery, where the entire Lawson family was buried in a single mass grave. Voices and the sounds of weeping have been heard in the graveyard, and local legend has it that if you drive out to the cemetery at night, park outside, sprinkle baby powder on the back of your car, and wait – the handprints of the Lawson family children will appear in the powder.

It's been nearly a century since Charlie Lawson went insane on Christmas Day and killed his entire family. The ghost stories associated with that event remain today as proof that those who live in the area where it all happened have never been able to forget that terrible day.

And Christmas has never been celebrated in quite the same way as it was before 1930.

SONGWRITERS AND POETS WERE AMONG THOSE who pounced on the story of the Lawson Family Massacre once news began to spread of the tragedy.

And it's easy to see why people were so morbidly fascinated by the brutal crime. Charlie slaughtered his family on Christmas Day, a date that was guaranteed to add a little sadness to any murder. He was a father who killed his children, which grabbed even more attention, especially since three of those children were less than five years old. Then there's the strange mixture of savagery and tenderness that he showed, bludgeoning the children to death and then lovingly placing pillows under their shattered heads. Although incest and insanity have both been offered as explanations for the murders, we'll never really know what made Charlie do it.

The horror of the massacre was stoked by the murder ballads that followed in its wake. The most significant was Walter "Kid" Smith, who crafted the first newspaper stories into the ballad verses that are best known today. Smith was a touring musician in North Carolina and Virginia. With two other musicians – fiddle player Posey Rorer and guitarist Norman Woodlief – from the North Carolina Ramblers, he went into the recording booth and laid down three tracks, one of which was his ballad, "Murder of the Lawson Family."

Here are some verses from the song:

It was on last Christmas evening,
A snow was on the ground,
Near his home in North Carolina,
Where this murderer, he was found.

His name was Charlie Lawson,
And he had a loving wife,
But we'll never know what caused him,
To take his family's wife.

They say he killed his wife first,
And the little ones did cry,
'Please Papa, won't you spare our lives?
For it is so hard to die.'

But the raging man could not be stopped,

He would not heed their call,
And kept on firing fatal shots,
Until he killed them all.

Buster Carter and Leweis McDaniels, who formed the Carolina Buddies and performed the best-known version of the Lawson family murder ballad.

Using connections Rorer had at Columbia Records in New York, he managed to get one of the top men there to listen to the song. After Rorer told the executive what a big story the murders were in North Carolina, he was convinced to let them turn it into a record.

Rorer then recruited a banjo player named Buster Carter and another guitar player, Lewis McDaniels, forming a new band called The Carolina Buddies. When the record came out, "Murder of the Lawson Family" was by far the most popular track. It was quickly issued as the "A" side of its 78rpm record.

The song became a regional success and began to be played on the radio, record players, and jukeboxes. Part of the song's power was in the matter-of-fact way the band told the tale. It's presented in the straightforward manner of mountain ballads, drawing emotion from audiences who heard the tragic story.

Mac Wiseman

A few other bands covered The Carolina Buddies song in the 1950s and 1960s, including The Stanley Brothers, The Country Gentlemen, and Doc Watkins. In 1966, Mac Wiseman released it as "The Ballad of the Lawson Family" and offered a version of the song that is bizarrely cheerful, considering the subject matter. It's a jaunty, toe-tapping tune – even when it comes to the part where Charlie's kids beg him not to shoot them.

Dave Alvin, who had formed The Blasters, included "Murder of the Lawson Family" on his 2000 album, *Public Domain*. He borrowed a melody from an old English folk song and added Smith's original lyrics. In an interview, he explained the power behind the ballad: "It's the murder of innocent children, which is pretty intense. And it has that final verse, which is kind of sentimentally sweet but at the same time gives the whole scene some kind of redemption."

Dave Alvin

The verse read:

They all were buried in a crowded grave,
While the angels watched above,
'Come home, come home, my little ones,
To the land of peace and love.'

Other versions have also been recorded, like the one by the band Sport Fishing USA in 2013. They added some of their own lyrics and a new melody, which turned it into an audience-pleasing rocker.

There's also a 2013 cover by Vandaveer, who also played with the lyrics, added some harmony vocals, and made their song their own.

As the years have passed, the ballad of the tragic family has continued to haunt audiences with its eerie story and heartbreaking lyrics.

BUT LISTENERS TO THE BALLAD WERE NOT THE only ones haunted by the past.

Buck, the massacre's only survivor, eventually married and started a family of his own. He and his wife, Nina, had a son and three daughters. His son, Arthur, was his namesake, and he named two of the girls for his murdered sisters.

Buck tried to have a good life, and while he had many happy times, he was terribly damaged by the events of Christmas Day 1929. He drank to forget, and when things got especially bad – usually around the holidays – he locked himself in a room with a bottle and played The Carolina Buddies record of "Murder of the Lawson Family" over and over again while he drank and wept.

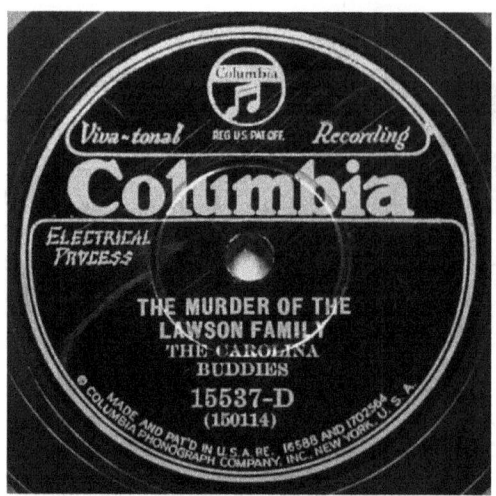

The Carolina Buddies record that Buck Lawson listened to over and over again before his tragic death.

Buck escaped death in 1929 but was not destined to grow old. On May 10, 1945, he and another man were riding in a work truck that became stuck in a deep crevice that had been cut in a road for repairs. Witnesses said they had not seen the warning signs and had accidentally driven into the construction zone. The passenger in the truck was seriously injured – Buck was killed instantly.

Even in death, though, he was haunted by his father's actions.

The first three paragraphs of his obituary were a description of the murders in 1929. Buck's life and death are not mentioned until the fourth paragraph.

Arthur "Buck" Lawson was laid to rest in the Browder cemetery alongside the family he had lost years before. In his lifetime, Buck never stopped believing that he had failed his mother and his siblings, so we can only hope that he found some comfort on the other side.

8. "THE MURDER OF GRACE BROWN"

IN THE SUMMER OF 1906, A YOUNG WOMAN NAMED Grace Brown – who was 20 years old, unmarried, and several months pregnant – traveled to the beautiful Adirondacks region of New York State to become a respectable married woman.

She had spent the last month in seclusion at her parents' farm, writing desperate letters to her boyfriend, the father of her unborn child, Chester Gillette. Convinced that her life would be ruined if her delicate condition became obvious, she begged her lover to marry her. In one letter, she wrote, "Oh Chester, please come and take me away. I am so frightened, dear."

And Chester did come to take her away. The pair traveled to Big Moose Lake, where they planned to be married and begin a new life together – or at least that's what he told Grace.

In truth, Grace would never be seen alive again.

GRACE BROWN GREW UP IN THE VILLAGE OF South Otselic, New York. She was the middle child and daughter of a successful dairy farmer and went by the nickname "Billy" because of her love for the hit song "Won't You Come Home, Bill Bailey." Grace attended school in the village, making it through the eighth grade. When she turned 18, she moved to nearby Cortland to live with her married sister, Ava, and to work at the new Gillette Skirt Factory.

It was there that she met Chester Gillette, the nephew of the factory's owner. Chester had been born in Wickes, Montana, to Franklin Gillette

Grace Brown

and Louisa Maria Rice. His parents were financially comfortable but deeply religious and eventually renounced all material wealth and joined The Salvation Army. After that, the family traveled around the West Coast, so Chester spent part of his childhood in Spokane, Washington, and lived in Hawaii during his teen years.

Chester did not follow his family into religious work. He attended Oberlin College's preparatory school, thanks to the generosity of a wealthy uncle, but left after two years in 1903. After leaving school, he worked at odd jobs until 1905, when he took a position at another uncle's skirt factory in Cortland, New York. Thanks to his family connections, he became part of local upper-class society but also began a romantic relationship with Grace, who was merely a "factory girl."

Although Chester claimed that he loved the pretty young woman, he seemed to be in no rush to settle down. This was largely because he considered himself to be several rungs above Grace on the social ladder. Chester had seduced her, and while good enough to sleep with, she was not the kind of girl he'd marry. He planned to pursue one of the daughters of the rich men in town. Those men were friends with his uncle, and with luck, he could marry into a wealthy family and never have to work in a factory again.

Chester began chasing other women on the side, including a wealthy young woman named Harriet Benedict, but his secret affair didn't stay secret for long. When Grace learned of it, she threatened to expose him publicly as a heartless seducer because Chester wasn't just sleeping with her, but he had gotten her pregnant, too. If her life were going to be ruined by a pregnancy, she told him, she would make sure that his life was also ruined.

Fearing her pregnancy would be discovered, Grace moved back home to her parents' farm, hoping she could convince Chester to marry her before it became evident that she was expecting. Over the next two months, she sent him letter after letter, pleading with him to come and take her away so that they could be married.

The letters seemed to wear Chester down, and in early July, he invited her to take a vacation with him to the Adirondacks. Grace, believing they were setting out on a sort of pre-wedding honeymoon, was ecstatic when Chester arrived at the hotel where they had agreed to meet. Grace had packed most of her wardrobe for the trip, ready to start a new life. Soon, they would be married and raising their child together.

Chester Gillette

But in her excitement, Grace failed to notice that Chester hadn't brought along the trunks and suitcases like she had. He'd only brought a single bag – as if his trip would be much shorter than hers.

During the journey to the Adirondacks, they registered at hotels with Chester using false names. They stayed one night in Utica, New York, where they left their hotel without paying. They continued by train to Tupper Lake, where they spent another night. Rain fell the next day, though, and ruined their plans for an outing on a nearby lake, so they returned south by train to Big Moose Lake.

On July 11, the couple checked in at the Glenmore Inn, where Chester registered as "Carl Graham." Since his suitcase was monogrammed "C.E.G.," he chose a name with the same initials. After leaving their bags in their room, Chester – carrying a tennis racket -- escorted Grace down to the lake, where they rented a rowboat.

What happened during the next few hours will never be known for sure. The pair was spotted on the lake several times that afternoon by other boaters. At one point, they were seen picnicking on a beach. When

The Glenmore Inn and Big Moose Lake

they failed to return at sundown, Robert Morrison, the man who rented them the rowboat, was not especially alarmed. Tourists often didn't realize just how large the lake was. Finding themselves too far away to make it back before nightfall, they sometimes rowed to the closest shore and spent the night in one of the cabins that ringed the lakefront.

But when the couple had not returned by late the next morning the following day, Morrison became concerned. A search party went out on the lake in a steamer, and they scoured the water and shoreline. They eventually came upon the rowboat, floating upside down in the water. Looking down into the depths of the water, one of the searchers spotted an object caught in the weeds at the bottom. Using a long, spiked pole, they managed to haul up the drowned corpse of Grace Brown.

Three days passed before Chester Gillette, still using an alias, was arrested in the nearby town of Inlet. At first, he claimed that Grace had drowned accidentally when the boat overturned. He later changed his story, claiming that she had deliberately thrown herself overboard. "She got up and jumped in the water – just jumped in," he said. The boat capsized, and he nearly drowned trying to save her before managing to swim to the shore. Neither explanation accounted for the terrible wounds on her head, which had been caused – according to the autopsy report – by some kind of bludgeoning implement, very possibly a tennis racket.

The question of what really happened to Grace remains in doubt, however, due to her body being embalmed before the autopsy was conducted. Isaac Coffin, the aptly named Herkimer County coroner, admitted on the witness stand that the damage to her head could just as easily have come when her body was recovered from the lake.

Chester's trial became a media sensation. District Attorney George Ward pulled out all the stops to secure a conviction. The authorities confiscated Grace's love letters to Chester from his apartment, and the prosecutor read them aloud in court. In the letters, she begged him to accept responsibility for her pregnancy. In her final letter, sent on July 5, she wrote that she was looking forward to the trip he'd promised her. She wished farewell to her childhood home and wished she could tell her mother about the baby. She wrote:

I know I shall never see any of them again. And mama, great heavens, how I do love mama! I don't know what I shall do without her. Sometimes I think if I could tell mama, but I can't. She has trouble enough as it is, and I couldn't break her heart like that. If I come back dead, perhaps if she does not know, she won't be angry with me.

When Ward read the letters aloud during the trial, reporters later noted that there wasn't a dry eye in the courtroom.

The trial was essentially over when Ward then brought a glass jar into the courtroom that contained the fetus that had been removed from Grace's body during the autopsy. Chester's lawyer loudly objected – his client had already admitted that he was the father – but the damage was

done. Despite the uncertainty surrounding Grace's manner of death, the jury only took six hours to find him guilty.

The New York Court of Appeals affirmed the conviction and Governor Charles Evans Hughes refused to grant clemency. Chester went to his death in the electric chair on March 30, 1908, still claiming that he was innocent.

Even though the case was notorious at the time – inspiring three different murder ballads – the sad fate of Grace Brown would've likely faded into history if it wasn't for author Theodore Dreiser.

Theodore Dreiser

For years, Dreiser had been poring over newspapers in search of a crime that embodied his personal obsessions with sex and social ambition in America. When he learned of the story of Grace Brown and Chester Gillette, he found the perfect material for a book. He even paraphrased many of his Grace's letters in his novel, quoting her final letter almost verbatim.

The result was his 1925 classic, *An American Tragedy*. It became an enormous bestseller and earned Dreiser a place as one of the literary greats. In 1931, he achieved even greater fame when the book was turned into a Hollywood film with the same name and then remade years later as the Academy-Award-winning "A Place in the Sun," starring Elizabeth Taylor and Montgomery Clift. The story of a trusting young woman and her murderous, social-climbing lover became more deeply entrenched in American culture.

The murderous actions of Chester Gillette also spawned a ghost story that has been haunting the Glenmore Inn – later called Covewood Lodge – ever since. For decades, guests and staff members at the inn on Big Moose Lake have been encountering the ghost of a young woman in old-fashioned clothing in the hallways, on the stairs, and even in some of the rooms. Her specter is often accompanied by doors that open and close, lights that turn on and off, and water faucets that twist open on their own.

But more often, the mysterious woman is seen outside, walking along the nearby beach. It was here where Chester and Grace rented the rowboat on that fateful July afternoon. The woman looks young, has brown hair in a bun at the back of her head, and wears a long, white dress that trails along behind her. She vanishes as she nears a rocky area along the shoreline, leaving no footprints in the sand.

Is it the ghost of Grace Brown? Those who have seen her believe that it is and that her spirit is still trapped at Big Moose Lake after being drowned by her unfaithful lover.

The ghost of a young woman who is believed to be Grace Brown still haunts the shoreline of Big Moose Lake.

MURDER BREEDS GHOST STORIES, BUT IT CREATES songs, poems, and ballads, too. At least three versions of a ballad called "The Murder of Grace Brown" have been inspired by the tragedy over the decades. They are so similar, though, that their lyrics will not all be printed here.

Here's a taste of the most popular one, which seems to focus on Chester Gillette and his regrets than on the life and death of Grace Brown:

*The dream of the happy is finished,
The scores are brought in at last,
A jury has brought in its verdict,
The sentence on Gillette is passed.*

*Two mothers are weeping and praying,
One praying that justice be done,
The other one asking for mercy,
Asking God to save her dear son.*

*All eyes are turned on the drama,
A-watching the press night and day,
A-reading those sweet pleading letters,
Wondering what Gillette would say.*

*He is now in State's Auburn dark prison,
Where he soon will give up his young life,*

Which might have been filled with sweet sunshine,
Had he taken Grace Brown for his wife.

But Cupid was too strong for Gillette,
It was playing too strong with his heart,
For the one that had loved him so dearly,
Yet from her he wanted to part.

Nearly as sad as the story of Grace Brown's murder itself, the ballad continued to be performed for many years before vanishing into obscurity, only remembered by true crime addicts and collectors of American murder ballads.

9. "THE LONESOME DEATH OF HATTIE CARROLL"

IT WASN'T A HEADLINE THAT MATCHED THE CLIMATE OF THE TIME, or at least it shouldn't have been. In 1963, the Civil Rights movement finally gained steam in America. In August, Dr. Martin Luther King, Jr. led as many as 250,000 marchers to Washington, D.C., where he delivered his historic "I Have a Dream" speech. It seemed the country was on the cusp of change.

But at the same time, an unconnected story also appeared in southern newspapers – one that had nothing to do with the rights of African Americans. That story reported on how a prominent white man from Baltimore was sentenced to only six months in prison after killing a black server at a society dance a few months earlier.

Many thought the man's abhorrent behavior at the dance should have earned him a much longer stretch behind bars but believed his position among the white elite allowed him to get off lightly. Right from the start, the young black woman's death was seen to symbolize every injustice that the marchers on Washington wanted to overturn.

The story of the murder got the attention of a young folk singer who sang two songs for the crowd that followed Dr. King to Washington. He had already penned two songs about racist murders in the past 18 months – "The Death of Emmett Till" and "Only a Pawn in Their Game." The second song was about the murder of black civil rights activist Medgar

Evers, who'd been gunned down in Jackson, Mississippi, just two months earlier.

That meant Evers' death was still a raw memory for the crowd when the folk singer stepped up to the podium at the Lincoln Memorial to sing. The activist's widow was there as one of the rally's speakers, and yet, here was this white singer speaking out to the predominantly black audience about a black man who'd been murdered just for being black. But the song was well-received, winning the singer applause and cheers as he slipped back into the crowd.

At the time, the singer was not the legendary performer we know today. He was then just 22 years old, had recorded just two albums, and would have to wait another two decades for his first chart hit. His career could have gone either way at that point, but his civil rights songs were driven by genuine outrage, and he was willing to risk his future by speaking out during those turbulent times.

That newspaper story about the murdered black woman and the white man who largely escaped justice made him angry, and in October 1963, Bob Dylan knew he had the subject of his next protest song.

HATTIE CARROLL DIED ON THE NIGHT OF FEBRUARY 8, 1963.

Hattie Carroll

She was working as a server in the bar of the Emerson Hotel in Baltimore that night. The 51-year-old grandmother had worked part-time at the hotel for the past six years, happy to help when extra staff were needed for a big gathering like the Spinster's Ball that was going on that Friday evening. It was a big night for the hotel – a white-tie charity dance with 200 guests from Maryland's most prominent families and the renowned Howard Lanin Orchestra providing the music.

Two of the guests, William Zantzinger and his wife, Jane, started their evening with a pre-dinner cocktail at the Eager House restaurant. The 24-year-old Zantzinger was the son of a wealthy tobacco family from southern Maryland. His parents could trace their ancestors back to both the state's first white settlers and a former governor of Maryland. His sister had been given two spectacular debutante balls, both of which had been covered in the *Washington Post*.

His wife, Jane, came from a similar family background, solidifying their many social and political connections.

According to accounts from others at the Eager House, William and Jane were already drinking heavily before they even sat down at their table and continued to drink during their meal. It wasn't long before they'd become so loud and unruly that the bar manager refused to serve them anything else.

But they didn't let being cut off slow them down. Jane made herself at home at another table and began drinking with a group of strangers. William, meanwhile, started stumbling after any of the servers who happened to be carrying trays of drinks, unsteadily – but deliberately – striking some of them with a wooden cane he was carrying for some reason. The cane was a cheap carnival souvenir rather than a necessary walking stick, but it was still heavy enough to inflict pain.

The Emerson Hotel in Baltimore

After they sloppily finished dinner, the couple moved on to the Spinster's Ball at the hotel. When they walked in, William announced himself loudly by shouting, "I just flew in from Texas! Gimme a drink!"

He was still fooling around with the cane, knocking it against a silver punchbowl whenever he wanted more booze, smacking a black bellhop on the rear, and running the tip of it up the leg of any pretty woman who walked by. As this was happening, he was also working his way through one bourbon and ginger ale after another from the open bar.

When the couple tried to go out onto the dance floor, they became tangled up and then tripped and fell to the floor. Irritated, William started hitting Jane on the head with one of his shoes. Some of the other guests intervened, one of whom later testified that he'd knocked William down after the obnoxious drunk took a swing at him.

After getting to her feet, Jane dusted herself off and allowed hotel staff members to take her to a room upstairs where she could clean herself up and calm down. William, though, staggered back to their table, where he continued to drink.

The longer he sat there, the darker his mood became. He approached Ethel Hill, a black server who was clearing a nearby table, and asked her about a "fireman's fund." She said she didn't know what he meant, and William snarled, "Don't say 'no' to me, you nigger, you say 'no, sir." He took a swing at her with his cane and then chased after her as she fled to the kitchen, striking her on the arm, thighs, and buttocks.

Working with Ethel that night were three other hotel servers – Marina Patterson, Grace Shelton, and Shirley Burrell. All three women witnessed William Zantzinger's behavior that night and later testified about what they'd seen. Marina later recalled:

I heard Mrs. Hill say, "What is wrong with you? Leave me alone.' Then I heard him say, 'Nigger, what's wrong with you?' Then I saw him whack her across the buttocks with the cane. She ran out of the room crying, 'Somebody help me! This man is killing me!'

Less than 10 minutes after this incident, William shoved his way through the crowd to the bar again, demanding another drink. Hattie Carroll, who was busy serving another customer, asked him to wait for one moment.

I'll quote Marina's testimony again:

Mrs. Carroll was fixing another drink, so she didn't serve him immediately. He said, 'Nigger, did you hear me ask for a drink? I don't have to take that kind of shit off a nigger.' He took the cane and struck her on the right shoulder. She leaned against the bar. Mr. Zantzinger stood at the bar for a while, then he picked up his drink and left. She seemed to have been in shock. She said, 'That man has upset me so, I feel deathly ill.'

Shirley Burrell confirmed Marina's account, adding that the blow to Hattie's arm had been so severe that she "couldn't understand how she could stand up." She said that after Zantzinger walked away, Hattie had slumped over against her.

A moment later, William was back at the bar. He yelled at Hattie, "Why are you so slow, you black bitch?" He swung the cane again and, this time, struck her solidly in the head.

Marina and Shirley helped Hattie into the privacy of the kitchen, where she burst into tears. Grace Shelton remembered that her right arm was still hurting, too, and that Hattie told her that she was unable to hold onto anything with that hand. Grace added, "Her speech became thick and garbled, and her words were running together." Hattie's right arm had gone numb, so the other women tried to massage it back to life.

Out in the bar, someone had called both an ambulance and the police. A guest, Hal Whittaker, snatched the cane from William's hands and broke it into pieces. He later testified, "I saw that lady being taken out on a stretcher, and I became upset. I didn't want him to use it again."

By now, Hattie had lost consciousness and was rushed to Baltimore's Mercy Hospital. Two police officers arrived at the hotel, and they arrested William, who loudly protested his innocence.

They were leading him out of the ballroom in handcuffs when Jane finally reappeared. Still very drunk, she tumbled down a short flight of stairs, knocking both her drunken husband and Officer Warren Todd onto the floor. Crawling across the tiles and grabbing William by the legs, she sobbed, "You can't take my Billy Boy away! He beats me, but I still love him!"

The police officers responded to this by arresting her, too, and dragging the couple off to the Pine Street Police Station. There, Jane was charged with disorderly conduct and was allowed to leave after posting a $28 bond.

Hopefully, she didn't drive herself home.

William was also charged with disorderly conduct, plus two charges of assault on Ethel Hill and Hattie Carroll. He was left to cool off in a cell for what remained of the night.

Early on Saturday morning, still wearing his dirty and wrinkled tuxedo and now sporting a black eye, William appeared before Judge Albert Blum in Municipal Court. At the time the hearing began, Hattie was still unconscious at Mercy Hospital, and Judge Blum had left instructions that he was to be immediately told of any change in her condition. William entered a not-guilty plea on all the charges against him and he was released on a $3,600 bond.

As he walked out of the courtroom that morning, Hattie was already dead, but the news didn't reach Judge Blum until it was too late. He later said that he never would've allowed such a low bail if he'd known he was

now dealing with a potential murder case. The police blamed the hospital staff for being too slow about passing on the information.

One of the last people – likely the very last person – to speak with Hattie was Yvonne Ross, another hotel worker, who'd ridden with her friend to the hospital. She later testified:

I stayed with her at the hospital for a while. She was unconscious. Then she woke up. The last thing I heard her say was 'Help me please.'

HATTIE DIED LESS THAN EIGHT HOURS AFTER BEING ATTACKED by the drunken William Zantzinger. As one eyewitness to the assault described it, "He was like a wild animal. After he had knocked her unconscious, he became even more belligerent. Now she's dead – all because she didn't serve him fast enough."

According to the hospital, Hattie had died from a brain hemorrhage, although her official cause of death wouldn't be released until after an autopsy. Matters were complicated because she also suffered from an enlarged heart and high blood pressure.

Once the news reached the authorities that Hattie was dead, another warrant was issued for William and for Jane, who had failed to show up at her disorderly conduct hearing. The *Baltimore Sun* reported the story of the attack with a headline that read, "Caning Suspect, Wife Sought State-Wide in Death of Barmaid. Charles County Man is Charged with Homicide." The story beneath noted that the police had failed to find Zantzinger at his home south of Baltimore and now "had no idea of his whereabouts."

However, William surrendered the next day, walking into Baltimore police headquarters with his attorney, Claud Hanley. He was arrested, handcuffed, and returned to the lock-up to wait for his next hearing.

When he appeared in front of Judge Robert Hammerman the next day, the court ruled that he would be held without bail until a trial was scheduled. But William's lawyers persuaded the superior City Court to overturn this ruling. That judge, Dulany Foster, set William's bail at $25,000 and allowed him to go free until the trial date. Maryland's state prosecutor, William O'Donnell, didn't oppose bail.

By now, George Gessell, the bellhop at the Emerson Hotel, had added his own assault complaint against Zantzinger, which means he was now charged with one count of homicide, two counts of assault, and one of disorderly conduct. Judge Hammerman insisted that William pay an additional $500 bond for the Gessell assault before he reluctantly released him.

Jane Zantzinger was also granted bail again – this time for $600 – and she now also waited for a trial date on her disorderly conduct charges.

The most charming couple in Maryland was now back on the streets.

HATTIE'S FUNERAL WAS HELD ON A CHILLY OVERCAST afternoon at the Gillis Memorial Church in West Baltimore, where Hattie had sung in the choir. Newspaper reports stated that at least 1,600 people were in attendance, only about half of whom were able to fit into the church for the service itself. White police officers, on hand to control the crowd, watched as organizers handed out grim flyers that asked a single question" "Who will be next?"

Although there were no white faces in the church pews, the National Council of Christians and Jews did send representatives to the funeral, as did the

Emerson Hotel. Messages of sympathy came in from across the South, confirming that Hattie's death had garnered national attention.

Reverend Theodore Jackson preached that Hattie's death would mean more to the city of Baltimore than any other it had seen. He shouted from the pulpit, "The ministers of this city, the doctors, the lawyers, all people should come together as never before and let people know that colored citizens are not going to stand for certain things. We are in the hands of a just God, but not in the hands of just people."

After a tearful performance from the choir, relatives were led to 34 cars waiting in the funeral procession. Hattie's body was taken to Baltimore's National Cemetery, where her husband James' military service allowed her to be buried, too. Crowds lingered outside the church long after the processional cars had disappeared, reluctant to end the services for a woman that most of them had never known.

They stood there under the cloudy sky for nearly an hour -- small groups of smartly dressed black mourners, a handful of grim-faced white ones, and even a small group of Muslim women with long scarves covering their hair. The sound of murmuring voices marked a polite exchange of words between people who might never have spoken to one another under different circumstances.

But the death of Hattie Carroll – a kind and pleasant woman who never drew attention to herself – had brought them together.

A SHORT TIME AFTER THE FUNERAL, WILLIAM ZANTZINGER had his next appearance in court. He was brought before Judge Basil Thomas of Baltimore's Central Homicide Court for a hearing that determined the charges against him were serious enough to refer the case to a grand jury.

The witnesses included Assistant Medical Examiner Dr. Charles Petty, who testified that Hattie's brain hemorrhage had been caused by the fright, fear, and anger of Zantzinger's attack.

Grace Shelton and Shirley Burrell offered their accounts of Zantzinger's behavior at the Emerson Hotel that night, describing what they'd seen. Shirley broke down and wept as she testified about the attack, adding that William had been loud, abusive, and belligerent all evening.

Deputy State's Attorney Charles Moylan – stung by rumors that his office had already decided to settle for a manslaughter conviction – insisted that detailed testimony from his witnesses was important because it established malice on the part of the defendant. He reminded the court that "Malice is the essential element that distinguishes murder from manslaughter."

A few days later, the grand jury formally indicted Zantzinger on a homicide charge, and a tentative date of March 28 was set for his trial – although no one believed it would happen that soon. His attorneys had already been maneuvering for a change of venue, and in mid-April, it was announced they'd been successful. The trial would be moved out of Baltimore to Hagerstown in western Maryland.

William Zantzinger during the grand jury hearing, where he was indicted for Hattie's murder a few weeks after her death.

WHILE THE LEGAL PROCEEDINGS IN HATTIE'S CASE KEPT grinding on, folk singers were taking notice of the story. Don West, a socialist campaigner and poet, had composed nine verses of a song he called "The Ballad of Hattie Carroll." He suggested that it be sung to the tune of "Wayfaring Stranger." Compared to the song that Bob Dylan would write six months later, West's effort is unbalanced and awkward, more concerned with showcasing the writer's conscience than adding any poignancy to the events that occurred. It bluntly described Hattie's story as one of "brutal murder" and told of a powerful, wealthy man who "flailed away" with his cane and Hattie was "beat to death."

Zantzinger's trial hadn't yet been scheduled when the song appeared, so no one knew yet whether the law would punish him as a murderer or not. Although West didn't name Zantzinger in the song, he did list Hattie Carroll's name in full, leaving no doubt about who the killer in the song had to be.

And while Dylan didn't use West's song as inspiration for his own, he did likely use a piece written by Roy H. Wood as a primary source.

Wood detailed what happened on the night of the Spinster's Ball and then sharpened his literary knife and went after William Zantzinger. He wrote, "Zantzinger's father is a member of the state planning commission in Maryland. Others of his relatives in the Devereux family are prominent in politics. The judge who released Zantzinger on bond has already permitted his attorney to claim that Mrs. Carroll died indirectly as a result of the attack rather than directly. There is speculation here that attempts will be made to get Zantzinger off with a slap on the wrist."

Wood was angry about the way Hattie was treated and wanted to make sure that his readers were angry, too. He took every chance to show that Zantzinger was a rich, spoiled thug but took the details of the attack to another level, implying that Zantzinger broke his cane on Hattie's back. He also clearly wanted his readers to question whether corruption played a role in the case, insinuating that the judge and Zantzinger's lawyers were dishonest.

Whether the colorful aspects of Wood's article were deliberate distortions or justifiable exaggerations, they played an essential role in shaping Bob Dylan's lyrics, and, thanks to that, Wood influences the way we all think about this story today. The things he decided to include in his writings in February 1963 have remained with us longer than he could have ever imagined.

FEARFUL OF HOW A JURY MIGHT REACT TO WILLIAM Zantzinger's actions on the night of the ball, his attorneys convinced him to opt for a court trial. On June 19, 1963, a three-person panel of judges assembled to hear the case. The panel was headed by Judge David McLaughlin and shared the bench with Irvine Rutledge and Stuart Hamill.

I don't have to tell you that all three judges were white.

Many of the members of Maryland's white aristocracy were present in the courtroom that day. Many guests from the Spinster's Ball had been summoned to give testimony and looked unhappy about being dragged into court. William Zantzinger, though, looked almost uncannily calm.

When state prosecutor William O'Donnell and his assistant, Charles Moylan, opened the case, they certainly didn't go easy on the defendant. O'Donnell referred to Zantzinger as "the lord of the manor, lord of the plantation," and Moylan claimed William had never been able to accept the defeat of the South after the Civil War and the end of slavery that it brought.

They built their case with witnesses like Marina Patterson, Grace Shelton, and Shirley Burrell and saved Charles Petty, the doctor who'd carried out Hattie's autopsy, as their final witness. He stated that Hattie's death was a direct result of the blow she'd received from Zantzinger's cane.

Either way, he gleaned all the details from Wood's account and the newspaper articles that documented the case. Wood's piece included the ages of the killer and his victim, the number of Hattie's children, the high-society nature of the dance, Zantzinger's wealth, the acreage of his tobacco farm, his political connections, and the suggestions of corruption in his trial. All those things ended up in Dylan's lyrics. Wood never used the words "murder" or "killed," though. Dylan's song couldn't say the same.

Bob Dylan was 22 years old when he recorded "The Lonesome Death of Hattie Carroll" in 1963. He performed at the March on Washington that year, along with Joan Baez.

Clinton Heylin, a well-known student of Dylan's music and career, often referred to "The Lonesome Death of Hattie Carroll" as "a million-dollar libel case waiting to happen." He noted that because it wasn't literally Zantzinger's blow with the cane that directly caused Hattie's death, he couldn't fairly be called a "killer." I'm not sure that's accurate, but there is no denying that Dylan took a risk linking Zantzinger to murder when he'd been convicted of only manslaughter, a much less serious crime.

But this was a murder ballad, a folk song that told the story of what happened – a privileged white man killed a black woman and got off lightly. It was what happened – even if you could make excuses that it wasn't the literal truth.

Zantzinger was quoted bad-mouthing Bob Dylan many times over the years, calling him "a scum bag of the earth" and sputtering that "I should have sued him and put him in jail." But if Zantzinger had been stupid enough to sue and give Dylan all the free publicity for the song he could ever want, he would've opened him up to more hate and ridicule than he could have handled. I mean, keep in mind that this is the guy whose wife bragged that "nobody treats his niggers as well as Billy does."

Though he never sued over the song, there is evidence that Zantzinger's lawyers threatened legal action against both Dylan and his record label when the song came out. The lawsuit never went anywhere, and Zantzinger remained bitter about it for the rest of his life.

Dylan first recorded "The Lonesome Death of Hattie Carroll" in October 1963 as part of the New York sessions for his third album, *The Times They Are A-Changin'*. While it may not have held up to the scrutiny of libel courts, it remains a classic when it's judged as art. It's the work of a superb songwriter who was already starting to leave his contemporaries behind.

One striking aspect of the song is that Dylan never feels he needs to spell out that Zantzinger was white and Hattie was black. In the volatile racial atmosphere of America in 1963, he knew that listeners would fill in that information for themselves.

The song could also be seen as being more about privilege than about murder, making it a privilege ballad disguised as a murder ballad. It's not just that an unknown poor person was murdered; it's suddenly become about all of us because of the way that the system is played by the rich and powerful. The courts are there to fix what happened to Hattie Carroll, but this is bigger than that, and we should all be concerned about it. This is the reason why the song continues to resonate with people after all this time.

Dylan himself also seemed to realize that the song was something special. It was the song that he chose to perform when *The Steve Allen Show* had him on for his first national television appearance in February 1964. In an existing clip from the show, Dylan seems nervous and fidgety while sitting next to Allen for a short interview. It's when he gets to sing the song – instead of just talking about it – that he regains his composure.

WILLIAM ZANTZINGER COMPLETED HIS SIX-MONTH JAIL sentence and was released about a month after Dylan appeared on *The Steve Allen Show*. However, his notoriety showed no sign of going away. In January 1964, Hattie Carroll's family filed a civil suit against him, asking for $1 million in damages. Newspapers – especially African American ones – continued to run letters that drew attention to the light sentence he'd received.

In October 1964, news appeared that Jane Zantzinger was planning a fundraiser for Republican presidential candidate Barry Goldwater, who'd led the opposition against President Kennedy's civil rights legislation. Despite Jane's protests that her husband had nothing to do with the event, one newspaper story was headlined "Killer of Hotel Barmaid Raising Funds for Goldwater." It wasn't a good look for anyone involved.

After a few years of continuing to run the family farm, Zantzinger switched to real estate. He had three children, divorced Jane, and then married again. In October 1983, the Internal Revenue Service seized the income stream that he was receiving from his mother's trust to settle $78,000 in unpaid income taxes, but it barely slowed him down. By 1991, he owned a nightclub, an antique shop, and an auction business called W&Z Realty. He drove a white Mercedes with vanity plates and cultivated a reputation as a good ol' boy who loved to have a good time and hosted an annual pig and oyster roast.

Every few years, a reporter would notice the anniversary of Hattie's death and approach Zantzinger for an interview, but he always turned them away. He did end up back in the newspapers in the early 1990s, though, when the *Maryland Independent* carried a front-page story that revived his image as a wealthy racist. According to the article, he'd been collecting rents of $200 a month for some beat-up old shacks that he hadn't actually owned since 1986. Charles County had confiscated the shacks because Zantzinger owed over $18,000 in unpaid property taxes. The six shacks were described as "reminiscent of slave quarters" and had no running water, no sewers, no outhouses, and no heat. They were occupied by – surprise, surprise – poor black families, who had to empty buckets of waste in the woods near the shallow well they relied on for drinking water.

William Zantzinger leaves court in cuffs in 1992 after being sentenced to 18 months in jail and fined $50,000 for "unfair and deceptive trade practices" in his real estate business.

It was estimated that Zantzinger had illegally collected over $10,000 from each family over the years. He'd even successfully sued a 61-year-old black tenant named John Savoy for unpaid rent of $240 on a shanty Savoy lived in but Zantzinger no longer owned.

Zantzinger was charged with deceptive trade practice, including one count of making a false and misleading oral statement. The maximum sentence was one year in jail and a $1,000 fine. Soon after this, he was indicted for rent theft, two counts of felony theft, and 50 counts of unfair and deceptive trade practices. Worse, the investigation discovered that he'd also wrongly collected at least $4,700 in other rents. He was arrested and released on personal bond.

The case went to court in November 1991, with Zantzinger pleading guilty to several misdemeanors and prosecutors dropping the felony cases against him in return. Evidence presented during his trial revealed that he had concealed his rental income during his 1988 divorce, explaining that he no longer held title to the properties. This destroyed any possible argument that he had continued to collect rents in good faith. The court also heard about his manslaughter conviction in Hattie Carroll's case, as well as three more recent court appearances for drunk driving.

Judge Steven Platt sentenced him to 18 months on work release in the country jail, plus 2,400 hours of community service with local charities, plus penalties and fines that totaled $62,000. This time, the judge denied his request for time to put his affairs in order, and William was led away in handcuffs to immediately begin his sentence – a sentence more severe than the one he'd received after causing the death of Hattie Carroll.

A few months later, the Maryland Real Estate Commission declined to renew Zantzinger's license and, to add insult to injury, fined him $2,000 just because it could.

William Zantzinger died in 2009 – and I think we can all agree that it was good riddance.

10. "NEBRASKA"

DURING THE DARKEST DAYS OF THE GREAT Depression in America, the public was looking for an escape. Many of them found it at the movies, in the booze that had recently been legalized again, and with radio, crime magazines, and newspapers, which they used to follow the exploits of the country's anti-heroes.

A nation that was sick of the government and the banks cheered on the outlaws and the bandits who were looting the institutions that the common folks saw as the enemy. The stock market crash forced millions out of work, and the banks foreclosed on the homes and farms of the poor. Why shouldn't John Dillinger, Baby Face Nelson, and all the rest get a little revenge for those who couldn't fight back themselves?

Legends and lore sprang up about the outlaws that had taken to America's highways to outrun the law. For instance, in stories about Charles Arthur "Pretty Boy," Floyd claimed he wasn't just a bank robber and killer but a Dust Bowl-era Robin Hood, stealing from the rich and giving back to the poor.

He wasn't, I can assure you. But the reason why so many people started to believe this story was true was because of the song written about him in 1939 by "This Land is Your Land" singer Woody Guthrie.

Pretty Boy Floyd died in a hail of bullets in an Ohio cornfield on October 22, 1934, while he was Public Enemy No. 1 on the FBI's "Most Wanted" list. The unassuming Oklahoma bandit – who liked to bake pies when he wasn't planning bank robberies – was a hard-luck country boy who turned to crime during the Depression. He was already a hero to farmers and the unemployed, who'd also been hit hard by the Depression, but the song turned him into a legend.

His path to crime really was a desperate one. Convicted of a St. Louis patrol robbery in his 20s, he served three years of a five-year prison sentence, during which his wife divorced him. Paroled in 1929, he vowed to go straight, but lack of work, failure of his family's farm, and several brushes with the law left him bitter. After his father was shot and killed during a quarrel with a local shopkeeper – and the killer was freed after pleading self-defense – Floyd seems to have snapped. Pretty Boy – as the papers started calling him – began robbing banks and spent the rest of his life a wanted man.

Woody Guthrie

Woody Guthrie's song "Pretty Boy Floyd" was recorded for his album *Dust Bowl Ballads*, which was sort of a *Grapes of Wrath*-themed tribute to the disaster in Oklahoma that occurred in the mid-1930s. Sandwiched in between songs like "Dust Can't Kill Me" and "Dust Pneumonia Blues," an action song about an American outlaw seemed like a breath of fresh air – pardon the pun – and made the song a hit.

But, of course, Woody Guthrie being who he was, the song was cleverly disguised as a protest song, taking aim at the brutality of the FBI and, by extension, the tyranny of the U.S. government.

And that quiet aspect of the tune was what brought it back as a protest song in 1968 when The Byrds included it on their album, Sweethearts of the Rodeo. Pretty Boy Floyd being portrayed as a "simple man of the people" made the song appealing to a whole new generation.

And he wasn't the only outlaw of the 1930s to make an impression through a murder ballad of sorts.

During the Great Depression, Bonnie Parker and Clyde Barrow's murderous love story captivated the nation. Not only were they a couple of dead-broke kids who were tearing down the establishment, but they were also an attractive young couple living as romantic outlaws along America's highways.

Bonnie Parker was a four-foot-11-inch, 90-pound, 19-year-old, former honor roll student who was already married to a man in prison for murder when she met petty criminal Clyde Barrow in 1930. The pair immediately fell for one another and were rarely separated for the rest of their short lives.

For three years – from 1931 to 1934 -- Bonnie and Clyde terrorized the Midwest and South with a brazen series of bank and store robberies, shootouts, and murders. But somehow, along the line, the young couple became folk heroes and sympathetic characters on the run from the law.

Maybe it was their good looks, or the comical selfies left behind in an abandoned hideout, or perhaps it was Bonnie's poetry, but the newspapers, detective magazines, and the public couldn't get enough of them.

Bonnie Parker and Clyde Barrow – Two of America's favorite outlaws in the 1930s.

Bonnie herself wrote the first ballad written about Bonnie and Clyde. Here's a bit of what she wrote and called "The Ballad of Bonnie and Clyde."

They don't think they're tough or desperate
They know the law always wins
They've been shot at before, but they do not ignore
That death is the wages of sin.

Some day they'll go down together
And they'll bury them side by side
To few it'll be grief, to the law a relief
But it's death for Bonnie and Clyde.

During their crime spree, they killed at least 13 people, including cops, and carried out an almost endless string of robberies and burglaries, but Bonnie was right -- the law did catch up with them in the end, and they did go down together.

In May 1934, they were ambushed on a lonely Louisiana road by six armed lawmen who fired over 100 bullets into their car.

And then, after the dust settled, Bonnie and Clyde were mostly forgotten. They might have stayed that way if it wasn't for movies and music. In 1967, Faye Dunaway and Warren Beatty revived their legend in a groundbreaking film and made the couple glamorous and sexy all over again.

Merle Haggard

And, of course, the music business took notice. Less than a year after the movie came out, country artist Merle Haggard released a song and an album called *The Legend of Bonnie and Clyde*, which opened the door for others.

More country ballads followed, but more recently, they've also shown up in rap and hip-hop music. These artists – like their earlier outlaw country counterparts – identified with Bonnie and Clyde as outsiders who were mistreated by the law. They portray the pair as fellow outcasts, just trying to survive and getting by because of their undying love for each other.

The most popular of these tunes is undoubtedly "Bonnie and Clyde '03" by Jay-Z and Beyonce. I have no idea what the real Bonnie and Clyde would think of that one, but regardless, it helped to keep their story alive.

But Depression-era bandits haven't been the only highway killers and thieves whose bloody history has been preserved through murder ballads. But in this case, no one has tried to paint these other killers as heroes.

HE WANTED TO LOOK LIKE JAMES DEAN.

No, that's wrong, he wanted to BE James Dean.

After he saw *Rebel Without A Cause*, Charlie became obsessed with the actor. He started styling his hair like Dean and dressed like Dean's character in the movie. Charlie related to the character he saw on screen -- the troubled, rebellious teenager who couldn't stay out of trouble.

Charlie believed the character was a kindred spirit of sorts, someone who had suffered from the same things that Charlie had.

He may have been a born loser and a no-good delinquent, but James Dean's character in the movie wasn't the kind of kid who'd leave behind the horror story that Charlie did. He wouldn't have gone on a murderous road trip through the badlands of Nebraska and Wyoming that ended with 11 people dead.

No, that was all Charlie. He terrified the public in 1958 by introducing them to a kind of rampage like nothing America had ever seen before.

CHARLES RAYMOND STARKWEATHER WAS BORN IN Lincoln, Nebraska, on November 24, 1938. He was the third of seven children born to Guy and Helen Starkweather. They were an ordinary, working-class family, and there was nothing about them to suggest that one of the Starkweather children would grow up to be a killer.

Charlie's father, Guy, was by all accounts a mild-mannered man. He had been a carpenter all his life but was often unemployed because of severe rheumatoid arthritis in his hands. During times when Guy couldn't work, Helen supplemented the family income as a waitress.

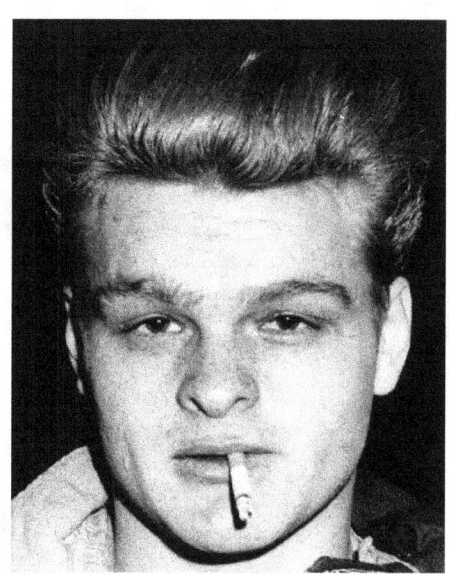

Charles Starkweather

Charlie attended Saratoga Elementary School, Everett Junior High, and Lincoln High School – but his school years were a time of torment for him. He was born with a mild defect that caused his legs to be misshapen, and he also had a speech impediment. These things led to constant teasing from his classmates. Desperately unhappy, he refused to apply himself to his studies, leading to him being labeled a slow learner. Worse yet, he was diagnosed with myopia, which drastically affected his vision for the rest of his life. He walked funny, talked funny, and had to wear glasses – all ammunition for the bullies who preyed on him at school each day.

But then Charlie found something that he excelled in – gym class. There, he found a physical outlet for the rage growing inside him. Charlie used his newfound physicality to fight back against those who had bullied him for years. They quickly found the tables had been turned, and Charlie went from someone they teased to someone they feared. Charlie, once considered one of the most well-behaved students in school, had become the student who was in trouble all the time. Students – and even faculty members – were afraid of him.

Around this time, Charlie attended his first showing of *Rebel Without A Cause* and became obsessed with modeling himself after James Dean, as well as other "rebels" he saw in the movies. He sported a black leather motorcycle jacket, black and white cowboy boots, and sometimes darkened his naturally red hair with black shoe polish.

In 1956, Charlie, then 18, met a 13-year-old named Caril Ann Fugate, a petite, pretty girl whose older sister had been the girlfriend of one of Charlie's friends. He developed a fixation on Caril Ann, and she returned his attention. She swooned over the older, rugged, handsome boy and spent every minute she could with him.

So that he could be closer to Caril Ann, Charlie dropped out of Lincoln High School in his senior year and started working at the Western Union newspaper warehouse. It was the perfect job for him since it was

Charlie and Caril Ann before the horror of their murder spree began

located near Whittier Junior High, where Caril Ann was a student. Being close by, he could visit her every day after school.

Charlie was, not surprisingly, a lousy worker. His employer later recalled that he had to be told how to do something two or three times before getting it right. But being stupid wasn't what made Charlie bad at his job – it was his obsession with Caril Ann.

Caril Ann inadvertently caused Charlie to be kicked out of his family home when she crashed his 1949 Ford into another car. Charlie was trying to teach her to drive. Guy Starkweather, the legal owner of the car, had to pay for the damage, and an altercation between the father and son erupted, ending with Guy forcing Charlie to move out.

Charlie quit his job at the warehouse and started working as a garbage collector. Angry, unhappy, and belligerent, he used the garbage route to scout out homes for robberies. He decided that he wanted to become a criminal and developed a personal philosophy that stayed with him for the rest of his life – it doesn't matter who they were when they were alive; dead people are all on the same level.

Charlie Starweather had no respect for the living or the dead.

Finally, his antisocial behavior turned murderous on the evening of November 30, 1957. Robert Colvert was a 21-year-old young man recently discharged from the U.S. Navy. Bobby had married his childhood sweetheart the previous year, and they were now expecting their first child. He worked nights at the Crest Service Station in Lincoln, pumping gas and dreaming about bigger and better things. Everyone who knew him described him as a kind man and excited father-to-be who, like his dad, enjoyed carpentry. He was easygoing and always quick to laugh. Unfortunately for Bobby, though, he crossed paths with a loose cannon.

Charlie stopped at the service station with plans to buy a stuffed animal for Caril Ann on credit, but Bobby refused him. Angry, Charlie stomped out of the place but returned around 3:00 A.M. with a shotgun. He demanded the money from the register – around $90 in bills and loose change – and then took Bobby with him. Charlie drove him to an isolated spot along Superior Street, where some kind of altercation occurred. Bobby, probably believing that Charlie was going to kill him, began fighting for his life and was injured in the fight. Charlie put the shotgun to his head and pulled the trigger. Then, he drove off, leaving Bobby dead in an empty field.

Later that Sunday, December 1, Charlie went into a thrift shop where he bought shoes, a jacket, shirts, undershirts, and jockey shorts. He paid for all of it with $10 in loose change that he pocketed from the robbery.

Charlie found himself empowered by committing his first murder. He had a new existence, he believed, and a new purpose in life – to kill those he deemed unworthy.

Bobby Colvert was the first. Although Charlie confessed the murder to Caril Ann, the police had no suspects. They suspected that Bobby had been killed by a transient, and, as a result, they didn't spend much time investigating it. Bobby was laid to rest on December 12, 1957, and forgotten by everyone but his friends and family.

Charlie had gotten away with his first murder.

THE THRILL FROM CHARLIE'S FIRST KILL LASTED until January 1958, when he lost his job. On Tuesday, January 21, he went to Caril Ann's house, supposedly looking for his girlfriend, although he must have known she was at school. His knock on the door was answered by Caril Ann's stepfather, Marion Bartlett. He was home with his wife, Velda, and their two-year-old daughter, Betty Jean. Neither of Caril Ann's parents cared for the moody and troubled young man, and since Caril Ann wasn't around to interrupt, they took the opportunity to tell Charlie to stay away from her.

Charlie responded – by shooting Marion and Velda to death. Worse, he killed Betty Jean, too.

Marion was shot in the head, and Velda was shot in the face and then bludgeoned with a rifle. It's unclear where Betty Jean was killed. Some believe she was initially spared, but her crying got on the nerves of both Charlie and Caril Ann, so she was stabbed to death. Others say that Charlie beat, stabbed, and strangled the little girl before Caril Ann got home from school.

Regardless of when they were killed, all three bodies were placed in outbuildings around the home – Marion in the chicken coop, Velda in the outhouse, and Betty Jean in a trash barrel.

Years later, Caril Ann would claim she had broken up with Charlie on Sunday, January 19. She would also claim that her family was dead when she arrived home, and Charlie told her she would be killed too if she didn't cooperate with him. That was her story, anyway, although based on many of her actions, I'm reasonably certain that it was something she came up with many years later.

The teenage couple lived in the house together for the next six days. The proximity of the three dead bodies didn't seem to bother them. Caril Ann turned away visitors and concerned family members, including her grandmother, sister, and brother-in-law, claiming the entire family was sick with the flu. She posted a "sick note" on the front door, allegedly signed by her mother, asking that the household not be disturbed.

It was only when Caril Ann's grandmother threatened to call the police to check on the family that the couple decided to go on the run.

August Meyer's farmhouse, where the couple took shelter before killing the man.

In Charlie's car, they drove 15 miles out of Lincoln to the small town of Bennet, where a friend of the Starkweather family named August Meyer lived. When they turned into his long driveway, though, Charlie's car bogged down in the mud. He and Caril Ann had no choice but to trek to the farmhouse on foot.

August Meyer was a lifelong bachelor, a quiet and friendly man who lived simply on his farm. He offered his horses to assist Charlie in pulling his car out of the mud, and the couple followed him to his barn to get some chains and ropes. But when they entered the barn, Charlie raised his shotgun and killed the longtime family friend by firing both barrels into his back. When August's faithful dog tried to defend his owner, Charlie beat the dog to death, breaking the stock on the shotgun.

Caril Ann later claimed the brutality of August's death – along with the beating of the dog – convinced her that her only option was to go along with whatever Charlie told her to do.

She helped him ransack the farmhouse for food and money, and then, with the car still buried up to its axles in the mud, they started walking along the road, hoping to catch a ride.

And they did, later that same night. A kind and unsuspecting couple -- Robert Jensen, 17, and Carol King, 16 – stopped when they saw the pair walking down the highway. Charlie was charming when they first got into the car but soon turned vicious. He ordered Robert to drive to an abandoned storm cellar in Bennet and then forced the couple out of the car and into the cellar. In that dark underground chamber, Charlie shot Robert six times in the head and then tried to rape Carol, stabbing her

The Ward house in Lincoln, Nebraska

once in the abdomen as she struggled. She managed to get free, but Charlie shot her down – or did he?

Later, Charlie confessed to killing Robert Jensen, but he claimed that it was Caril Ann who, in a jealous rage over seeing Charlie's reaction to the pretty young woman, shot and killed her. Caril Ann claimed that she stayed in the car while Charlie did all the killing. Who was telling the truth?

The couple fled from Bennet in Robert's car and returned to Lincoln. The plan was to find a suitable house where they could hide out. On January 28, Caril Ann chose the house while driving near Lincoln's Country Club. It belonged to C. Lauer Ward, a wealthy industrialist. He and his wife, Clara, had one son, Michael, and thankfully, he was away at school. Like Caril Ann, Michael was only 14.

They slipped into the house and tied up Clara and her hearing-impaired maid, Lilyan Fencl. Charlie and Caril Ann took turns sleeping so that one of them would always be standing guard. At some point, both hostages were stabbed to death, and Charlie also snapped the neck of the family dog. Clara was stabbed in the neck and chest, and Lilyan was tied to a bed and stabbed.

Who killed them? Charlie later admitted to stabbing Clara once, but he accused Caril Ann of inflicting the rest of the wounds on her body. He also claimed that Caril Ann stabbed Lilyan, too.

When Lauer Ward returned home that night, Charlie was waiting. He shot him in the head and killed him instantly.

Then, with Caril Ann's help, he gathered up all the cash and jewelry he could find, and they loaded it into the Wards' 1956 Packard. They fled Lincoln, leaving victims eight, nine, and ten behind them. They planned to head for Washington state, where one of Charlie's brothers lived.

It was the murder of the wealthy businessman, his wife, and their maid that created outrage in the community. Every law enforcement agency in the region began a house-by-house search for the killers. Governor Victor E. Anderson contacted the Nebraska National Guard, and the Lincoln police chief called for a block-by-block search of the city. Frequent sightings of the two were often reported, but the teenage killers stayed one step ahead of the law.

Charlie realized that the Wards' Packard was too high-profile, and they needed to find a new vehicle. They got lucky about 10 hours outside Lincoln when they saw a traveling salesman named Merle Collison sleeping in his Buick outside Douglas, Wyoming. Charlie tapped on the window to wake him up, then demanded he get out of the vehicle. The salesman did everything Charlie told him to do, but the couple killed him anyway. Charlie later stated that his gun jammed and that it was Caril Ann who finished Collison off.

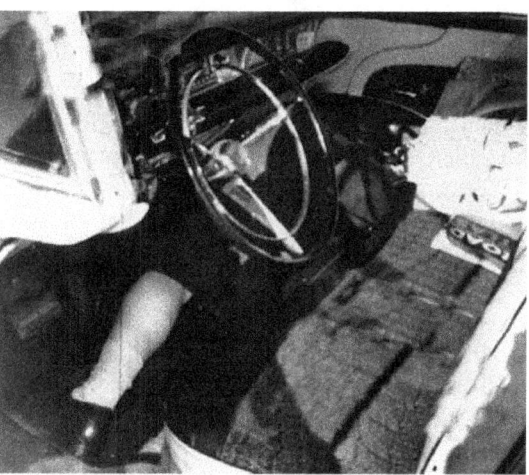

Merle Collison's body — a man that Charlie claimed was murdered by Caril after his own shotgun jammed.

Charlie climbed behind the wheel of the Buick and tried to start it. But the car had a push-pedal emergency brake, something new to Charlie. He managed to start the car, but it stalled as he tried to drive away.

Seeing two cars on the side of the road, a passing motorist named Joe Sprinkle pulled over to help. Charlie, confused by the new parking brake, asked Joe for assistance. But Joe noticed Collison's body stuffed in the car, and suddenly, there was a gun pointed at his face. Joe Sprinkle wasn't afraid of much. Outweighing Charlie and standing at least a head taller, Joe decided to put up a fight, and he managed to wrestle the gun from the teenage killer.

At that same moment, Natrona Deputy Sheriff William Romer arrived. As he was stepping out of his vehicle, Caril Ann suddenly jumped out of Collison's car and ran toward the deputy, screaming, "He's going to kill me! He's crazy! He just killed a man!"

Charlie, now unarmed, jumped into the Packard he'd tried to abandon and roared away, heading toward Douglas. After being told by Caril Ann that the escaping man was Charles Starkweather, Romer stayed behind and radioed for help. A roadblock was immediately set up at the Douglas city limits. Charlie blew through it, leading the authorities on a 100-mph chase through the town streets. Officers fired shots at the Packard, punching holes in the metal body. Just east of town, a shot shattered the back window, and Charlie slammed on the brakes, coming to a screeching halt. He sat motionless behind the wheel for a few stress-filled moments as officers called out threats and fired warning shots, and then he surrendered.

Flying glass from the shattered back window had nicked Charlie's ear and right hand, leading him to believe he had been shot. This cold and brutal killer, who had no value for the life of anyone else, apparently valued his own enough to give up when he thought he might die.

Converse County Sheriff Earl Heflin later told the press, "He thought he was bleeding to death. That's why he stopped. That's the kind of yellow son of a bitch he is."

Charlie later claimed he only gave up because he was out of ammunition.

THE NEXT DAY, JANUARY 29, 1958, CHARLIE APPEARED before a Wyoming justice of the peace to be charged with the murder of Merle Collison. Governor Milward Simpson had already publicly announced that if Charlie were convicted and sentenced to death by a Wyoming jury, he would commute the sentence. Simpson was opposed to the death penalty.

Faced with this dilemma, the Wyoming state's attorney let it be known that he would defer to Nebraska prosecutors. Governor Simpson, as anti-death-penalty as he was, quickly signed extradition papers to send Charlie back to Nebraska, a state whose governor had no aversion to using the electric chair.

And like that, Charlie was back in Nebraska two days later. He stayed in jail until May, when his trial began. Against his wishes, his attorneys attempted an insanity defense, but the jury didn't buy it. On May 23, 1958, he was found guilty and sentenced to death for the murder of Robert Jensen.

Caril Ann's entanglement with the legal system would be much more complicated. Nervous, upset, and said to be in a state of shock at the time of her surrender, she had to be sedated at the jail in Douglas. The following morning, she cried for her mother and wondered why she couldn't call her parents. Sheriff Heflin – whose shot had shattered the back window of Charlie's car – initially believed that Caril Ann had no idea her family was dead. He was present on January 31 when Caril Ann was told her family was dead and saw her break down.

But he didn't realize yet what a great actor Caril Ann would turn out to be.

Even Charlie first insisted that Caril Ann was a hostage and had nothing to do with the crime spree. However, Natrona Deputy Sheriff William Romer – the officer Caril Ann surrendered to – disputed this. He said that Caril Ann told him that her parents were dead and that she had watched them die. When Sheriff Heflin found this out, he searched through the items taken from Caril Ann when she was arrested and discovered newspaper clippings about her family's death had been in her pockets. Nebraska prosecutors responded to this information by charging the young woman with murder.

By the time Caril Ann went to trial, Charlie had changed his story, clearly stating that his girlfriend had played an active role in the murders and had personally slain some of the victims herself. When her trial began in November 1958, she became the youngest woman in U.S. history to be charged with first-degree murder.

In the courtroom, Caril Ann's attorneys continued to claim that she was held hostage by Charlie. He threatened to kill her family, and she was unaware they were already dead. But Judge Harry A. Spencer – and the jury – didn't believe her. She'd had too many chances to escape, yet she never did. Caril Ann was convicted of murder and sentenced to life in prison.

Caril Ann in a patrol car after her surrender and arrest. She'd always claim she was held hostage by Charlie but the jury at her trial didn't believe it and she was sent to prison.

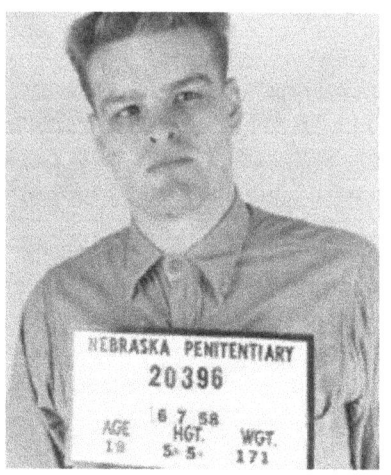

Charles Starkweather went to the electric chair on June 25, 1959.

Charlie wasn't that lucky. At 12:04 A.M. on June 25, 1959, he was executed in the Nebraska electric chair. Half an hour before the execution, the doctor who was supposed to pronounce Charlie dead, B.A. Finkel suffered a fatal heart attack.

Charlie was indifferent towards his execution. He offered no last words but wrote in a letter from prison to his parents: "Dad, I'm not real sorry for what I did, for the first time me and Caril had more fun."

He was unrepentant to the very end.

Charlie was buried in Wyuka Cemetery in Lincoln along with five of his victims – the Bartlett family and the Wards.

WHILE IN PRISON, CARIL ANN WAS CONSIDERED a model inmate. She was paroled in 1976, after serving nearly 18 years, and left Nebraska for Lansing, Michigan. She changed her name and lived a quiet existence as a janitorial assistant at a local hospital. Except for a 1996 radio appearance that she made after the state refused to pardon her, she never spoke about the events of 1958. She married in 2007 but was widowed after an auto accident only six years later.

The murder spree of Charles Starkweather and Caril Ann Fugate was the first of its kind in post-World War II America. It was also the first significant crime incident of the television era. Reporters and journalists flooded Wyoming and Nebraska, broadcasting to viewers the horrible details of the violence left in the couple's wake. Thanks to the sensational reporting, the people of Nebraska and the surrounding region lived in a state of terror while they were on the loose.

Unlike many other killers that have been glamorized over the years, Charlie wasn't all that interesting. He wasn't particularly smart, and he struggled with his feelings of inferiority, evidenced by his romancing of a 13-year-old girl. Starkweather killed out of anger and envy and a demand to be noticed. He despised the "normal" lives of the people he killed because their normality was what he wanted for himself. He wanted to be seen as a tough guy, but he was just a bully who enjoyed causing pain for others.

Caril Ann's role in the murder spree was much more complex. She was barely 14 when the rampage began, but she'd been involved with Charlie for months. She could have left Lincoln with him as a desperate means to stay alive after seeing her family slaughtered – or she could have also been a willing participant until it seemed their capture was inevitable.

Caril Ann Fugate was paroled in 1976. Her role in the murder spree has always been questioned.

If what she claimed about being manipulated and held captive by Charlie was true, then how do we explain what happened before her family was killed?

She claimed she broke up with Charlie on January 19, 1958, but she knew he had killed service station attendant Bobby Colvert almost two months earlier. She'd later say that she only knew that Charlie robbed the service station. She didn't know about the murder. That is impossible, however. The murder was covered in newspapers and talked about around town. So, why did she wait so long to break up with him – if she actually did? And why didn't she go to the police then? She could have saved ten lives if she had.

The biggest issue with Caril Ann's story is one that confused investigators then and now – why didn't she escape when she had the opportunity? According to her version of events, she waited in the car while Charlie killed Robert Jensen and Carol King in the abandoned storm cellar. If the keys were in the car, why didn't she leave? If Charlie had taken the keys, why wouldn't she have escaped on foot? When they returned to Lincoln, they slept in shifts at the Ward house. Why didn't she run – and possibly save the lives of Clara Ward and Lilyan Fencl – while Charlie was asleep?

In 2012, a copy of an investigative file was discovered, which had been compiled by a Lancaster County deputy sheriff in Nebraska named

Robert G. Anderson. In the report, he stated that Charlie and Caril Ann had stopped at a service station near Roca, Nebraska, on January 27, 1958, around 1:00 P.M. While Charlie was talking with a mechanic about repairing a tire, Caril Ann had gone into an attached diner and ordered four hamburgers for the road.

According to the waitress on duty, she sat down at the counter and was very calm and nonchalant. She waited about 10 minutes for the burgers to be cooked and never once indicated that she had been kidnapped or was in any kind of distress. The waitress added that three men were sitting at the counter, too, and she didn't say anything to them either.

That was, by the way, the same morning that August Meyer was murdered, and soon after leaving the diner and service station, the couple also murdered Robert Jensen and Carol King.

Caril Ann always insisted that she never played a part in the murders, but there is no one left alive who can confirm or deny her statements. There seems to have been good reason – in my opinion – why the judge in her case, law enforcement officials, prosecutors, and jury at her trial didn't believe her side of the story.

Do I think that Caril Ann Fugate would have been involved in a multi-state murder spree if she hadn't been influenced and manipulated by Charles Starkweather? No, I don't.

But do I think she had a role in the murders? Yes, I do. She was a very young and impressionable girl, and Charlie knew precisely how to make her do what he wanted.

But there's one more question worth asking – would Charles Starkweather have gone on a rampage across Nebraska and Wyoming if he didn't have Caril Ann – the love of his life – at his side? Maybe, or maybe not.

I sometimes wonder what would have happened if the two of them had never met, if Charlie hadn't tried to buy that stuffed animal at the service station, or if…

Well, there's no sense in continuing. They did meet, and 11 people died for their love -- a reckless, terrifying, utterly destroying kind of love that managed to ruin the lives of everyone it touched.

IT WAS WRITTEN AND RECORDED IN A SMALL, rented farmhouse in Colt's Neck, New Jersey. The singer and songwriter retreated there after his fifth studio album was released in October 1980, which brought Bruce Springsteen his greatest commercial success. But he wasn't as happy as he should have been. The newfound attention led him to take an inward look at what it meant to be an entertainer. The success of the album, *The River*, led to "very conflicted feeling about being so separate from the people I'd grown up around and that I wrote about," he later recalled.

Bruce's pain was rooted in a lonely childhood. He had been poor his entire life, and now suddenly, he's "Bruce Springsteen." He felt like his past was making his present complicated, and at the old farmhouse, he knew he had to try to understand how to get past what was making him feel so isolated.

Bruce Springsteen at the Colt's Neck, New Jersey house where the Nebraska album was recorded.

For Bruce, freedom had always come through writing, and this time, he based his writing on the books he read and the films he watched while hiding out on the farm. He delved into history books, searching for stories to inspire his songs. He read a biography on Woody Guthrie and titles like *A People's History of the United States* and Ron Kovic's autobiography, *Born on the Fourth of July*. He read noir books by James M. Cain and Jim Thompson and the gothic short stories of Flannery O'Connor and watched films like John Ford's adaptation of *The Grapes of Wrath*.

While he filled notebook after notebook with possible songs, the album didn't come together until late one night when he was channel surfing and stumbled across *Badlands*, Terrence Malick's film about Charles Starkweather, whose murder spree in 1957 and '58 galvanized the country.

The title cut from what would become his 1982 album *Nebraska* was the result of his fascination with the murders and stands out among the 10 dark and mournful songs that make up the record.

*I saw her standing on her front lawn,
just twirling her baton,*

*Me and her went for a ride, sir,
and ten innocent people died.*

*From the town of Lincoln, Nebraska,
with a sawed-off .410 on my lap
Through to the badlands of Wyoming,
I killed everything in my path.*

Springsteen later recalled telephoning a reporter from Nebraska who had worked on the story of Starkweather and Fugate. That conversation, he said, focused him on the feeling of what he wanted to write about.

In a killer, Bruce had found his muse. He wrote "Nebraska" in the first person, from Starkweather's perspective. And it's disturbing. It's an unhurried ballad that shows how unrepentant Starkweather was about the murders. He's not raving mad, but he's profoundly insane, and you can hear it.

*I can't say that I'm sorry for the things that we done,
At least for a little while, sir, me and her,
we had us some fun.*

*They wanted to know why I did what I did
Well, sir, I guess there's just a meanness in this world.*

In a surge of creativity, Bruce wrote 15 songs in just a few weeks. Then, on a cold January night in 1982, he sat down in a small bedroom with an orange shag rug on the floor and recorded all the songs on a 4-track cassette machine – just Springsteen, an acoustic guitar, and a harmonica. He mixed the songs onto a cassette tape that he carried around in his back pocket for days.

Springsteen's E-Street Band later tried to record what he had on the cassette, but bigger and bolder wasn't what he was looking for, especially with the most desolate songs he'd recorded in the old farmhouse. Among those that proved successful with a full-band arrangement turned up later on other records, like "Born in the U.S.A," "Pink Cadillac," "Glory Days," and "Downbound Train," which, in my opinion, is so tragically sad that it probably should have made the cut for *Nebraska*.

For this album, though, Springsteen decided to master the songs on his cassette and put them out as they were. The songs sounded a little muddy, imperfect, and unfinished – all the things that shouldn't be put out as an album.

But Bruce put the album out anyway.

Nebraska became one of Springsteen's most critically acclaimed albums, and many consider it his "masterpiece." For Bruce, it was exactly what he wanted it to be – he'd had some success, but he did what he wanted to do. He made the records he wanted to make, not the ones that the critics or the record company wanted him to make.

And if *Nebraska* really is Springsteen's greatest album, then it couldn't have happened without a murder ballad about two teenage killers who wreaked havoc along the lonely highways of the American Great Plains.

11. "RIDERS ON THE STORM"

"THERE'S A KILLER ON THE ROAD."

If you've listened to *L.A. Woman*, the final album recorded by The Doors – and if you haven't, why not? – then there is no way you don't remember what's become one of their classic tunes, "Riders on the Storm." A strange mixture of psychedelic rock, jazz, and art rock, it's been referred to as a precursor to gothic music wave that was still a few years in the future.

It's also an eerie song, with added sound effects of rain and thunder and an unsettling doubling of Jim Morrison's lead vocal with a spoken whisper track underneath. As engineer Bruce Botnick later said, "It adds this mystery to the song."

But that wasn't all that was unsettling about it. "Riders on the Storm" turned out to be the last song Morrison ever recorded. When the album was finished, he left L.A. for Paris and either died on July 3, 1971, or he went permanently off the grid – whichever you'd like to believe.

There are also those lyrics. It's believed that most came from one of Jim's many notebooks of poems, but the inspiration for the song – and possibly that poem – came from real life.

It was inspired by one of the most sinister spree-killers in history. His reign of terror began on December 30, 1950, and over the next two weeks, he went on a senseless rampage. He kidnapped nearly a dozen people, including a deputy sheriff, and murdered six of them in cold blood, including three children.

During those 14 days, the killer – a born loser named Billy Cook – terrorized the highways of the American Southwest and earned a permanent place in murder ballad history.

BILLY COOK WAS BORN IN 1929 AND GREW UP NEAR the southwestern Missouri town of Joplin. His early years were tough, growing up during the Depression, and he had to make do with money, food, and clothing divided up between seven brothers and sisters. His father, Will, was a laid-off coal miner with no education, and after losing their house following the death of Cook's mother, he moved himself and his kids into an abandoned mine shaft.

Billy "Cockeyed" Cook

They barely scraped by, but Cook's father eventually decided he didn't want to be responsible for all those children, so he hopped a freight train out of town and left them to survive on their own. The authorities found them huddled in the old mine, dressed in rags, scrounging for food, and living like animals. They became wards of the state, but soon, all were either adopted or sent to foster homes – except for Billy.

There was, everyone agreed, something not quite right about Billy. He rarely spoke; he menaced younger children at the state home and had a sinister-looking deformity of the right eye that never allowed the lid to close all the way. It earned him the unflattering nickname of "Cockeyed." He was eventually taken in by a woman who did it purely for the government payout, and she and Cook never got along.

But she didn't have to tolerate him for long. As he got older, Billy began staying out all night, shoplifting, vandalizing homes and businesses, and getting into other kinds of trouble. He ended up spending most of his formative years at a reform school after he told a judge he'd prefer it to foster.

Billy believed he'd simply been born bad, and he embraced it. While locked up, he tattooed the words HARD LUCK across the knuckles of both

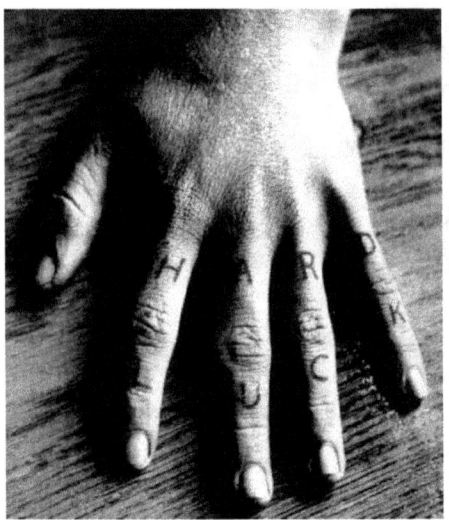

Billy Cook's "HARD LUCK" tattoos on his knuckles.

hands. He was released after serving his time, but almost immediately, he robbed a cab driver of $11 and stole a car. Quickly arrested, he was sent back to the reformatory, where he was supposed to stay for the next five years. Among other juvenile offenders, though, he earned a reputation as the most dangerous inmate in the institution. This led to a transfer to the Missouri State Penitentiary, where he finished his sentence.

Even at this fearsome prison, Billy stood out among the inmates, once beating a man so severely with a baseball bat that he almost died. The other man had made the mistake of laughing at Cook's drooping eyelid.

Billy was finally released in 1950. He returned home to Joplin, looking for his father or his siblings, but he didn't stay there long. He left town and started hitching rides across the Southwest, ending up in Blythe, California. He found a job as a dishwasher – the only legitimate job he ever had – but became bored and started wandering again.

His next destination was Texas, and somewhere along the way, he'd picked up a .32-caliber, which he kept tucked away in his pocket – just in case.

By now, Cook had little use for anyone and, frankly, hated everyone. The violence and despair of his youth turned to rage, and eventually, it boiled over. On December 30, he kidnapped a motorist near Lubbock, Texas, locked the man in the trunk of his car, and drove off with his captive. Fortunately, the driver managed to use a jack handle to open the trunk from the inside. He held it down until Cook turned off the highway and onto a secondary road. Convinced Cook planned to kill him, the driver jumped out when the car slowed down and escaped.

Billy Cook, though, kept driving. He traveled the lonely stretch of highway between Claremore and Tulsa, Oklahoma, before the stolen car ran out of gas. He left the vehicle on the side of the road and started walking. It wasn't long before he saw a 1940 Chevrolet coming in his direction. Cook waved frantically – as if he'd experienced car problems – and smiled grimly as the Chevrolet slowed to a stop.

The driver of the car was a man named Carl Mosser. Carl, his wife, Thelma, and their three small children were on vacation, traveling from Decatur, Illinois, to New Mexico.

The Mosser family from Decatur, Illinois made the mistake of offering a ride to Billy Cook. It proved to be a fatal mistake.

The friendly family was happy to offer Billy a ride.

It's hard not to wonder why a couple would pick up a hitchhiker with their young children in the car, but that was a very different time. The Mossers believed they had nothing to fear. They simply wanted to help a young man who seemed down on his luck.

Billy repaid their kindness by pulling a pistol from his pocket and forcing Carl to drive – and keep driving. They drove west across Oklahoma and crossed into Texas. Carl, desperately worried about his family, could only hope that his brother, Chris, who lived in Albuquerque and was expecting them, would become concerned and alert the authorities when they didn't arrive when planned.

By the time they'd reached Wichita Falls, Texas, Carl was frantically trying to think of some way to get rid of the maniac sitting next to him in the passenger seat. He thought he saw his chance when the car started to run low on gas. He convinced Cook to stop at a service station for gas and food, and when he stopped at the pump, he directed the elderly attendant to fill the tank. When he asked, on Cook's orders, for sandwiches to be delivered to the car, the attendant told him that he'd have to go inside for that.

Carl went into the station, accompanied by Cook. It was then that Carl grabbed Cook and tried to pin him from behind. Frightened, the attendant pulled an old revolver and waved it at the two struggling men. He ordered Carl to let Billy go, and Carl quickly tried to explain what was

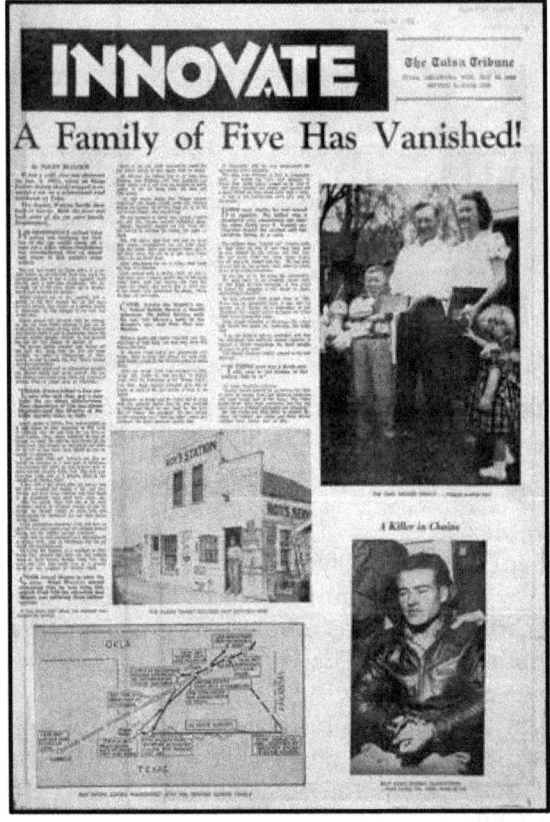

happening. Too scared to help, the older man ordered both of them out of the station. But Carl wasn't giving up. He grabbed Billy again, and they continued to fight until Cook broke away and pushed Carl through the station's front window. He landed outside on his back, surrounded by shards of broken glass. Billy grabbed him by the shirt and ordered him back to the car.

The terrified attendant locked himself inside the station as the two men got back into the Chevrolet. But then he suddenly gained the courage to chase after the car after Billy and the Mossers drove away. Billy saw him coming and fired several shots at him. With that, the attendant's newfound bravery vanished, and he stopped his pursuit.

Cook, now seething with rage, forced Carl to keep driving. They passed through Carlsbad, New Mexico, and then reversed course to El Paso, Texas. The terrifying journey continued to Houston and Winthrop, Arkansas. From there, he directed Carl to his old stomping grounds of Joplin.

By this time – after 72 hours of terror and trauma – Thelma had reached her limit. She became hysterical and started to cry. This started the children wailing, and unable to shut them up, Billy gagged all of them but Carl.

They continued driving pointlessly around Joplin for hours, once drawing the attention of a police officer – or so Billy believed. Now tired of the family, Billy turned his gun on the Mossers and killed them all. He

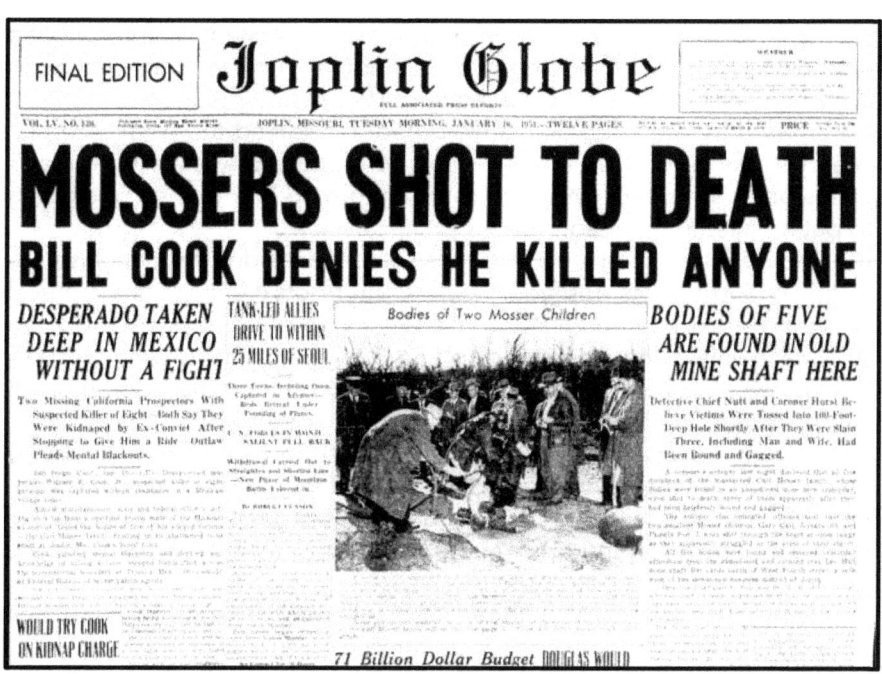

dumped their bodies in a place he knew well – the old abandoned mine shaft that he and his siblings once called home.

Billy drove off in the Chevrolet, and he vanished for a time, but unfortunately, he didn't stay gone for long.

A FEW DAYS AFTER BILLY KILLED THE MOSSERS, their Chevy was found abandoned along Route 66 near Tulsa. It might have avoided attention if someone hadn't looked inside and saw the blood all over the interior. The authorities were notified, and officers who raced to the scene found not only the bullet holes that had been punched in the seats, but they also found something Billy Cook had mistakenly left behind.

Although the bodies of the Mosser family wouldn't be found for nearly a week, the police did find the crumpled receipt for the .32-caliber pistol that Billy had bought when he left his dishwasher job in California. His name was printed clearly on the paper, and with an identity linked to the blood-soaked car, the authorities began a massive manhunt for the missing family – and for Billy Cook.

Soon, Billy surfaced again, back in California. When he ran afoul of a deputy sheriff, Billy kidnapped him at gunpoint and forced the officer to drive him around while he bragged about executing the Mosser family.

After about an hour, Billy grew bored and forced the deputy to pull over, get out of the car, and lay down in a ditch. Billy cuffed the man's hands behind his back and then calmly informed him that he was going to put a bullet in his head.

The deputy braced himself for the shot, but it didn't happen. Instead, he heard Cook's footsteps fading away as his boots crunched in the gravel along the side of the road. He would never know why he was spared.

Meanwhile, Cook managed to flag down a motorist named Robert Dewey, who stopped to give him a ride. Billy opened the door and got into the passenger seat, but they'd only traveled a short distance before Billy shot the man without warning. Although he was wounded, Dewey fought back. As the pair struggled, the car left the road and careened out into the desert. Finally, Billy managed to get his gun free and ended the fight with a bullet to the other man's head. He pulled the body from the car and dumped him into a ditch.

By this time, an alarm had been raised all over the Southwest, so Cook decided to cross the border into Mexico. He made one last stop, kidnapped two men at a diner, and brought them along to Santa Rosalia, a few miles over the border.

Amazingly, Billy was recognized by the local police chief, Francisco Morales. He simply walked up to Billy, snatched the pistol from his belt, and placed him under arrest. Before federal authorities in Mexico knew what was happening, Morales rushed Billy to the border and turned him over to FBI agents who were waiting there.

Billy's arrest set off a mad scramble among state officials. Despite the slaying of the Mosser family in Missouri, he was turned over

Billy Cook being turned over to the American authorities by Mexican police.

to the California authorities and was tried for the murder of Robert Dewey. Cook expressed as little regret about Dewey's death as he did about the others, and a jury convicted him and sentenced him to death.

And what were his last words uttered on the way to his death? "I hate everybody's guts, and everybody hates mine," he reportedly said.

Billy Cook died in the gas chamber at San Quentin on December 12, 1952.

AND THEN THINGS TOOK A CURIOUS TURN.

A Comanche, Oklahoma, undertaker named Glen Boydstrun came up with an interesting idea about what to do with Billy's body after the execution. Glen was old enough to remember the crowds that had once turned out to see the bullet-riddled bodies of Depression-era bandits like Pretty Boy Floyd, so he decided to try his luck at putting Billy's body on display in Comanche, even though the town had nothing to do with the killer or his victims.

Glen contacted Billy's father, Will Cook, in Joplin and made a deal with him. He'd pay for a proper burial for Cook's son if Cook would allow him to claim the body at San Quentin. Cook agreed, so the undertaker immediately drove to California, collected the corpse, and rushed back to Oklahoma.

Just three days after he'd died in the gas chamber, Cook's body, outfitted in a suit and tie, was placed on display in Comanche. Glen was disappointed with the first day's turnout, so he added loudspeakers and, like a sideshow barker, urged people to see the "last American desperado." Thousands came on the second day, including busloads of schoolchildren. In all, as many as 12,000 curiosity-seekers paid to see the body before Billy's brothers and sisters hired a lawyer, got the body away from the huckster and their no-good father, and took it to Joplin.

Billy Cook was buried in the dark of night at Peace Church Cemetery, a wooded burial ground outside of town. According to a 1952 *Joplin Globe* article, a brief service was held with flashlights and lanterns, and about 15 people were in attendance. Billy was buried in an unmarked grave, hoping to avoid local scrutiny. Just as the grave service ended, a reporter wrote, "the cry of a small child could be heard in the chill of the night air."

This was the first hint that there might be something spooky going on with Billy Cook and the Peace Church Cemetery, but it wouldn't be the last.

Peace Church Cemetery near Joplin, where Billy Cook was laid to rest in an unmarked grave. But does he rest in peace?

It's not uncommon today to go to the cemetery and find things like flowers, notes, and candles left in various spots that people believe might be the location of Cook's unmarked grave. It has been rumored that local teenagers have congregated in the graveyard many times to try and contact Billy's spirit. In 1987, three 17-year-old boys from nearby Carl Junction were discovered to have killed several animals and then murdered a 19-year-old acquaintance by beating him to death with a baseball bat. At their trial, their defense claimed they had been engaging in satanic rituals and had been influenced to commit the murder by the spirit of Billy Cook. The jury wasn't buying it, and they were convicted of murder.

Despite what the jury believed, many people believe that Billy doesn't rest quietly in the old cemetery. Over the years, stories have circulated about a shadowy figure that has been seen lurking on the grounds and wandering among the trees. Whoever this figure is, it seems lost and confused, and some have remarked that he appears to be angry about something.

If this lingering spirit is that of Billy Cook, then his anger becomes clear. In life, Billy hated everyone and everything, and, likely, his hatred about being born hasn't gone away, even in death.

BUT BILLY COOK DIDN'T JUST INSPIRE LOCAL GHOST stories. His dark influence was first felt in the 1953 thriller *The Hitch-Hiker*, which was co-written and directed by Ida Lupino. The film tells the story of two buddies, Roy Collins and Gilbert Bowen (Edmond O'Brien and Frank Lovejoy), who set out on a weekend fishing trip. But things don't turn out as planned after they make the mistake of picking up a hitchhiker named Emmett Myers (William Talman, who played Hamilton Burger in the *Perry Mason* TV series), who turns out to be a murderous psychopath. Myers kidnaps the men, forcing them to drive him to Mexico. Along the way,

Collins and Bowen find their attempts to flee are hampered by Myers's creepy ability to literally sleep with one eye open.

When writing the film, Ida Lupino interviewed the two men who were Billy Cook's last captives, and she even visited Cook in San Quentin shortly before his execution. She said later, "I was afraid of him. I could not wait to get the hell out of San Quentin."

Her film was released in March 1953, just a few months after Cook's execution, but that release didn't come without challenges. Thanks to the Motion Picture Production Code -- which controlled the depiction of sex and crime in the movies at the time -- Lupino had to decrease the number of Cook's on-screen killings. The Code also prevented her from using Cook's real name in the film, but she did exercise some creative liberties with the capture of the film's villain, spicing up the real-life, undramatic arrest with two fistfights and a shootout.

When the film was released, it was marketed with a chilling line: "When was the last time you invited death into your car?"

THE UNSETTLING FEELING OF "INVITING DEATH INTO your car" was something that Jim Morrison hoped to capture in "Riders on the Storm." Some of the lyrics seemed lifted directly from Billy Cook's bloody exploits:

> *There's a killer on the road,*
> *His brain is squirming like a toad,*
> *Take a long holiday,*
> *Let your children play.*
> *If you give this man a ride,*
> *A sweet memory will die,*
> *Killer on the road...*

The Doors in 1970, just before recording their final album, which featured "Riders on the Storm"

When *L.A. Woman* – the last album from The Doors – was recorded, it had only been five years since they'd recorded their first album. They're considered one of the groundbreaking bands of the late 1960s and early 1970s, yet their existence was a blur. They went from being a popular club band to national superstars once their first album hit the airwaves, and "Light My Fire" became a massive hit. Their first three albums were so popular – and so good – that it wasn't long before they went from clubs and small auditoriums to giant sports arenas.

And Jim Morrison didn't handle it well.

As the popularity of the band rose, Jim turned into a self-destructive, often belligerent drunk who frequently showed up onstage so wasted he was barely able to perform. The low point came in Miami in March 1969, when he allegedly exposed himself onstage, leading to his arrest and beginning a fall from grace that was as rapid as his rise to fame. The Doors were banned in many cities, and Jim spent much of the following year dealing with messy legal proceedings and trying to stay out of jail.

In 1970, the band made a comeback with their album Morrison Hotel and a scaled-back tour of smaller venues. It was successful, and while it helped to erase some of the taint of Miami, Jim was physically worn out and mentally exhausted by the time the band got together to record *L.A. Woman*.

And it wasn't just Jim. The rest of the band were dragging, too. They were uninspired, taking drugs out of boredom, and only Ray Manzarek seemed to want to be there.

At first, things seemed to be no different from their other recording sessions, with Paul Rothchild as producer and Bruce Botnick in the engineering seat at Sunset Sound in Hollywood. But things quickly soured. Tension with Rothchild had been building for some time, and he wasn't in the mood to record a band that clearly didn't have their songs together or a lead singer who was too unreliable to cut tracks.

The rehearsals went on for about a month, but Rothchild later called them "a joke." The band straggled into the studio. Jim didn't show up half the time, and everyone seemed angry with everyone else. Rothchild later recalled they only had four or five songs that were defined enough to play as songs at that point. The most complete were "L.A. Woman" – which Jim had written as a tribute to his girlfriend, Pamela Courson – and "Riders on the Storm."

While Rothchild claimed later that he called both "great songs," he didn't seem to get the band to play them decently. They rehearsed and rehearsed, but nothing came together. Finally, he told Botnick that he couldn't do it anymore, and he walked out.

Rothchild wasn't the only one who felt liberated when he walked out the door. Things started to come together for Botnick and the band once they were free from Rothchild's criticisms, especially with "Riders on the Storm," which the producer had referred to as "bad cocktail music."

Botnick moved their rehearsal space, and everyone started to relax. Within days, they were ready to record, and the album was finished less than a week later.

When they first recorded "Riders on the Storm," Botnick described it as a "nice light song" that really came together when they started mixing it. With the rain and thunder effects and the doubling of Jim's voice, it turned into something dark and troubling. There was nothing "light" or "cocktail music" about it when they were finished.

The final mix only took four days, but Botnick remembered something strange that had happened during the process. They were mixing at what became Signet Sound when the San Fernando Earthquake of February 9, 1971, occurred. Botnick remembered in an interview: "The control room glass was floor to ceiling, so you'd look straight out to the studio as if there wasn't a wall there. It was spectacular, but unfortunately, with every earthquake aftershock, you had this glass wall that was 10 feet high and 30 feet long moving and swaying – it was really spooky. We'd have to leave the building between mixes."

When the album was finished, Jim left for Paris. It was unclear if he planned to return, make more music with The Doors, or drop out to write poetry full-time. At that point, though, no one was too worried about it.

The album was released in April 1971 and became an immediate hit. The first single was "Love Her Madly," but FM radio jumped on the title cut along with "Riders on the Storm."

The Doors were at the top of their game again, but Jim never came home to enjoy it. Whether he died or disappeared on his own – there's evidence to suggest either might have happened – he hasn't been seen since, but his musical legacy lives on.

As does a song written about a killer whose hatred and rage could only be quenched by death.

12. "PSYCHO"

"WHAT THE HELL IS THIS?"

That had to be the question asked by anyone who heard the strange country and western song that came and went without much fanfare in the summer of 1968. It was released on a small Nashville record label, so not many people heard it, but those who did must have been unsettled and confused in equal measure.

The song was performed by a fading singer who needed a hit and was written by a successful songwriter who could afford it to be a flop. And it was. It received little airplay, and the distribution was mediocre at best.

It should have vanished entirely, but over time, it somehow gained a small cult following, and its inclusion in an anthology of oddball songs rescued it from oblivion. Neither the singer nor the composer lived long enough to see this unlikely development.

And it didn't hurt that it had one very famous fan. In 2007, none other than Bob Dylan himself brought up the song during an interview. "It never got much airplay," he said, "but has become quite a bit of a cult classic, as is Eddie Noack himself."

Eddie Noack was the fading performer who tried to use the song as a comeback, and Leon Payne wrote it. The peculiar lyrics are addressed to "Mama," and while the tone of it is mild, the mood is tense – a first-person story of murder in which the killer never seems to break a sweat, despite what he's describing in the song.

*I seen my ex last night, Mama,
At a dance at Miller's store,
She was with that Jackie White, Mama,
I killed 'em both, and they're buried,
Under Jenkins' sycamore.*

It's a chilling admission, but not unexpected in a song called "Psycho." The title came from the abbreviated term for "psychopath," and it had become a recognizable term about eight years earlier when Alfred Hitchcock had directed a film that used the same title. It was shorthand for a killer driven by deviant urges, especially one who is seemingly sane on the surface, like Norman Bates, whose best friend had been his mother.

Hitchcock's film was based on a book – also called *Psycho* – which was inspired by the story of a real-life killer whose story contained elements that were too macabre for the page and screen in the 1960s. That true story had spawned the book, the film, and this weird little song.

The songwriter, Leon Payne, was a history buff with a taste for true crime and the unusual. He came up with the lyrics after a conversation with his pedal steel player, Jackie White – who gets name-checked in the first verse – about everything from Richard Speck, serial killer Albert Fish, and the inspiration for Psycho – a Wisconsin man named Eddie Gein.

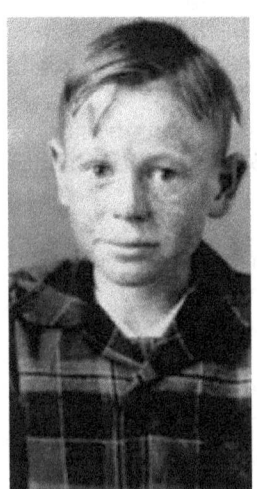

A young Edward Theodore Gein

EDWARD THEODORE GEIN GREW UP ON A FARM A few miles outside of the small town of Plainfield, Wisconsin. His father, George, was a hard-luck farmer with little talent for working the soil and a taste for alcohol. He was a drunk and a bully, but he was no match for his wife, Augusta.

Augusta was a terrifying woman who hated alcohol, men, and anything to do with sex. How she managed to become pregnant with her two sons, Eddie and Henry, remains a mystery. She considered the small town where they lived a terrible place and kept her sons on the farm away from the sinful influences of women and carnal love.

In 1940, George Gein dropped dead from a heart attack. Most likely, he was not sorry to go.

The years spent with Augusta had undoubtedly taken their toll on him.

The two boys were left alone with their mother, and soon Eddie was even deeper under her terrible spell. Henry tried to move away from the farm and have a normal life, but being rebellious came with a price. In 1944, he was found dead on the Gein farm. The young man had allegedly died from a heart attack.

Apparently, when he had fallen over, he bashed in the back of his head.

Eddie finally had his mother all to himself -- but that also came with a price. In 1945, Augusta had a stroke and was confined to bed. Eddie waited on her night and day when she screamed at him and belittled him for hours. Then she grew quiet and told Eddie to crawl into bed with her while she whispered to him as he slept. Eddie prayed that she'd never die and leave him alone.

Augusta Gein

Because, you know, a boy's best friend is his mother.

Eddie's prayers failed him, and Augusta died in December 1945. Eddie was now 39 and alone to fend for himself. It was at this point that

Eddie Gein's isolated farmhouse outside of Plainfield, Wisconsin. (Right) Eddie Gein in 1957

he began to descend into madness.

For a while, no one seemed to notice. Even in a town as small as Plainfield, Eddie was a loner and rarely ventured off the farm. He only showed up in town when he needed to run an errand, perform some handyman chores, or stop in for an occasional beer at Mary Hogan's tavern. No one seemed to think that he was any stranger than before. He had always been an odd little man who needed a bath and often laughed inappropriately at some of the strangest things. But he didn't seem to be any different than he'd been when his mother was still alive.

It would be later – after the horrors of his farmhouse were revealed – that Eddie's peculiarities seemed to stand out. Local folks would later recall his barroom discussions of articles that he had read in men's magazines -- stories of Nazi atrocities, island headhunters, and sex-change operations.

Tavern owner Mary Hogan

His jokes were a little odd, too. When Mary Hogan, the tavern owner, suddenly disappeared, Eddie began saying – with his weird little grin -- that she was staying overnight at his house. Mary had vanished from the roadhouse, leaving nothing but a puddle of blood behind, and many thought Gein's jokes about the poor woman were tasteless but just wrote them off to him being a weirdo.

Eddie would never hurt anybody, the locals thought. He was a strange little guy who disliked the sight of blood. He wouldn't even go deer hunting with the other fellows in town.

That's what everyone in Plainfield said – until Bernice Worden disappeared.

She vanished on November 16, 1957. Late that afternoon, her son, Frank, returned to town after an unsuccessful day of deer hunting and stopped by the hardware store that his mother owned and operated.

Strangely, Bernice wasn't there. She had apparently just walked out, leaving the front door unlocked and the back door standing open. Frank then discovered something terrifying -- a trail of blood leading from the store's front counter to the back door. A quick search revealed a receipt that had been left behind on the counter. The receipt was for a half gallon of antifreeze.

It had been made out to Eddie Gein.

Worden's Hardware Store in Plainfield (Below) Bernice Worden

Frank notified the police, and sheriff deputies went to Eddie's farm to question him about Bernice's whereabouts. He had not been expecting company, as was evidenced by what they found in the summer kitchen behind the house.

In that ramshackle little building, they discovered the body of the missing Bernice Worden. She was naked and hanging by her heels from an overhead pulley. She had been beheaded, disemboweled, and was dressed out like a butchered deer.

Eddie had been in the process of tanning her hide and had used the skin of her face to create what appeared to be a mask.

The stunned and sickened officers immediately called for reinforcements. A short time later, more than a dozen lawmen were combing the farm and exploring the contents of what would become known as Eddie Gein's "house of horrors." What they found that night was like nothing that had ever been seen before by American law enforcement.

The house was in a state of filthy chaos. The only room that was clean and orderly was the former bedroom of Eddie's mother. He had left it just as it was when she died. It was sealed off from the squalor of the rest of the house.

The nightmarish scene inside of Gein's house disturbed even the most hardened police officers who entered the place.

The rest of the house was a nightmare -- but it went beyond just being messy.

The police found lamp shades that had been fashioned from human flesh, and they gave off an eerie, yellow glow. A box was discovered that contained nothing but human noses. A belt had been made from female nipples. A shoe box found under a bed contained a collection of dried female genitalia. There were chairs that had been upholstered in human skin. Soup bowls were made from the sawed-off tops of human skulls. A human head was found in a box. The faces of nine women, carefully mounted, were hanging on one wall, looking down at furniture that had been constructed out of human bones.

Inside a crusted, bloody bag was the head of the missing tavern owner, Mary Hogan.

But those were not the only disturbing discoveries found in the house. The most unsettling was a vest that had been fashioned and sewn from a female torso, complete with breasts. The skin had been taken from a middle-aged woman and tanned like deerskin. Eddie later confessed that he often put on the vest at night and danced in the moonlight on his front lawn.

During the many hours of confessions that followed, Eddie admitted to the murders of two women -- Bernice Worden and tavern owner Mary

The gruesome items found in Gein's house — and the stories of his "murder farm" — made headlines across the country.

Hogan. The rest of the gruesome remains in the house had been scavenged from the local cemetery. For years after the death of his mother, Eddie had been slipping into the Plainfield cemetery at night and robbing graves.

The gruesome stories about Eddie Gein and the horrors of his farm became a national sensation, even after he was eventually sent to a state mental hospital, where he spent the rest of his life.

For months after Eddie was locked away, neighbor boys threw rocks through the windows of his farmhouse, allowing locals and out-of-state curiosity-seekers a better view of the interior. Eventually, notice was posted that the contents of the house and the farm itself would be auctioned off. The townspeople were in an uproar about the bad publicity, but there was nothing to be done about it — or so it seemed at first.

On the night of March 20, 1958, Eddie's home mysteriously caught fire and burned to the ground. Arson was suspected, but no one cared. The people of Plainfield were just delighted to see it gone.

Plainfield residents thought the destruction of the farmhouse would finally keep people away, but they were wrong. It didn't stop the

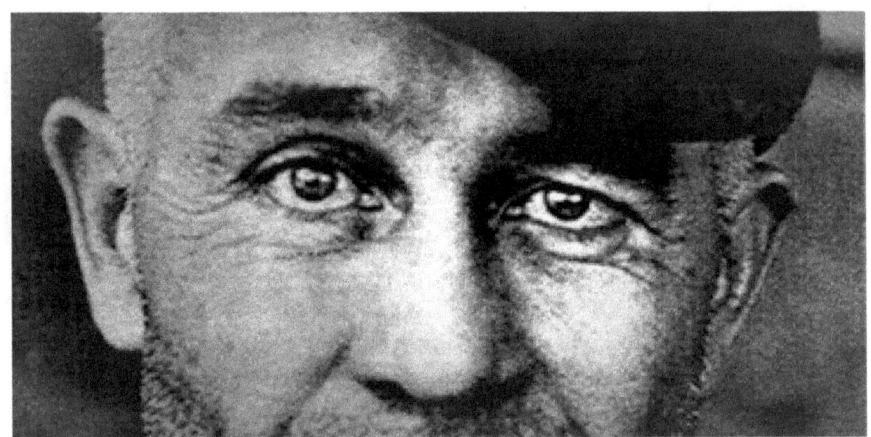

procession of cars that drove slowly past the place or the curious who came to witness the auction of the remaining property. Scrap dealers purchased Eddie's rusted farm equipment. The land was sold to a real estate developer who erased all traces of the farm and planted new trees on it.

People still look for the farm today – much to the dismay of those who live in Plainfield – but there's nothing to see.

For years after the auction, the car that Eddie was driving on the day of Bernice Worden's murder – now dubbed the "Ed Gein Death Car" – was put on display in sideshows across the country.

When it was first shown in July 1958, it was displayed in a canvas tent with a huge sign proclaiming, "See the car that hauled the dead from their graves! Ed Gein's crime car! $1,000 reward if it's not true!"

That first weekend, more than 2,000 people paid the 25-cent admission to see it. Plainfield residents and officials for the Wisconsin Association for Mental Health were outraged, while the carnies just loved the free publicity from all the complaints.

By the time Eddie Gein died in July 1984, he had become a legend – the Mad Butcher of Plainfield.

He was buried in the Plainfield Cemetery – the same place where he'd done his nocturnal grave robbing for years – and not surprisingly, souvenir-seekers chipped away pieces of his gravestone. What was left was stolen in 2000, and his grave has been unmarked ever since.

But Eddie's story didn't end there.

His twisted crimes went on to inspire many horror films — many of them bad — as well as three classics: *Psycho, The Texas Chainsaw Massacre*, and *Silence of the Lambs*.

And, of course, it inspired one very unusual song.

'PSYCHO" WASN'T THE ORIGINAL FIRST-PERSON MURDER song in country music history. Porter Waggoner released "The Cold, Hard Facts of Life" in 1966. That same year, Johnny Paycheck released his own homicidal Adultery revenge song, "I've Got Someone to Kill." But despite their lurid nature, the songs still had all the familiar country themes of love gone wrong, the empty whiskey bottle, and the killer's sorrow over what he'd done. Even Johnny Cash's "Folsom Prison Blues," which had lyrics like "I shot a man in Reno, just to watch him die," ends with the cold-hearted act only bringing grief and regret.

Eddie Noack's "Psycho" was something different.

It starts on a grim but conventional note with a double homicide triggered by jealous rage, but then things start coming completely off the rails:

I woke up in Johnny's room, Mama,
Standing right by his bed,
With my hands near his throat, Mama,
Wishing both of us was dead.

With six verses, three choruses, and one key change, the song recounts a series of less and less comprehensible murders. The killer recalls them vaguely, like in a trance, highlighting the compulsive need to commit the crimes. "You think I'm a psycho, don't you, Mama?" says the chorus, and then the narrator counters with a Norman Bates-style smirk: "If you think I'm psycho, Mama, you better let them lock me up."

The final verse ups the ante when the narrator murders a child but then claims to have no memory of the incident:

You know the little girl next door, Mama?
I think her name is Betty Clark,
Oh, don't tell me that she's dead, Mama,
Why I just seen her in the park.

And then, "Psycho" reveals the other trick that it has up its sleeve. After one last "You think I'm psycho don't you, Mama" chorus, we learn that Mama – who never responds throughout the song – is also dead. The whole song had been a monologue to a corpse. As the track fades, we hear Noack's deadpan voice trailing off with, "Mama, why don't you get up? Say something to me, Mama."

Leon Payne's subtle writing added to Eddie Noack's vocal, set "Psycho" apart from the slew of other morbid novelty tunes that often end up on campy anthology records.

I'm looking at you -- "They're Coming to Take Me Away, Ha-Ha!" by Napoleon XIV.

But if it hadn't been for just that kind of anthology record, "Psycho" would probably be lost forever. In 2016, a label called Omni began putting out collections of country weirdness called the *Hillbillies in Hell* series. "Psycho" is a lurid standout from goofiness like Wayne, Pat, and Keith's diabolical singalong "I'm Tired of You Satan" from 1966 or Billy Barton's 1958 nonsense, "The Devil, My Conscience, and I."

The collections are trashy fun, but the fan base for them is regrettably made up of primarily non-country fans who see the albums as a mockery of the genre's sincerity – which is fair if you get a load of most of the material that's included.

However, that's why adding "Psycho" into the mix is a little unfair. Noack was past his prime but still a respectable artist, and Payne was a member of the Nashville Songwriter Hall of Fame with a string of hits. What were they doing mixed up with the suicide, insanity, and Devil crowd?

It's a good question, but it's one that wasn't much different from the one asked by critics when Hitchcock made *Psycho*. Today, it's a classic, but when it came out, many complained that Hitchcock had degraded himself with what was essentially an exploitation film. The director's answer to that was that he was merely trying to stay viable by adjusting to changing tastes. It's very possible that Noack and Payne had similar motivations –if darker and more explicit music was a thing of the future, then they needed to embrace it.

Both men were respected in their fields. Payne had written standards like "I Love You Because" and "Lost Highway," and Noack had once called country "the only true American music" and refused to degrade himself by branching into rock-n-roll. Neither man would've poked fun at the genre he loved. The B-side to "Psycho" was a song written by Noack called "Invisible Stripes." It's a character study of an ex-convict struggling to survive outside of prison. It's the kind of socially relevant, thoughtful song Noack hoped he'd be remembered for.

He wasn't. In fact, he'd barely be remembered for his music at all. It turned out that "Psycho" couldn't have found a better artist to perform it than Eddie Noack – who'd best be remembered for the things that happened to him outside of the recording industry than the work he'd accomplished within it.

EDDIE NOACK WAS BORN IN HOUSTON, TEXAS, IN 1930. He was an only child, and his parents split up when he was a small boy, leaving him to be raised primarily by his mother. She later remarried, but mother and son had a strong bond that had been created by years of struggle during the Depression.

Eddie Noack

He was only a teenager when he embraced his love of writing and music. He wrote for his high school newspaper, learned guitar, and began to play and sing. By the time he graduated, he was set on becoming a professional songwriter and performer.

He soon entered the booming country music business and began playing shows at a variety of local venues. From the start, his literary interests set him apart from other artists. He used the money he made with gigs to finance a degree in English and had a deep knowledge of

Eddie's career was off to a great start in the country music business of the 1940s, but tragically, the good times wouldn't last.

country music as a historically rich art form. It became his dream to contribute to the genre in every way he could.

In 1948, Eddie recorded some original tunes for Gold Star Records, an early home for country, blues, and Cajun legends like George Jones, Lightnin' Hopkins, and others. It seemed as though nothing could stop his rise to fame.

Eddie's songs began to chart locally, and the industry noticed. He was taken under the wing of influential producer Harold "Pappy" Dailey, who signed the 23-year-old to Starday Records, the most acclaimed country label in Texas.

While a two-year stint in the Army put his career on hold, he returned to become an in-demand songwriter. In 1956, Hank Snow had a hit with a ballad written by Eddie called "These Hands," and he escaped Texas for the big time. He moved to Nashville in 1959 and signed with Mercury Records as a songwriter the following year. Still a young man at 30, Eddie was ready to launch the career that he'd dreamed about his entire life.

And that's when everything fell apart.

What happened next is hard to say, but Eddie fell hard – and fast. His songwriting stalled after "These Hands," which, ironically, is about a man looking back on a life of disappointments. He couldn't seem to come up with a commercial follow-up to the hot song, and he simply lost all momentum. His backers soon abandoned him and went in search of more promising artists. He quit performing and tried to focus on his songwriting, but success eluded him – even when he went back to singing again.

Mercury Records let his contract expire, and Eddie spent the rest of his career drifting through an ever-changing number of small labels, cutting demos, selling records out of his trunk, and playing venues that became a little smaller and a little dirtier with each passing year.

In 1962, he hit bottom working for a company that made vanity records for wannabe songwriters for a fee. The customers mailed in the music and lyrics, and Eddie performed the songs. A handful of records were then sent out.

His career had taken a devastating nosedive, which had him hitting the bottle even harder than he had in the past. Even when Eddie managed to get signed by a label called K-Ark, things didn't improve. Years later, in an interview, the label's head, John Capps, recalled, "Eddie would just hang around. He was heavy into drinking and just down and out."

Although no definitive biography of Eddie Noack was ever written, accounts agree that the ordinarily friendly and dependable man became increasingly crippled by dark moods and drink in the late 1960s. A few years later, the mood swings were diagnosed by a doctor as a manic-depressive disorder, which Eddie had inherited from his mother. Treatment for such disorders is common today, but at that time, Eddie and other sufferers were typically dismissed as moral failures, especially in conservative places like Nashville in the 1960s. They were romanticized as rebels or pitied as Hank Williams-style hellraisers whose battles with the bottle and hard living were money-making grist for the country music song mill.

But Eddie didn't fit into either of those categories. He also never sought help for his condition, likely because of the shame attached to his condition at the time.

By this time, Eddie was at the lowest point in his life.

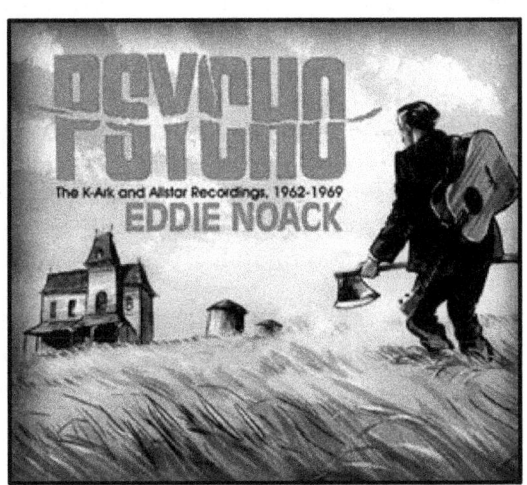

AND IT WAS AT THIS LOW POINT THAT EDDIE RECORDED "Psycho." His motivations are unknown, but it's likely that he just figured he had nothing to lose. Maybe it was a prank – a middle finger to the country music industry that he felt had abandoned him.

Or perhaps he hoped that something startlingly different – his version of an old murder ballad – would jumpstart his dead career. Or was he drawn to the dark themes of the song because of how his life had turned out?

After "Psycho" failed to take off for Eddie, he soldiered on at K-Ark. He issued another forgettable single and then unexpectedly returned to the murder and madness theme of his previous record with a spooky single called "Dolores" in 1970. It's essentially a Noack-penned rewrite of "Psycho," framed as a worried husband's warning to his wife about staying home because there's a killer on the loose. It only had four verses – and no chorus – and told an eerie tale:

Please stay inside tonight, Dolores,
Lately there's been violence on the streets,
The moon is full but hearts are dark, Dolores,
Danger in every stranger you meet.

There's a killer in the neighborhood, Dolores,
A man show sees a girl and goes berserk,
And you're just the kind of woman that he preys on,
And my mind stays so upset it's hard to work.

It's hard to understand why Eddie would have returned to this kind of theme unless "Psycho" sold better than we know. Otherwise, why would he have taken another stab – so to speak – at a first-person murder song unless he was trying to prove that his writing skills were just as good as those of Leon Payne? It was well-written but too close to the style of his earlier song to make much of an impression, especially since this song also has a twist ending where we learn the killer is, of course, Dolores' husband, who has killed his wife by mistake. "Dolores, how could I know that it was you?" he asks and then the song fades out with him humming insanely to himself.

The best part about the song is the in-joke that no causal listener could understand – that Eddie's first marriage, which happened when he was 22 and lasted for only a year, was to a woman named Dolores.

"DOLORES" FARED NO BETTER THAN "PSYCHO" DID, and when it came out, Eddie was trying once again at marriage. That year, he exchanged vows with his fourth wife, a Tennessee woman named Maudean McDonald. The pair seemed mutually devoted, even happy, but just like Eddie, Maudean had her own share of secrets in her past.

She had also spent part of her childhood with one parent, her father because her mother had been institutionalized for years. She'd also been married three times – once to an ex-Marine who was not long abusive but had brutally murdered a waitress and mother of three just three weeks after Maudean filed for divorce.

Eddie and Maudean during what seemed to be the good times in their marriage.

Soon after that, Maudean's 15-year-old son from another marriage took his own life. The young man had left a pitiful note behind with a line that included, "Don't cry over me because I'm not that good for anybody." His words suggested a deep depression, as did his method of suicide – a bullet to the chest, which literally broke his heart.

The end of Eddie and Maudean's marriage came a few days after Christmas 1974. The couple argued about the direction of Eddie's career, and he snapped at his wife, "You're just standing in my way!"

Clearly not in her right mind, Maudean retrieved a .38-caliber revolver that Eddie kept in his glovebox for protection and told him, "I'll never stand in your way again," and shot herself in the chest. She died instantly.

Eddie never recovered from Maudean's death or its tragic circumstances. Wracked with grief, he would sometimes lay on her grave and cry. He also kept her bloody nightgown in a dresser drawer until his death.

After that, he mostly called it quits. Musicians and music buffs occasionally sought him out and always found him gracious and generous, yet his talent and his health were gone. He managed to survive by eking out a living transcribing sheet for other songwriters and drinking to forget in local bars.

Tragedy touched Eddie again on May 11, 1977 – less than three years after Maudean's death – his beloved mother committed suicide in the exact same way, firing a .38-caliber bullet through her heart.

His conviction that the two women he loved most ended their lives because of him ripped away whatever spirit he had left. He died alone on February 5, 1978, with nothing left to lose.

Eddie, of course, didn't live to see his song become a cult classic, rescued from obscurity by the country weirdness of the *Hillbillies in Hell* records. "Psycho" was occasionally resurrected by artists like Elvis Costello, who heard it and recorded his version for a 1981 county homage called *Almost Blue*.

Other covers have followed, but what's striking about all of them is how little new content has been added to these later recordings. They're basically what Eddie Noack released in 1968 – an unknowing nod to just how good that little-known country singer had actually been.

13. "MIDNIGHT RAMBLER"

IN 1969, THE ROLLING STONES WERE AT THE TOP OF their game, and their latest album, *Let It Bleed*, was being hailed as their greatest one yet. By this time, the band had already earned a reputation for trouble. They were seen as the flip side of The Beatles -- menacing characters who didn't want just to hold your daughter's hand. They wanted to take her out, get her drunk, have their way with her, and dump her back on your front porch.

So, when the Rolling Stones added a song to *Let It Bleed* called "Midnight Rambler," no one was surprised to learn that what Keith Richards called a "blues opera" was a loose biography of a serial killer.

It was written by Richards and Stones' frontman Mick Jagger while they were on holiday in Italy, staying in a bright, sunny little town called Positano, which was very unlike the dark atmosphere of the song.

Did you hear about the midnight rambler,
Well, honey, it's no rock 'n' roll show,
Well, I'm a-talkin' about the midnight gambler,
Yeah, the one you never seen before.

In the lyrics, Jagger took on the persona of a killer stalking his victim. The character refers to himself as the "midnight rambler" and seems to relish his notoriety, just like real-life serial killers often do.

But this wasn't a song about serial killers in general. The two artists had a particular killer in mind, one who had confessed to his many crimes just a few years before the song was written.

His name was Albert DeSalvo, and he claimed to be the infamous "Boston Strangler," who had murdered at least 13 women between 1962 and 1964. A newspaper headline had once described the killer as the "Midnight Rambler," and Richards and Jagger used that moniker to bring their semi-fictional character to life.

Albert DeSalvo

THE SEX OFFENSES BEGAN AROUND 1960.

Around the Cambridge, Massachusetts, area, a smooth-talking man in his late twenties began going door-to-door looking for young women. If an attractive woman answered the door, he introduced himself as a talent scout from a modeling agency that was looking for fresh, new faces. If the woman fell for his line and invited him inside, he would produce a tape measure and proceed to check out her assets, using every opportunity to "innocently" fondle them.

Dubbed the "Measuring Man" after several of the women reported him, he ran out of luck in March when the police caught him trying to break into a house. He confessed to the burglary and, without any prompting, also admitted to being the "Measuring Man."

The burglar's name was Albert DeSalvo. He had been born in 1931 and had experienced a nightmarish childhood. Growing up, his abusive father brought home prostitutes and had sex with them in front of his children. When his wife complained, he beat her. One of Albert's most vivid early memories was seeing his father knock out all his mother's teeth, then break her fingers one at a time by bending them backward until they snapped. Albert himself was frequently brutalized by his father, who, on one occasion, clubbed him with a lead pipe when the boy didn't take care of an errand for his father at the expected speed.

It's likely not a surprise to learn that Albert developed his own early taste for violence. As a child, he once stated that his favorite pastime was to put a starving cat in a wooden crate with a puppy and watch as the cat scratched the puppy's eyes out. He was only 12 when he had his first run-in with the law after beating up a newsboy and robbing him of a few dollars. Soon after, he was sent to reform school after getting caught breaking into a house and stealing some jewelry.

He was in and out of reform school over the next couple of years, but after serving time for car theft, he was released in 1944 and enlisted in the Army. He was sent overseas, where he married a German girl and returned to the United States in 1954.

Less than a year after his return, though, in January 1955, he was indicted on a charge of carnal abuse after molesting a nine-year-old girl. Albert walked free when the mother decided not to press charges. He received an honorable discharge from the military and settled with his wife and child in Malden, Massachusetts. He supported them with various blue-collar jobs and by committing petty burglaries.

And then came his "Measuring Man" assaults.

Diagnosed as a sociopathic personality, the judge sentenced Albert to 18 months in jail, but he was released after 11 months for good behavior.

Not long after his release, Albert progressed from sexual assault to rape and began a new crime spree throughout Massachusetts, Connecticut, Rhode Island, and New Hampshire. He talked his way into the homes of countless women while posing as a utility worker in a set of green work clothes. Dubbed the "Green Man," he assaulted as many as 300 women across New England between 1962 and 1964.

At the same time, 13 rape victims in Boston had also been murdered. The initial victims of what the press called the "Boston Strangler" were older, ranging in age between 55 and 85. Each had willingly allowed her killer into her apartment, fooled by his story of being sent there by their landlord. Besides raping and strangling the women, the killer also violated their corpses, often shoving bottles and other objects into their vaginas. In most cases, he also left a "signature" behind. Using whatever he had strangled the victim with – often a nylon stocking – he knotted a decorative bow under her chin.

Near the end of 1962, the killer's methods changed. He began preying on much younger women, most in their twenties, and his murders became more bizarre. At one scene, he left his victim propped against the headboard of the bed, a pink bow tied around her neck, a broomstick

Some of the victims linked to Albert DeSalvo. DeSalvo was never convicted of the "Boston Strangler" murders, but he died in prison in 1973 after being stabbed by another inmate.

inserted in her body, and a "Happy New Year" card resting against one foot.

In October 1964, a young woman who had been assaulted by the "Green Man" reported that a man posing as a detective had entered her home and raped her. From her description, detectives were about to identify her attacker as Albert DeSalvo. When his photograph was published in the newspaper, several women came forward and also identified him as the "Green Man" who attacked them. He was arrested on rape charges and was sent to Bridgewater State Hospital for psychiatric observation.

It was there that Albert met and befriended a convicted murderer named George Nassar, to whom he bragged about his career homicidal career as the "Boston Strangler." It was only then that the authorities discovered that they had unwittingly captured the notorious killer.

Albert, though, was never punished for the "Strangler's" crimes. Thanks to a deal struck by his attorney, F. Lee Bailey, he was sentenced to life for the "Green Man" rapes and committed to the Bridgewater State Hospital, which was an institution for the criminally insane. Following an escape and a quick re-capture, however, he was transferred to a maximum-security prison in Walpole, where he died in 1973 after being stabbed by a fellow inmate.

This finally seemed to mark the end of the story of one of the most infamous killers of the 1960s – but it wasn't.

FOR YEARS AFTER ALBERT DESALVO'S DEATH, THERE was speculation about whether he was actually the "Boston Strangler." It wasn't difficult to link him to the "Green Man" assaults. Those were merely a step up from what he'd been arrested for in the past, but the murders seemed different. If DeSalvo really had committed nearly 300 rapes, why had he only murdered 13 of his victims, only in Boston, and then left a signature at each of the crime scenes? It didn't seem to make sense that he'd committed the rapes using one modus operandi and committed the murders using another.

George Nassar, who some believed was the real "Boston Strangler" – but DNA evidence would prove otherwise.

Some have pointed to George Nassar as the real culprit. It's been suggested that he and DeSalvo worked out a deal to split reward money if one of them confessed to being the "Boston Strangler." The two conspired with Nassar, describing the murders in detail, and then DeSalvo confessed to F. Lee Bailey, reciting the information given to him by Nassar. Thanks to DeSalvo's ability to describe the murders in detail, Bailey believed him – and so did the police. After hours of questioning, during which DeSalvo described murder after murder, the details about his victims' apartments, and what they wore, the authorities were convinced they had the killer.

Even though Albert confessed, there was no physical evidence to link him to the murders. Doubt remained among some officials, so the police brought the "Strangler's" one surviving victim, Gertrude Gruen, to the hospital to see if she could identify the man she had fought off when he attempted to strangle her. To observe her reaction, detectives brought two men for her to look at – the first was George Nassar, and the second was Albert DeSalvo. Gruen said that the second man, DeSalvo, was not her attacker, but when she saw Nassar, she felt there was "something upsetting, something frighteningly familiar" about him. DeSalvo's wife, family, and friends were elated because they had never believed he was capable of committing murder.

It didn't matter anyway, of course, since because there was no physical evidence that linked him to the murders, he was never tried in any of those cases. Naturally, this kept the conspiracy theories alive and making the rounds for the next 50 years or so.

Many refused to believe DeSalvo had been the "Strangler," and speculation continued for decades. Some cited inconsistencies in DeSalvo's confession, and while there were a few, in many cases, he offered details that had been withheld from the public. In his 1971 book, *The Defense Never Rests*, F. Lee Bailey stated that DeSalvo got one detail right that one of the victims was wrong about -- DeSalvo described a blue chair in the woman's living room. She stated it was brown. Photographic evidence proved DeSalvo was correct.

Dr. Ames Robey, medical director of the Bridgewater State Hospital, insisted that DeSalvo was not the killer, as did Middlesex District Attorney John J. Droney, FBI special agent and profiler John E. Douglas, a forensic psychologist named Michael Baden, and journalist Elaine Sharp, who took up the cause of the DeSalvo family to try and clear Albert's name as the "Boston Strangler."

Too many lies had been told during the investigation of the case, the doubters claimed – but they soon found that there is one thing that never lies.

In July 2013, the Boston Police Department announced that they believed they had DNA evidence that linked DeSalvo to Mary Sullivan, the final victim of the "Boston Strangler." She had been raped and strangled in 1964. After obtaining DNA from DeSalvo's nephew, the Boston PD said it was a "near certain match" to DNA evidence found on Mary's body and a blanket taken from her apartment. They soon obtained a court order that allowed them to exhume Albert DeSalvo's body.

After extracting DNA from DeSalvo's femur and some of his teeth, it was determined that DeSalvo was, in fact, the man who killed and raped Mary Sullivan.

Albert DeSalvo was, without a doubt, the "Boston Strangler."

DNA, you see, is the one thing that never lies.

THE SONG BY THE ROLLING STONES CALLED "MIDNIGHT Rambler" was not the first tune about the murders committed by Albert DeSalvo. In 1965, a band called The Standells referred to the murders in their Boston-themed song, "Dirty Water." It included the line:

Have you heard about the Strangler?
I'm the man, I'm the man.

Also hoping to make a few bucks off the notoriety of the crimes, Astor Records, a small label from Cambridge, Massachusetts, reportedly paid DeSalvo $50 for the rights to release a song under his name. Supposedly spoken by DeSalvo himself, the resulting 1967 novelty record was called "Strangler in the Night," its title a play on Frank Sinatra's 1966 hit single, "Strangers in the Night." It was actually composed and narrated by Boston journalist Dick Levitan, with musical accompaniment provided by a local band called The Bugs – which was not to be confused with The Beatles, of course.

And then, two years later, came the Rolling Stones and "Midnight Rambler."

The Rolling Stones had been around officially for only about five years when *Let It Bleed* was released. The band had been created by Brian Jones, a shag-haired blond guitarist who later died tragically at the age of only 27. Brian had always loved music, and although his parents pushed him toward a career in classical music, he became a devotee of American blues music instead.

Eventually, he met up with Mick Jagger and Keith Richards, and the resulting chemistry -- after some personnel changes -- gave birth to the Stones. After some initial success in the UK, they followed The Beatles to America, hoping to duplicate the way they had won over audiences in the States.

But it didn't happen easily. Their first two records – covers of old blues tunes – tanked, and their American tour fizzled after their single "Little Red Rooster" was banned by many radio stations because they believed it was obscene. Even the group's first performance on *The Ed Sullivan Show* in 1964 went so badly that Sullivan himself remarked, "I promise they'll never be back on our show."

But things changed dramatically for the Stones after the release of their first big singles, "The Last Time" and "(I Can't Get No) Satisfaction." By then, it was 1965, and the British Invasion was in full swing. Hit singles

The Rolling Stones in 1969

helped put The Rolling Stones on the same level as The Beatles. The public was soon split into two opposing camps, each arguing constantly about which band was better. The competition seemed to bring out the best in both bands. New instruments like the sitar and the dulcimer found their way into both Beatles and Stones recordings. Brian Jones could pick up just about any instrument and master it within minutes. The Stones were neck and neck with The Beatles' creative output until 1967, the year The Beatles released *Sgt. Pepper's Lonely Hearts Club Band.*

That year brought the "Summer of Love," and psychedelic music was hitting the airwaves. It was a new era for music, and The Beatles once again led the way with an innovative collection of songs that was unlike anything else on the radio at the time. The Stones would have to venture into the unknown waters of psychedelic music and away from their blues roots if they were going to keep up with the changing times.

Newfound fame had brought new relationships to the band, and these new associates provided unusual avenues of escape for the often-bored musicians, who had, by now, tasted just about every pleasure of life that the world had to offer. So, why not venture out beyond this world and toward the next one?

This is when The Rolling Stones began their foray into the dark side, playing and creating music influenced by people like filmmaker Kenneth Anger, introducing songs like "Sympathy for the Devil" and, for our purposes here, "Midnight Rambler."

The song has often been presented as a sort of "biography song" about Albert DeSalvo, but the lyrics never refer directly to him. Jagger only implies it when he sings, "Well, you heard about the Boston…" but an instrumental scream cuts him off.

The Stones began playing the seven-minute "blues opera" in 1969 and throughout the 1970s at their concerts. Each time they did, it was a showstopper. Mick Jagger created an eerie atmosphere as he took the role of the killer, thrashing the floor toward the end of the song as the audience screamed along.

These shows were enhanced by a custom rig that lighting director Chip Monck created for the 1969 U.S. Tour. It was the first lighting system to travel with any rock band, and the Stones used it to great effect for not only this song but all the dark material they debuted that year. At the climax of "Midnight Rambler," the lights on the stage turned deep red, giving the appearance of Mick being bathed in blood.

The Rolling Stones onstage performing "Midnight Rambler."

After debuting "Midnight Rambler" onstage on July 5, 1969, the band performed it regularly in concert through 1976. Performances of the song frequently turned into operatic-length jams during which Jagger crawled all over the stage, lashing the floor with his belt. One notable performance in 1969 – running just over nine minutes – was recorded for the 1970 album *Get Yer Ya-Ya's Out!* This version features Mick Taylor on lead guitar, in addition to Jagger, Richards, Wyman, and Watts. Versions of the song from 1975, featuring Ronnie Wood instead of Mick Taylor, are some of the longest live renditions of "Midnight Rambler" ever, clocking in at almost 15 minutes.

The Stones brought back "Midnight Rambler" for their shows starting in 1989, and it's remained a powerful concert favorite ever since – even though memories of the murders committed by the "Boston Strangler" have faded with the passing years.

14. "I DON'T LIKE MONDAYS"

THE MORNING OF JANUARY 29, 1979, WAS A BRIGHT AND sunny Monday morning in San Diego, California. Students were arriving at the Grove Cleveland Elementary School, smiling, laughing, and greeting their friends as they walked up the street or climbed out of the cars that had dropped them off.

But in a matter of moments, everything about that morning suddenly changed when gunfire rang out from a house across the street from the school. Principal Burton Wragg and custodian Mike Suchar were immediately killed. Eight children and a responding police officer were wounded.

Who was shooting? And why were they shooting at a school? Such a thing seemed unbelievable in 1979, but it happened, and the person behind the rifle was not a man in military gear or a disaffected youth in a long black trench coat – it was a 16-year-old girl named Brenda Ann Spencer.

When she was asked later what would make her shoot at a school filled with children, she offered an infamous reply that would go down in history, be immortalized in song, and provide a disturbing glimpse into a deeply troubled life.

BRENDA ANN SPENCER WAS BORN IN APRIL 1962 to Dorothy and Wallace Spencer, who'd been married eight years earlier in Chula Vista,

California. They had three children – Brenda was the youngest – but after Dorothy discovered that her husband had cheated on her with multiple women, she filed for divorce in January 1972. Brenda's siblings went with their mother when she moved out.

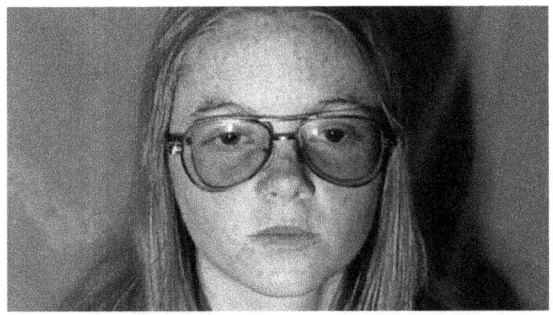
Brenda Ann Spencer

Brenda stayed in San Diego with her father, with whom she had a turbulent and likely abusive relationship since Brenda and her father shared a single mattress in the bedroom of their rundown, filthy home. They lived in poverty, but Wallace always seemed to have enough money for booze and guns. He was an enthusiastic collector, and his daughter seemed to share his interest. She also, according to people who knew her – because she really didn't have friends – dabbled in drugs and petty theft and was also frequently absent from Patrick Henry High School, where she was enrolled.

When she did show up, she often sought attention by describing herself as a "radical" and referring to police officers as "pigs." She cheered when she saw television news about cops being killed or wounded and often talked about how she wanted to kill a policeman by "blowing them away." Some classmates described her as "crazy" and reported being scared of her.

And they were justified in feeling that way. After being referred to a psychiatric clinic due to excessive truancy, she was diagnosed as suicidal. In December 1978, another psychiatric evaluation recommended that Brenda be admitted to a mental hospital for depression, but her father refused to give his permission. Two weeks later, he gave Brenda her Christmas present – a Ruger semi-automatic .22-caliber rifle with a telescopic sight and 500 rounds of ammunition. Brenda later said, "I asked for a radio and got a rifle." When asked why he'd given her that, she replied, "He bought the rifle, so I'd kill myself."

Around this same time, Brenda proved her skills as a photographer by winning first prize in a Humane Society competition. However, she continued to be generally uninterested in school. Teachers later recalled frequently inquiring if she was awake during class.

The Grover Cleveland Elementary School

Brenda seemed wide awake one afternoon in late January 1979, though, when she announced to classmates that she was going to do something big to get on TV.

Unfortunately, that's exactly what happened.

ON THE MORNING OF JANUARY 29, STUDENTS BEGAN lining up outside Grover Cleveland Elementary School, which was right across the street from the Wallace home.

The Spencer house, across the street from the school. Brenda opened fire from the front window.

Brenda watched them from her window with the Christmas gift from her father in her hands. The rifle had been loaded with the bullets he'd also given her. Brenda took a breath, aimed the rifle out the open window, and opened fire first on nine-year-old Cam Miller since he was wearing blue, Brenda's favorite color. Her next bullet struck Principal Burton Wragg, who'd been in the process of opening the school gates. Wragg was shot and killed as he and teacher Daryl Barnes tried to get the children behind cover. Brenda also killed custodian Mike Suchar as he tried to pull a student to safety. A 28-year-old police officer, Robert Robb, had responded to a call for assistance and was wounded in the neck when he arrived.

Miraculously, none of the children were killed, though Cam Miller and seven others were injured. Further casualties were avoided only because the police obstructed her line of fire by moving a garbage truck in front of the school entrance.

After firing 36 times over the next 20 minutes, Brenda put down the rifle and barricaded herself inside the house for the next six hours. Police negotiators called the house repeatedly, but Brenda refused to surrender. She told the police that the children and adults she'd shot were easy targets, and when she left her house, she planned to "come out shooting." But she didn't. She eventually surrendered peacefully, but only after a negotiator promised her a Burger King Whopper if she came outside.

At her trial, Brenda's attorney considered pursuing an insanity plea, but the judge wasn't buying it. Brenda was only 16 at the time of the shooting, but when prosecutors decided to try her as an adult, she pled guilty to two counts of murder and was sentenced to concurrent terms of 25 years to life in prison.

Under the terms of her sentencing, Brenda became eligible for parole in 1993. At the hearing, she told the board that she'd hoped the police would kill her that day – she'd been suicidal. She

When reporters asked Brenda to make sense of why she shot at the students and teachers at the school, she replied, "I don't like Mondays."

was denied parole that year and continued to be denied at subsequent hearings in 2001, 2009, and 2022. Her next opportunity for parole will be in 2025, the year of the publication of this book.

When Brenda Spencer opened fire on those students in 1979, there was no such thing as a "school shooting." It wasn't something that Americans had seen before, and her actions marked a significant turning point in our nation's history. Some have called Brenda the "mother" of the many school shootings that have occurred since then. San Diego Deputy District Attorney Richard Sachs noted that Brenda "hurt so many people and has had so much to do with starting a deadly trend in America."

Brenda eventually expressed regret about what she did that January day in 1979, blaming herself for the deadly shootings that have followed in her wake. At the time, though, I'm confident in saying that she had no idea of the horror that was to come – or even understood why she shot at the kids that day.

The reporters who repeatedly asked her for comments couldn't understand either. They struggled to make sense of a girl who had no hesitation before shooting at a group of children who were waiting outside their school. They begged her to make sense of it – why did she do it?

Brenda replied: "I don't like Mondays, so this livened up my day."

WHEN NEWS OF THE SHOOTING AT GROVER Cleveland Elementary School in San Diego went out on the Associated Press wire, the scruffy lead singer of an Irish band called the Boomtown Rats, Bob Geldof, was sitting in the campus radio station at George State University in Atlanta. He was getting ready to do an interview with a student deejay and happened to pick up the story and read it.

Bob Geldof and the rest of the Boomtown Rats

The story included the quote from Brenda that offered her explanation for the shooting. Thinking that not liking Mondays as a reason for doing something so awful was utterly senseless, Geldof wrote down the phrase "I don't like Mondays" and let it spin around in his head for a day or so before he turned it into a senseless song that illustrated the madness of the quote.

Geldof is the unreliable narrator in the song as he tells the story of an atrocity over an upbeat tune. It's a maniacal song; there's no question about it. Adding the danceable tune behind a story of a massacre is as bizarre as Brenda's excuse had been, so Geldof managed to accomplish exactly what he intended.

However, once the song was recorded, he started having second thoughts. Nervous about how the song might be perceived, he tried to bury it on side two of the band's next album, but the label wanted to release it as a single. "You're mad, that's not a hit," Geldof told them.

But it was released anyway in July 1979 and shot up to number one on the UK charts for the next four weeks. It even ended up winning Single of the Year at the British Pop and Rock Awards and became the biggest hit the Boomtown Rats ever had in their native Ireland.

Although it didn't make the TOP 40 in the United States, it still received extensive airplay – outside of San Diego – despite the efforts of the Spencer family to get it banned.

Today, the song remains a modern-day murder ballad, an oddity about a shooting spree instead of anything resembling a hit.

For Bob Geldof, it remains something that may not necessarily be a regret, but at least something he still thinks about from time to time with sadness. A few years after the song came out, he'd received a letter from Brenda Ann Spencer, mailed from her prison cell.

"She wrote to me saying that she was glad she'd done it because I'd made her famous," Geldof admitted, "which is not a good thing to live with."

15. "SUDDEN IMPACT"

WHEN FORMER CARNIVAL BARKER ANTON LAVEY founded the Church of Satan on April 30, 1966, it marked a startling change in the attitudes of society. Suddenly, this once feared and forbidden belief system was part of American popular culture. Its appeal to rock stars and celebrities like Jayne Mansfield and Sammy Davis, Jr. introduced it to mainstream audiences for the first time.

But the Church of Satan was just one of the new countercultures of the late 1960s. There was also the Civil Rights movement, new kinds of rock music, the hippie movement, and more – all of them helping to shift the country away from the conservative and religious traditions that had long been accepted as "normal" to Americans.

There was an immediate backlash from conservatives, especially when it came to Satanism, which was the most frightening new counterculture of all since fear of witches and the Devil could be traced back to the Puritans, the Salem Witch Trials, and the literal founding of the nation.

Beginning in the 1970s, Christian evangelists started speaking out against the rise of "diabolical forces" in the country. This marked the start of what would become known as the "Satanic Panic," although it wouldn't earn that label until the following decades when it turned into a catastrophic movement that ruined both lives and careers.

One of the most galvanizing moments in the history of the "Satanic Panic" movement was the publication of a book called *Michelle Remembers*. It was co-authored by a psychiatrist named Lawrence Pazder and his patient, Michelle Smith, whom Pazder began an affair with and later married. And while this is highly unethical, it's nothing compared to the damage the pair would cause with their bogus book.

Anton LaVey founded the Church of Satan in 1966, opening the door for what would become the "Satanic Panic" in the 1980s.

Perhaps more responsible for the panic that occurred was the book, *Michelle Remembers*, by Michelle Smith and Dr. Lawrence Pazder.

The book was allegedly an autobiography, and it not only popularized ritual sex abuse cases but it also helped religious fundamentalists cook up stories about cults and devil worship that were accepted – with zero evidence – by the mainstream media.

Michelle Remembers itself is ridiculous. It documents Michelle's "repressed" memories from childhood, which surfaced when she began therapy with Pazder. The stories in the book, which Michelle allegedly experienced, were right out of exploitation B-movies and included cameo appearances by Jesus and the Virgin Mary, who showed up just in time to save Michelle from a ritual that was attended by Satan himself. When it was over, they erased the young girl's memories until the time was right – that time being, of course, the 1980s.

Years later, *Michelle Remembers* was exposed as pure fiction, but by then, it was too late. For years, it had been accepted as truth and used as a guide for law enforcement agencies, courts, doctors, religious groups, and concerned citizens who believed what they'd read was true.

During the "Satanic Panic," the McMartin Preschool trial sent shockwaves across the country. At a school in California, children began to accuse daycare workers of sexual abuse on behalf of a satanic cult. While any claims of abuse had to be investigated, the allegations that were made included witches flying on broomsticks, rituals conducted in black robes, secret tunnels under the school, and actor Chuck Norris being a member of the cult. When the trial ended in 1990 – with no criminal convictions – it was the most expensive trial in American history, and there was no point in it whatsoever.

Like *Michelle Remembers*, the claims made during the McMartin trial were later wholly debunked. Once again, though, it was too little, too late for many of those involved.

The Pazder and Smith book and the McMartin case were probably the most famous incidents that occurred during this time of Satanic anxiety in the country. However, there were many others, and it spilled over into popular culture --- movies, games, books, magazines, television, and more than anywhere else into rock music.

By the 1980s, occult symbols and satanic song titles were deeply entrenched in heavy metal. Every hard rock band seemed to be laboring under the impression that having a pentagram on their album cover or mention of the Devil in some lyrics was a more effective marketing gimmick than posing with a naked model in leather and chains. As bands became more outrageous with their celebration of satanic imagery, society's moral watchdogs became increasingly indignant about what they saw as rock music's insidious influence on their impressionable fans.

Once fundamentalists could repress their rage about rock music no longer, they launched an aggressive campaign against scores of iconic bands, accusing them of deliberately planting subliminal satanic messages in their music – messages that could only be understood when the albums were played backward.

Backmasking is a recording technique that involves hiding a message in a song by recording it backward. It had been around for years, and fans knew about it – especially the folks who believed in the "Paul is Dead" conspiracy about The Beatles but never thought much about it. Musicians who acknowledged its use defended it as a gimmick to sell more records, but that was all.

But for evangelists, politicians, and right-wing parent groups, it became the hot-button topic of the day. They alleged that backmasking was a deliberate attempt to "brainwash" young people with hidden advertisements for sex, drugs, and, of course, Satan. One fundamentalist author, Jacob Aranza, cited unnamed expert sources in 1984 who confirmed that backmasking was a subliminal technique that converted rock fans to the occult without their conscious knowledge.

The hysteria over backmasking began in April 1982, when Dan Rather and the *CBS Evening News* aired a story about supposedly hidden Satanic messages in pop songs.

Rather played an infamous backward track that allegedly appeared in Led Zeppelin's "Stairway to Heaven," as well as garbled pieces of songs by bands like Electric Light Orchestra and Styx. Many viewers were shocked by what they heard in the report, and fundamentalist groups blamed the record companies, who were undoubtedly part of the satanic conspiracy.

Led Zeppelin IV, which featured "Stairway to Heaven," which was frequently accused of having hidden messages.

Hilariously, Electric Light Orchestra admitted they did have recordings on their albums that contained hidden messages – although none of them were satanic. On their album Face the Music, the song "Fire on High" had a secret message that wasn't all that secret since it's obviously garbled when played normally. When played backward, the message said, "The music is reversible, but time is not. Turn back! Turn back! Turn back!"

Jeff Lynne from ELO

The B-52s — one of my least favorite bands — used the same approach to subliminal humor by placing a backward track in "Detour Through Your Mind." When the track is reversed, the listener can hear Fred Schneider's voice say, "I buried my parakeet in the backyard. No, no, you're playing the record backward. Watch out, you might ruin your needle."

Funny, sure, but ELO was still in the hot seat with so-called "satanic messages." It was claimed that their song "Eldorado" contained a section that went, "He is the nasty one. Christ, you're infernal, It is said we're dead men. All who have the mark will live."

It was clear as a bell — if you played it backward and used a lot of imagination.

Jeff Lynne laughed at the suggestion that this message was real. "It doesn't say anything of the sort," he said in an interview. "That was totally manufactured by the person who said it. Because anybody who can write a song forward and have it say something else backward is some kind of genius, and I ain't. At first, I was upset by the accusation. But now I think it's funny. I was just going to say again, categorically, that we are totally innocent of all those claims of devil stuff, it's a load of rubbish."

After that, ELO turned it into a sport. On the back cover of their third album, they reversed all the band member's names in the album credits. There is a series of dots and dashes on the album that spells out ELO in Morse code. The opening song of the album was appropriately called "Secret Messages," and at the start of it, a keyboard methodically tapped out ELO again in Morse code. After the keyboard, a backward track can be heard with the phrase "come again." There's even a voice that intones secret messages to help the first-time listener discover the location of the secret track. When it was reversed, it said, "Welcome to the big show." There's another backward track at the end of the album — a very cordial "Thank you for listening."

Not everyone saw the humor in ELO's Secret Messages album. Those who had always blamed the excesses of rock-n-roll for all of society's ills continued to come up with other garbled word salads of phonetic sounds as evidence of the Devil's work.

Satanic messages were allegedly hidden in "Hotel California," an Eagles song that's spooky all on its own. Fundamentalists also came after Cheap Trick for backmasking in their song "Gonna Raise Hell." The band had the last laugh, though. On their *Heaven Tonight* album, they inserted a high-speed subliminal message in the track "How Are You?" When the garbled words were slowed down, they became "The Lord's Prayer."

Other groups targeted included the Cars, whose "Shoo Be Doo" reversed was supposed to state "Satan" 11 times, and Jefferson Starship, whose song "A Child is Coming" supposedly contained the hidden message of "son of Satan." It was claimed that the song "Snowblind" by Styx allegedly contained the command, "Satan, move in our voices." Black Oak Arkansas was targeted for their song "When Electricity Came to Arkansas," which reportedly hid the message, "Satan, Satan, Satan. He is God, God, God." What's great about this one is that the album was recorded live, which means the grunting syllables would have had to be well thought out in advance and then pronounced very clearly and phonematically – in front of a live audience – to give the hidden message. It would take a genius to do that, and we're talking about Black Oak Arkansas here, so I think we can safely disregard that one.

As it turned out, no song was safe. In April 1986, evangelist Jim Brown convinced Ohio teenagers to burn their records of television's *Mister Ed* theme song – although how many copies could there have been? -- because he somehow persuaded them that a reversal of "A Horse is a Horse" contained the words "Someone sung this song for Satan."

The 1980s were a very strange time.

I THINK WE'VE ESTABLISHED THAT SOME "HIDDEN" messages were less garbled than others – and some were even comically deliberate – but there was never any proof that a conspiracy existed to brainwash fans of rock music. However, many people were willing to ignore the evidence and to take the conspiracy so seriously that lawsuits were filed, alleging that the messages were actually killing people.

In October 1984, 19-year-old John McCollum shot himself in the head with a .22-caliber handgun after listening to several Ozzy Osbourne albums, including *Blizzard of Oz*, which featured the song "Suicide Solution." When the police arrived on the scene, they found the young man with the gun still in his hands. He was also wearing headphones, which suggested to investigators that his death had been spontaneous

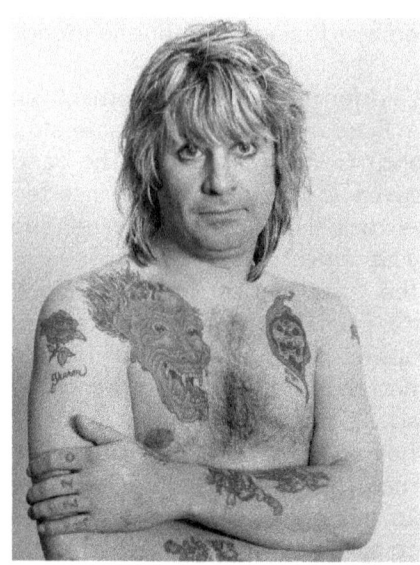

Ozzy Osbourne in 1984

and linked to the music he'd been listening to when he shot himself. That was tough to prove, but the fact that he had an alcohol problem and suffered from depression was not.

However, his angry, grief-stricken parents ignored those things and blamed Ozzy for their son's death. Upset by what they claimed was the rock star's irresponsible and reckless indifference to the effects of his music, McCollum's parents initiated legal proceedings against Osbourne and his label, CBS Records. It was one of three similar lawsuits that Ozzy was forced to defend himself against at the time.

Two other teenagers had killed themselves in similar circumstances, also allegedly under the influence of Osbourne's satanic spell. When the McCollum case came to trial in January 1986, the media – as well as the radical religious right – saw it as a critical test case.

Dressed conservatively in a tailored suit, Ozzy took the stand to protest that the song was, in fact, inspired by his own self-destructive drinking habit and was intended as a warning against over-indulgence. The word "solution" in the title, he said, referred to alcohol, not the ending of one's life, as a solution to life's problems. In other words, alcoholism was a form of suicide. Osbourne also argued that his image as a devil-worshipping occultist was just a part of his act. He had no wish to convert the youth of America to Satanism. Rock was entertainment, nothing more.

Unimpressed, the prosecution alleged that Osbourne had hidden subliminal messages in an instrumental section of the song, which encouraged listeners to "Get the gun – shoot," a suggestion that the singer strenuously denied. Under pressure from relentless questioning, Ozzy barked at the prosecutor, "I swear on my kid's life I never said 'get the fucking gun!'"

Neither the judge nor the jury could make out what was being said in the passage in question, which was totally obscured by guitar feedback, bass, and drums, so they turned to the experts from the Institute for Bio-Acoustics Research to dig into it a little deeper. The IBAR techs subjected "Suicide Solution" to intense scrutiny in their laboratory, filtering it through state-of-the-art sound equipment to isolate Ozzy's mumblings, which they claimed had been recorded at one and a half times the standard rate of speech, presumably to avoid detection by the casual listener. Their report concluded that the "meaning and true intent" of the subliminal lyrics "becomes clear after being listened to over and over again." The offending lines were said to be, "Why try, why try? Get the gun and try it! Shoot, shoot, shoot," followed by a demonic laugh.

Anticipating the argument that the defense might offer, that these words were ad-libs, the experts revealed that they had identified something far more sinister in the track – the presence of high-frequency signals that had been developed to aid the assimilation of information by the human brain. They couldn't have ended up in the recording by accident.

This was disputed by the defense, who argued that Ozzy had been messing around at the mixing desk and the so-called "lyrics" were merely a sound effect. Besides, he was free under the First Amendment of the U.S. Constitution to write and record anything that he wished, unencumbered by the worry that someone might misinterpret what he had said.

The judge agreed, and the court of appeal concurred that the Devil might have all the best tunes, but his lyrics are unintelligible, so there's no risk to any of his fans.

WHILE SUCH LAWSUITS MAY HAVE CLOSED THE BOOK on the satanic conspiracy of backmasking, rock music wasn't yet out of the crosshairs of the religious right.

In 1988, Geraldo Rivera offered a ridiculous episode of his already absurd talk show called "Devil Worship: Exposing Satan's Underground." Watching it now is hilarious, but when it aired, there were far too

Geraldo Rivera in 1988

many people who believed what they were watching was true. One section of the show portrayed teenagers who listened to heavy metal music as blood-drinking, grave-robbing, "Hail Satan!" degenerates. To "prove" it, several murders were featured that allegedly linked young killers to devil worship.

Tommy Sullivan, who murdered his mother in New Jersey. The authorities blamed heavy metal music for the crime.

The most notorious featured in the show was the case of Thomas Sullivan, a 14-year-old from Milton, New Jersey, who had killed his mother with his Boy Scout knife, set a fire in the family home while his father and brother slept, and then committed suicide with the knife he stabbed his mother with. His father and brother made it out of the house alive, but Tommy's body was found the next morning in a neighbor's backyard. His wrists and throat were slashed.

According to Morris County Prosecutor Lee S. Trumbull, Tommy's actions had been spurred by his fascination with the occult, books he'd read about the Devil, and his love for the band Black Sabbath. This announcement was made, by the way, without any evidence to prove it was true.

But even the suggestion of Satan was good enough for Geraldo, and he used the Black Sabbath connection as an excuse to get Ozzy Osbourne as a guest on the show via satellite. But when he was asked about the connection between his music and so-called "Satanic crimes," Ozzy was abruptly cut off before he could comment on the accusation or offer any kind of defense.

Accusations like this didn't end with Geraldo, and while some lawbreakers were metal fans who were also interested in Satanism, the music wasn't what turned them into criminals. It seemed that it might've been more productive to check out their home lives or their mental health, but those kinds of things weren't sensational enough for the press.

Things got even uglier before the panic died out – including when James Vance tried to sue Judas Priest in 1985 after he and a friend, Raymond Belknap, tried to commit suicide after listening to the band's *Stained Glass* album. The boys shot themselves – Vance survived, Belknap didn't. Ultimately, Judas Priest and their label were able to avoid legal responsibility in the case. However, freaked-out parents and moral campaigners were still convinced that heavy metal was turning their children into suicidal Satan worshippers.

But there was one song that came out in 1985 that didn't inspire anyone to become a homicidal or a suicidal Satanist. This song was written to tell the story of a murder that happened during the summer of 1984, when a 17-year-old drug dealer named Ricky Kasso murdered his friend, Gary Lauwers, in some woods outside of Newport, New York, while blasted out of his mind on LSD.

The coroner's report would later say that Ricky stabbed his friend 36 times and sliced out his eyes. It was a brutal and insane attack, and for weeks after the murder, Ricky led local teenagers into the woods to show them Gary's body and brag about what he'd done. This was disturbing but perhaps not as distressing as the fact that none of these kids told the police.

But, of course, they found out anyway, and thanks to the brutality of the slaying, the authorities labeled it as "Satanic." Sensational stories spread through rumors and newspaper reports about how the Devil told Ricky to kill his friend and about how Gary was tortured and then murdered in an occult ritual.

Then there was what two other teenagers who were present at the murder heard Ricky say before he murdered his friend – "Say you love Satan," Ricky allegedly ordered him.

And once Ricky was arrested wearing a heavy metal band t-shirt, the last nail was hammered into his coffin.

Satan was alive and well in New York, and he was busy convincing his fans to slaughter their friends.

IN THE WAKE OF THE MURDER, THE ENTIRE COUNTRY seemed to be enthralled with devil worshipper Ricky Kasso. One of the things that seemed to enthrall people the most was how the teenager who dubbed himself the "Acid King" came from such an ordinary background.

Richard Allan Kasso, Jr. was born on March 29, 1967. His father was a local high school teacher and football coach at affluent Cold Harbor High School in the suburb of Northport on Long Island. His father once described his son as a "model child and a young athlete," but when Ricky started using drugs, his once-promising future devolved into a nightmare.

By the time he was in junior high, Ricky was in trouble for petty theft and drug use. He was often kicked out of the house, living on the streets and sleeping in cars, garages, and at the homes of friends. His drug use mainly included marijuana, PCP, and LSD, all of which he tended to keep

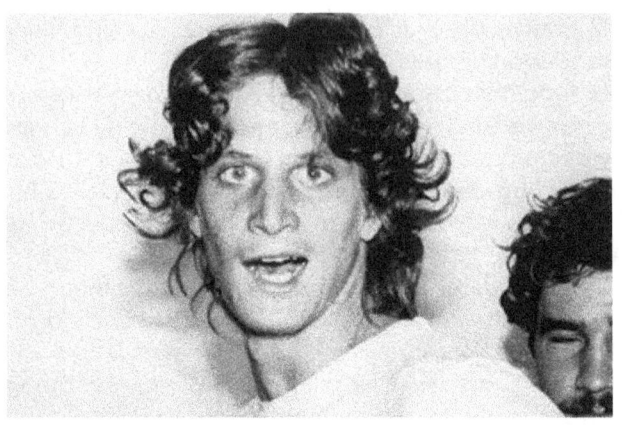

Ricky Kasso, who became notorious for committing a "Satanic" murder in 1984.

for himself but occasionally sold drugs in Northport to pay for his own supply. On at least one occasion, his parents admitted him to the South Oaks Psychiatric Hospital in nearby Amityville, New York, for drug rehabilitation and psychiatric care, but it proved to be a failure.

As a teenager, it was claimed that Ricky began dabbling in the occult – a not-uncommon fascination for many kids at the time. You can take my word for that.

Anyway, according to classmates, Ricky would "go to cemeteries and hang out, smoke bags of angel dust, and try and get in touch with the Devil." That was about as close as he got to performing "occult rituals." However, he did celebrate Walpurgisnacht – the pagan feast held on April 30 when spirits are supposed to gather – at the "Amityville Horror" house in 1984. He also told friends about his interest in Anton Lavey's book, *The Satanic Bible*, and he was arrested in 1983 after he was caught digging into a colonial-era grave in a local cemetery.

About a month after the arrest, he contracted pneumonia and was treated at Long Island Jewish Hospital. While he was there, his parents tried to convince doctors to involuntarily commit him for psychiatric treatment, but they refused. The psychiatrists who examined him stated that Ricky exhibited antisocial behavior but was neither psychotic nor a danger to himself or others.

Boy, they sure got that one wrong.

THE CONFLICT BETWEEN RICKY KASSO AND GARY LAUWERS, which eventually ended in murder, began in early 1984. One night at a party, Gary stole several bags of PCP from Ricky's jacket while he was passed out on a couch.

Ricky confronted him a short time later, prompting Gary to immediately return five of the bags and promise to pay for the ones that he'd already used. Before this, the pair had been friends, but now things were tense between them, and words had turned into physical confrontations on a few occasions in the following months.

By mid-June, though, Ricky seemed like he'd let go of his irritation with Gary. One night – probably June 19 – Ricky was hanging out at a small gazebo in Cow Harbor Park, listening to music on a radio borrowed from a friend, and invited Gary to get high with him and two other friends, Jimmy Troiano and Albert Quinones.

Gary Lauwers

The group walked to Aztakea Woods, set up camp, and took several hits of what they believed to be mescaline. The tablets were "purple microdots," and while they were erroneously believed to be mescaline on the street, they were likely LSD. They also smoked a few baggies of PCP while trying to start a small fire. However, all the available firewood was too wet, and they couldn't get it to burn until Gary used his socks and the sleeves from his ragged denim jacket as kindling.

However, according to Jimmy Troiano, Gary didn't offer those pieces of clothing voluntarily.

They were all tripping on the LSD when Ricky demanded that Gary remove his clothes and "donate them to the fire." When Gary only offered those few pieces, the two began to argue, and things escalated into violence. Ricky scuffled with Gary, bit him on the neck, and then stabbed him in the chest. Ricky then reportedly stabbed Gary in the back and demanded that he say that he loved Satan. Gary was said to have instead replied, "I love my mother," before finally giving in to Ricky's demands. Jimmy said that Gary then tried to run, but Ricky caught him and continued stabbing him in the back until he fell.

Jimmy and Albert then helped Ricky carry the body of their friend deeper into the woods. After finding a place to leave the corpse, Ricky was said to have bent over the body and chanted something about the

Devil. In his drug-fueled haze, he thought he saw Gary's head move, so Ricky began stabbing him in the face.

The other two boys fled the woods in terror, and Jimmy later said that he vividly recalled hearing Ricky laughing behind them as they ran.

NO ONE MISSED GARY LAUWERS AT FIRST.

He ran away from home so often that he'd been gone for weeks before any adults started to wonder where he might be. But the local teenagers? They knew exactly where Gary was.

After the murder, Ricky bragged about the murder to friends and even brought several kids who doubted the story to see the body before he and Jimmy returned to the woods to bury the mutilated remains in a shallow grave. More days passed, and eventually, someone talked. On July 1, an anonymous tip was received by the police about the location of the body.

On July 4, detectives used police dogs to search Aztakea Woods, and they soon discovered the missing Gary Lauwers. His body was badly decomposed, and his face had been destroyed beyond recognition. He'd been stabbed at least 36 times, and a knife had been used to slash open his eyes.

The authorities found Ricky and Jimmy passed out in a car the following day and arrested them both.

The murder immediately became a media sensation, and reporters – drawn by the occult and the "Satanic Panic" – descended on the Long Island town in droves. Everyone seemed to be shocked that teenagers from such an upscale suburb had committed such a brutal crime – until Satan was added to the mix, of course.

Once rumors reached the press that Ricky was a "Satanist," it all made sense. News stories became wilder and wilder. Most presented Ricky not as a fucked-up teenager who was high most of the time and tried to get attention by talking about the Devil but as a member of a murderous devil cult, even though there was no evidence of it.

The coverage by newspapers and television was bad, but worse was the press release by the police department that claimed Ricky regularly took part in satanic rituals with the cult – members of which never materialized. Most of the elements of the press release – just like the news stories – were eventually proven to be untrue.

Even his father chimed in, telling the press that his son frequently read books about witchcraft and wore shirts with satanic symbols on them.

Ricky Kasso was arrested wearing a shirt that allegedly had "satanic symbols" on it, which was, in fact, simply an AC/DC logo.

Those symbols? It was the logo for Ricky's favorite band, AC/DC. He'd been wearing that shirt when he was arrested, and this naturally led to an alleged connection between the murder, the Devil, and heavy metal music. That connection turned out to be as legitimate as other claims that were made about the murder.

The sinister reality of Gary's murder was that Ricky Kasso was a messed-up, mentally ill teenager who had acted on his own, not in the name of some formidable cult, the Devil, or the music that had been associated with the Devil for so long.

The only evil in the case was what was inside of Ricky.

The jury acquitted Jimmy Troiano at his trial. His lawyer argued that he'd been so high on the night of the murder that he'd been incapable of distinguishing between reality and the effects of the drugs.

Ricky, though, never stood trial for Gary's murder. Two days after his arrest, he hanged himself with a bedsheet in his jail cell.

IN THE WAKE OF THE MURDER, THERE WERE A HANDFUL of songs that were inspired by the terrible events in the Aztakea Woods.

Sonic Youth released a song called "Satan is Boring" in 1985, and The Dead Milkman put out "Bad Party" in 1989. Faster Pussycat offered "Crying Shame" that same year, and while there were others, most of them seemed to be trying too hard – using song titles and even short-lived band names for the shock value and not as what we'd consider a modern-day murder ballad.

Big Audio Dynamite

Interestingly – at least in the first decade or so after the murder – none of the songs that Ricky Kasso inspired were released by heavy metal bands. My guess is that such bands were already being hammered by ministers, the media, and angry parents looking for scapegoats and weren't going to touch Ricky with a 10-foot pole.

Instead, the first song about the "Say You Love Satan" murder, as it had started to be called, was titled "Sudden Impact," and it was released by the British band Big Audio Dynamite, which was formed by Mick Jones from The Clash.

Trust me when I tell you that this is *not* The Clash.

Party down, eat your friend, b-movie stories never end,
Rock the house, shoot your mum,
Cheap thrills wrapped up in bubblegum
Get down, burn the cat, the hardcore life is where it's at,
Love boat, sub attack, beware of sudden impact.

Burnt out case from the neighborhood,
Converge one night deep in the wood,
The bat from hell arrived that night,
To make that picnic out of sight,
Satanic rights to a tune they knew well,
To make the party rock like hell,
Hold tight the ride begins,
Macho men with pimply skin.

I haven't been able to find any information about why they were inspired to write the song or what connection they were looking for when it came to the murder.

Oddly, even though there are clear references to a "satanic night in the woods," some recent interpretations of the song claim that it's actually about "rapid social change, cultural collision, and the disorientation that comes with these shifts." The analysis goes on to state that the song encourages listeners to "disrupt the status quo and cause shockwaves in both personal and societal contexts."

I'm not sure if the writer was unaware of the murder that occurred shortly before the song was written and released or if this is simply a case of a band that has distanced itself from a song that has a very messy backstory.

If that's the case, I can't say that I blame them.

16. "DIANE"

THE FIRST TIME YOU LISTEN TO THIS SONG, YOU CAN'T help but notice the ominous introduction – muffled, plodding drums and a bass line that almost imperceptibly speed until joined by a distorted guitar that finally launches the tune. The tempo nearly doubles, but the rhythm is one of painful despair.

It's 1980s hardcore – a form of post-punk known for its speed and intensity – but a little looser and more melodic. When the guitar retreats a bit and a voice emerges from the noise, the words are subdued, almost like a voice-over, delivered with restraint, as if more emotion might distract from the bone-chilling message they wanted to deliver.

Hey little girl, do you need a ride?
I've got room in my wagon, why don't you hop inside?
We could cruise down Robert Street all night long,
But I think I'll just rape and kill you instead

The chords and beat never change. The barrage of drums, bass, and feedback eases slightly for each verse, then erupts again. The chorus is only a single word, and it repeats like a loop throughout the entire song, drowning you in the pain that's being unleashed by the singer, who becomes more desperate as the song continues.

That single-word chorus is the song's title: "Diane."

It's difficult to explain the intensity of hearing that woman's name repeated over and over when you're only reading about it. You really need to find the song and listen – as I hope you've been doing with this book all along – and hear that name sung in groups of three, drawn out slightly with every third iteration. The repetition of the name's two syllables becomes simply a dirge-like wail that gets under your skin.

The singer then returns for the second of three verses, maintaining the same conversational composure at first, but then he begins to crack. On the final line, his low-key delivery becomes a shriek:

Oh, won't you come and TAKE A RIDE WITH ME?

The relentless chant of "Diane" follows, and then a guitar cuts in with a break that's built entirely on rising and falling chords, like a banshee's cry. Part of the power of the song comes from the singer's decision to deliver the vocals from the killer's point of view – and yet, it's *not* the killer's point of view. Instead, he sings the killer's words, but the emotion comes from his own perspective as if he is being forced to watch what is happening – and by listening, we're sharing his experience.

In the final verse, the killer breaks down again, and the scream that comes in the song's last line is a wailing cry of pain:

We could lay in the weeds for a little while,
I'll put your clothes in a nice, neat pile,
You're the cutest girl I've ever seen in my life,
It's all over now, AND WITH MY KNIFE...

The sentence is unfinished, but the deed is clearly done. However, we can choose to look away if we like. This is not a song that exploits a murder or glorifies a killer. It's a compassionate song and an attempt to portray unbearable emotion through words and music.

I've never been a fan of Hüsker Dü – the band who released this song in 1983 -- but this song is one of the most agonizing in this book. It's a perfect modern-day version of the "murdered girl" ballads that have been around for centuries, but this time, the musicians themselves became the delivery method of utter agony.

CATHARTIC EXPRESSION WAS SOMETHING THE BAND had been known for since the beginning. It was formed in St. Paul, Minnesota, in 1979, where guitarist and vocalist Bob Mould was enrolled at Macalester College. He worked part-time at a local record store, where he met drummer Grant Hart and bassist Greg Norton. The three musicians had diverse tastes, but all shared a love for hardcore punk rock. They got their start as one of the countless bands inspired by punk that sprang up in the

Hüsker Dü

Midwest at the beginning of the 1980s but became something else in the years that followed.

The trio began rehearsing in Greg Norton's basement and decided to call themselves Hüsker Dü after a 1950s Danish board game that translates to "Do you remember." They developed a blistering wall of sound as hardcore took hold, and angry kids began blasting deafening sounds in suburban basements across the country. They were impressed by the aggression and stripped-down passion of hardcore but were skeptical about it in the long term. This might explain why their early records didn't have much purpose or personality, but again, that began to change.

By the early 1980s, Hüsker Dü had developed a strong regional following, and they released their first single in 1981, followed by their debut album, *Land Speed Record*. A year later, they recorded their first studio album, *Everything Falls Apart*. By then, they had been touring relentlessly across the United States in a van, playing at small clubs. Along with The Minutemen, R.E.M., Black Flag, and The Replacements, Hüsker Dü formed the core of a group of independent rock band that carved out a reputation for touring constantly and getting their records played on college radio stations.

Hüsker Dü shows became known for being a non-stop barrage, with the band members rarely speaking to the audience and one song going into the next without interruption. Along with touring, the band was doing a lot of recording, releasing their *Metal Circus* EP in 1983. This 19-minute, seven-song release marked a change for the band – a more enriched sound, stronger melodies, and more personal lyrics. It marked the point when Hüsker Dü left standard hardcore behind and developed a unique voice of its own.

There are no weak tracks on this EP for Hüsker Dü enthusiasts. There are moments of punk, incendiary tracks like "Out on a Limb," which is built around a buzz-saw guitar, and thornier songs about helplessness, self-abuse, and desperation. But it was Grant Hart's "Diane" – inspired by the 1980 murder of a 19-year-old St. Paul waitress -- that lingered with listeners.

The varying themes of the songs on this album became typical for Hüsker Dü. As their music matured, they traded their blended, abrasive noise for personal tunes that were candid and vulnerable but, like punk, offered in direct and unsentimental ways. The band's fusion of new, catchy tunes with harsh accompaniment opened new expressive possibilities for the band – but it didn't always go smoothly.

Grant Hart and Bob Mould frequently clashed as the band went through changes. The two began as collaborators, became competitors, and ended up as enemies. Grant's temperament was much more easygoing than Bob's was. Bob was tall and menacing, and his onstage persona was one of no-nonsense seriousness.

Grant, on the other hand, was shaggy-haired, wore hippy beads, and drummed barefoot. He'd come from a working-class background that he described as "dysfunctional but not abusive." When he was 10, he lost his older brother, a budding drummer and music fan, in a fatal car accident. He inherited his brother's drum kit, and music became both his passion and his escape. He learned drums, guitar, and keyboard and played in several garage bands before meeting Bob and Greg. Grant preferred 1950s and '60s pop to the metal and progressive rock of the FM radio era – influences that affected Hüsker Dü's sound. When he met Bob at that St. Paul record store, both were rock fans who'd been newly won over by punk.

The two also shared more than just musical tastes and ambition, however. Both were secretive about their sexuality – Bob was gay, and Grant was bisexual – and as Hüsker Dü became a viable band, they kept their sexualities quiet and used alcohol and speed as a guard against insecurity. While the hardcore scene was left-wing and tolerant, it was also very masculine, and anti-gay rhetoric and violence were part of the scene.

Grant later turned to heroin, and his addiction was a significant factor in the band's acrimonious break-up in 1988. Bob, though, keeping in character, quit drinking that same year without slip-ups or relapses – he just quit. Grant never really shook his dependence, and he died from liver cancer at only 56.

But during the heyday of the band in the mid-1980s, he created one of the most searing "murdered girl" ballads of the twentieth century.

DIANE EDWARDS WAS AN AVERAGE TEENAGE GIRL with an average teenage job waiting tables at a Perkins Pancake House in West

Diane Edwards

St. Paul in 1980. There was little about her life or, sadly, her death that would make her the subject of a true crime story. Her murder, when remembered at all, is generally just listed among the events that led to the capture of her killer. According to Bob Mould, Grant knew her. In 1980, the year she was slain, Hüsker Dü was less than a year old.

Diane's murderer, Joseph Ture, Jr., was born in St. Paul in 1951. He had an unstable childhood – his parents divorced when he was 10 – and he spent time in institutions. He disliked his stepmother and called his birth mother an "unfit parent," so he obviously had a problem with women. A detective later referred to him as "a very mixed-up character with a bad bringing-up. Life was not easy for him. I don't feel sorry for him, but I can see why he kind of didn't like women."

The trauma and resentment of his childhood festered as he got older, especially when it came to his attraction to women. He'd ask girls out and then become enraged when they turned him down. He developed an intense hatred of rejection – and a desperate need for revenge. He joined the Marines but washed out before he finished basic training.

After that, Ture became a drifter, spending lots of time in diners and chain restaurants, where he took notes about the female workers that he liked in a series of small notebooks. He stalked and pursued them, sometimes finding women's addresses by tracing their license plates. But even this disturbing behavior failed to earn him a second look from the women he encountered. Sandy-haired with stylish 1970s sideburns, he wasn't conventionally unattractive, but something about him just seemed to repulse women.

Perhaps they could sense that something awful lurked beneath the surface of this otherwise innocuous man.

In 1978, Ture broke into the home in a remote area of St. Cloud, Minnesota, seeking revenge against a 16-year-old waitress named Susan Huling, whom he'd pursued. Not only had Susan rebuffed him, but she told her mother, Alice, about it, who confronted the 27-year-old Ture and called him a "pervert."

Once inside the house, Ture killed Susan, Alice, and two other children with a shotgun. Susan's 11-year-old brother survived the attack by pretending to be dead.

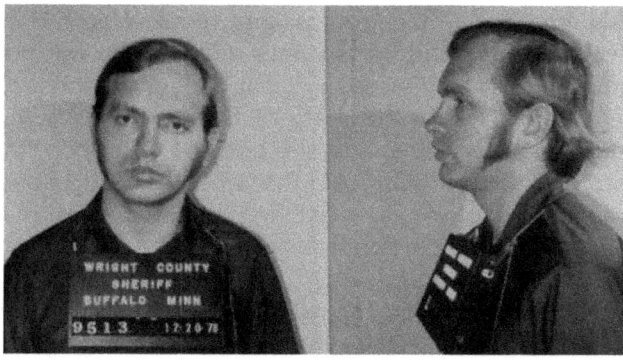

Joseh Ture, Jr.

In 1979, Ture went after another waitress, 18-year-old Marlys Wohlenhaus. He slipped inside her family home and bludgeoned her to death.

That same year, he killed 20-year-old Joan Bierschbach, another waitress, and this time, he abducted her and kept her captive in a cabin outside of St. Cloud for several days before she died. He later told a prison cellmate that she had recited the Lord's Prayer every time he raped her.

Between the murders, Ture committed several assaults and rapes, unable, or unwilling, to control his sinister urges.

On Friday, September 26, 1980, Diane Edwards was walking home from her waitressing job. She hadn't been able to get a ride that night, so she decided to walk the seven blocks that would take her home.

Joseph Ture was waiting for her. He had been watching her at the restaurant all evening, and the police later found her name in one of his notebooks.

At 9:05 P.M., a group of teenage girls saw Ture force Diane into a 1975 Ford Galaxie and speed away, but they were unable to recall the license plate number on the car or identify the abductor.

Two weeks later, Diane's nude body was found in a ditch in rural Sherburne County. According to a confession he later recanted, Ture raped Diane in the car, stabbed her, drove to the dump site, and then raped her again. She may have already been dead by then. He left her clothes in a pile next to her corpse and fled the scene.

In 1981, Ture was sent to prison for rape and, while behind bars, was convicted of Diane's murder. What followed was a decades-long legal nightmare of written confessions, retractions, and eventually convictions for the Huling and Wohlenhaus murders. He was never charged with the murder of Joan Bierschbach, but he remains the lead suspect.

Tragically, the notoriety of the other murders overshadowed what happened to Diane, and she became little more than a footnote in the story. Grant Hart later said that when he heard about Ture's crimes, they made him "physically sick," and he complained that there was never as much information about Diane's murder as there was about the other women.

Perhaps this was the reason why he decided to write the song, which provided the only enduring reminder of Diane Edwards' death.

Grant Hart

IT'S UNKNOWN IF GRANT KNEW HOW CLOSELY HIS SONG mirrored the traditional murder ballads of the past – from its skeletal narrative to its unclear motive.

One of the closest in theme was "Pretty Polly," the darkest of the murdered girl ballads that had been carried to the New World by early settlers and then transformed into an American song. Like the ballads we discussed in earlier chapters, "Pretty Polly" describes the slaying of an innocent young girl by a devious suitor. Lured into the woods with vague promises of love, he instead shows her the grave he dug the night before and then buries her in the hole.

Popularized as an Appalachian folk tune, it was first recorded in the 1920s, and versions of it still exist today. It's a story that leaves much to the imagination of the singer since no reason is ever offered for Polly's murder. Because of this, many performers added a reassuring ending where the killer, haunted by his crime, turns himself in to be hanged and suffers eternal damnation.

Unlike "Diane," "Pretty Polly" alternates points of view between the killer, the victim, and an unnamed narrator, depending on who performed the song. But both ballads are clear about the madness of the unhinged killer, who informs both the victim and the listener of his intentions early on. In both cases, this announcement inspired dread in the listener, who must sit through the rest of the song knowing its outcome and the fate of the victim.

Grant's own dread and despondence eventually became too much for him. If writing and performing "Diane" was meant to be a way to process the horror and brutality of the murder through art, then, over time, it became too much. Ignorant listeners asked him if the song was "pro-rape," while zealous fans sang along to the chorus with an enthusiasm that betrayed the original desperation in his writing. Grant found himself torn between defending the song from people who didn't understand it and admonishing audiences at solo gigs to remember that it was a true story about a real person. In 2010, he told one such crowd, "The most significant thing about her life was her death."

Eventually, he dropped "Diane" from live shows altogether.

17. "DEATH VALLEY '69"
REVISITING CHARLIE MANSON

FOR THREE YEARS AT THE END OF THE 1960S, THE Manson Family terrorized Southern California and, in a way, the rest of America. Manson's notorious crimes have been linked so closely to the turbulent era during which they occurred that '60s chronicler Joan Didion was prompted to say: "Many people I know in Los Angeles believe that the Sixties ended abruptly on August 9, 1969."

Personally, I'm not sure that I blame Charles Manson for killing the 1960s, but I do blame him for The Carpenters, Bread, Seals and Croft, and all the other weak music we had to endure in the first half of the next decade that was a push back against the rock era of the previous one.

But if Charlie did kill the 1960s, he also inspired two songs that were released a decade apart. They were both written and performed by iconic rock artists of consecutive generations. One was a rocker by an enduring singer and songwriter who reinvented himself probably a dozen times over the years, and the other was an anarchic anthem by a group of underground anti-heroes.

But both songs address the same horrific murders that had perhaps a greater impact on our culture than anything else in the latter half of the twentieth century.

FROM 1969 TO 1972, CHARLIE MANSON AND HIS FOLLOWERS brutally murdered at least 11 people – but probably more. The terrifying murders, which were committed with ritualistic overtones and left behind bloody markings on walls, were documented in my other music-related book, *A Song of Dance and Death*, so we won't go into too much detail here.

But the Manson murders – especially the slaughter of actress Sharon Tate, who was eight months pregnant, her friends, and businessman Leno LaBianca and his wife – became an instant part of macabre folklore. This happened in part because of their many connections to the counterculture, Hollywood, and rock-n-roll. Or, in the case of Leno and Rosemary LaBianca, they were successful "establishment" types – or "pigs" in the parlance of the Family.

Charlie Manson – the man blamed for killing the 1960s

And then there was Manson himself – a semi-literate criminal who'd spent most of his life in prison. While he was seething with anti-authoritarian hostility, he also had a dominating charisma that he used to exploit the need the youth of the time had for a leader or a guru.

It all came to a deadly and blood-soaked end, but Manson remains an enduring and highly flawed icon that has influenced film, television, literature, and, of course, music. In fact, his impact on the last 60 years or so of our history is more profound than we'd even like to admit.

As a cultural force, the cumulative accomplishments of the social movements of the 1960s – civil rights, anti-war, environmental, and more – undeniably altered the country; they also created a barrier between those who praised and those who criticized the changes they brought. There was also a sense of loss and betrayal felt by those who had been deeply invested in the fully transformed society that the hippie movement had promised – a freer, gentler, peaceful world that never came to be and ended up being mocked by conservatives and cynics alike. Many blamed this loss, literally and symbolically, on Charlie Manson and his murderous behavior.

Members of the Manson Family in the California desert

On the surface, Charlie gave the Family exactly what the hippies wanted for themselves – free love, communal living, and music – but then the vile acts they carried out, committed less than a week before Woodstock, caused such destruction in the social fabric that it could never be repaired.

Before true crime was a section in the local bookstore, only a handful of titles existed. The one most commonly found in middle-class homes of the 1970s was *Helter Skelter: The True Story of the Manson Murders* by Vincent Bugliosi. Written by the Los Angeles County District Attorney – with help from Curt Gentry – who tried and convicted Charlie and eight of his followers for the Tate-LaBianca murders, Helter Skelter was a riveting piece of crime reporting, and even now, it's still regarded as a classic, despite its many flaws. Reading the book became a rite of passage for young people, who had been denied access by their parents and had to devour it in bookstores, at the houses of their friends, or in their own homes when they could read it in secret. The book's black-and-white crime scene photos were discreetly "whited-out" – a respectful gesture that has long since vanished – and a simple message at the front of the book that read: "The story you are about to read will scare the hell out of you."

For all the things Bugliosi got wrong in the book, that was one thing that he definitely got right.

The book read by the most dedicated Manson buffs, though, was *The Family* by Ed Sanders, which came out in 1971, three years before *Helter Skelter*. The author was a poet and member of the satiric rock band The Fugs. He not only offered a highly critical countercultural take on Manson but also uneasily became friends with Family members who were still living at Spahn ranch – the remote Hollywood film set for hundreds of B-movie westerns and the place where the Family squatted for most of 1969 and 1970. Some of those he befriended were later convicted of murder. It's a book that truly evokes the strange and unsettling aura of the times.

Both books offer vivid examples of the links between the murders, Hollywood, and the music business. The Manson story is riddled with connections to film, from its Benedict Canyon and Los Feliz crime scenes to Sharon Tate's husband Roman Polanski's films with murder and occult themes, like *Repulsion* and *Rosemary's Baby*. Manson had schemed to become some kind of star after his release from prison in 1967, and while he preferred becoming a rock star, he said that movies would also be okay. Throughout 1968 and 1969, he and the Family haunted movie studios and the homes of film stars in hopes of breaking into the business, but he eventually abandoned the idea in favor of breaking into music instead.

And it was with rock-n-roll that Charlie's malignant influence was felt the most and where it lingers to this day. It was in prison when Charlie, a competent singer and guitarist, decided that music was going to rocket him to stardom once he was released into the wonderland of California in the 1960s. His failure to break into the business – despite having some surprisingly high-profile artists supporting his efforts – played a critical role in his change from sex-and-drugs savior to a bloodthirsty nutcase.

Although he was brought to the attention of Terry Melcher – the son of actress Doris Day and producer for The Byrds – Charlie failed to impress him, and the rejection damaged his fragile ego. Melcher lived in Benedict Canyon with his girlfriend, actress Candice Bergen, and when they moved out, the house was leased to Roman Polanski and Sharon Tate. On the night of August 8, Charlie

Terry Melcher

sent four of his followers to the house and told them to kill everyone inside. I don't think it was by chance that he sent them to Melcher's house – not realizing that Terry no longer lived there.

Charlie had met Melcher through Dennis Wilson in 1968. The handsome drummer from the Beach Boys had picked up a pair of hitchhikers and had taken them home, not realizing both were members of the Family. When he returned home late that night after a recording session, he found his house was infested with attractive young women – and their guru-like leader. A dark period followed for Dennis, during which the Family took up residence at his home and, over the next few months, helped themselves to at least $100,00 worth of his belongings and cash while also pressuring him to help Manson with his music career.

Beach Boy Dennis Wilson

For a time, Dennis became caught up in the madness and promoted and recorded the would-be star. He called Charlie "the Wizard" but eventually became afraid of him. He later erased the recordings of Charlie's music, saying, "The vibrations connected with them don't belong on this earth."

Once Dennis couldn't take any more, he had the Family evicted, and he cut off all contact with Charlie. Extortion attempts followed, but when Manson threatened his young son, an angry Dennis – who'd never run from a fight – beat Charlie bloody. Even so, Dennis became increasingly fearful for his life in the months that led up to the murders.

Charlie was angry about losing his best music business contact, but he was also angry about the way that Dennis had used one of Charlie's songs for the B side of the 1968 Beach Boys single "Bluebirds Over the Mountain." Dennis had substantially rewritten the song, trying to make it commercially viable. He had also taken sole writing credit for it, which was fair considering all the money the Family had cost him. Originally an anthem to the death of the ego with sadistic overtones called "Cease to Exist," Dennis changed it to an unlikely love song called "Never Learn Not to Love," which included the usual Beach Boys harmonies.

There are few artifacts of Charlie Manson that are as haunting as this song. The Beach Boys cut the record during a rough patch in their career when their troubled but gifted songwriter, Dennis' brother Brian, had withdrawn after the traumatic collapse of what he believed was his finest work, the psychedelic *Smile*.

"Never Learn Not to Love" was the only Manson song that saw wide release before his final incarceration. It was even performed on the popular *Mike Douglas Show*, which Dennis sang with stoned sincerity.

But Charlie shouldn't have worried about missing his big break in the music business because the single flopped. However, demands for money continued, and threats of violence escalated until Dennis received .45-caliber bullets delivered to his home by a Family associate. The intimidation took its toll, and Dennis found himself living in a state of fear that only ended after Manson's arrest in late 1969.

"I'm the luckiest guy in the world," Dennis later said, "because I got off only losing my money."

THE DEATH KNELL FOR THE MANSON FAMILY BEGAN ON August 21, 1971, when five members and a white supremacist from the Aryan Brotherhood stole 143 rifles from a gun shop in Los Angeles. The plan was to use the weapons to free Manson by breaking him out of jail or to hijack a 747 jet and kill one passenger every hour until he was released.

A silent alarm in the gun store alerted the police, and an argument over whether to kill the store's staff and customers delayed the thieves long enough to torpedo their escape in their gun-filled van. The police arrived, and a brief shootout occurred, during which, amazingly, no one was killed.

The arrests and convictions that followed the foiled robbery removed most of Manson's most hardcore followers from the streets, as did the 1972 slayings of a young former Marine and his wife in Stockton, California. Both were shot to death. The husband's body – which was also decapitated – was found buried next to a hiking trail, and his wife was discovered in a freshly dug grave in the basement of a rental home. Two Aryan Brotherhood members and two female followers of Manson were charged with murder, and all were later convicted. Most disturbing was that the police found the dead couple's infant daughter in the care of the Manson women.

Dennis Wilson had to have realized that he was even luckier than he initially thought he was.

Neil Young

ANOTHER MUSICIAN WHO SPENT TIME WITH CHARLIE Manson – and the writer and performer of one of the two songs featured in this chapter – was Neil Young. He was both a folk singer and a creator of feedback-drenched rock, and he became a link between the counterculture movements of the 1960s and 1970s. And in 1974, he released a scathing track – inspired by Manson and the Family – that was part of an album about those changing times.

Young had consecutive hits in the early '70s with *After the Gold Rush* and *Harvest*, which were mostly mellow folk-rock albums that maintained his persona as a thoughtful creator of ballad rock. However, as the 1960s got smaller in the rearview mirror, Young's mood changed, and he wrote and recorded a trio of edgy, introspective albums that were designed to please nobody but Neil Young. If people bought them, well, that was just a bonus.

Between 1973 and 1975, he released *Time Fades Away, On the Beach*, and *Tonight's the Night*. They were tough, confrontational rock albums that were unleashed on a public that was expecting the earnest folk-pop songs that Young was famous for, like 1972's "Heart of Gold" or even his obvious message songs like "Southern Man" from 1970. Instead, fans got dark ruminations on things like drugs, disappointments, and the downside of fame. These things were nagging at Young as the new decade kicked into high gear.

On the Beach was the least musically raw and filled with despair of the three albums, but its lyrics still had a bitter bite to them.

A key track on the album was called "Revolution Blues."

Well, we live in a trailer at the edge of town,
You never see us 'cause we don't come around,
We got twenty-five rifles just to keep the population down,
But we need you now, and that's why I'm hanging around.

By 1974, when the album came out, the Manson Family had mainly faded from the headlines. The Tate-LaBianca killers were behind bars, and their death sentences had been commuted to life imprisonment after California abolished capital punishment in 1972. A 10-month trial had kept Americans on the edge of their seats as the gruesome details of the crimes were exposed, and Charlie made headlines by disrupting the proceedings and making threats. His remaining followers kept vigil on the street outside the courthouse. Manson carved an "X" into his forehead, and Family members, after insisting for months that they acted independently from their leader – all did the same. On the day when the verdict was read, they all shaved their heads.

Mysterious deaths occurred during and after the trial. One Manson follower was found dead with a bullet in his head. Those who were present told the police – who had no idea they were talking to Family members – he'd been playing Russian Roulette but failed to explain how the gun had been fully loaded and wiped clean of prints.

Another Family associate was found dead in a London hotel, his wrists and throat slashed. It was ruled a suicide because, once again, the police were unaware of a connection to the Family.

In the middle of the trial, one of Manson's defense attorneys – who had been forced on Charlie because he'd wanted to defend himself – vanished. Weeks later, his decomposed corpse was found.

Some of these deaths may have been suicides or accidents but, at the time, tweaked the paranoia of a country and left the police chasing possible links between the Family and these deaths and many others.

By this time, though, with the bulk of his most loyal followers behind bars, Manson's media presence started to become dull. Over time, he became less of an evil archetype of the era and more of a morbid curiosity from a different time.

Separated from their master, most of his other followers -- the teenage runaways who came under his influence at the most vulnerable and easily manipulated time of their lives – regained their sense of self and gradually recovered from their shared nightmare.

SOME WOULD SAY THAT YOUNG'S THREE ALBUMS – AS WELL as "Revolution Blues" – were an odd choice for a man whose career was at a crossroads in the early 1970s.

Young was a veteran of the '60s band Buffalo Springfield but was best known as one-fourth of Crosby, Stills, Nash, and Young. He had launched a successful solo career in 1968 with and without his band, Crazy Horse. By the time the decade came to an end, he was, in his own words, a "rich hippie." But despite his wealth and all his accolades, he had become discontented, especially within the confines of the country-edged singer-songwriter genre that he'd helped to create.

He was also plagued by tragedy. In 1972, he was badly shaken by the overdose death of Crazy Horse guitarist Danny Whitten. The tour that followed was a wobbly affair, with Young – often drunkenly -- debuting new material with looser, more hard rock arrangements than his fans were used to or sometimes wanted to hear. Then, he hit bottom the following year when his friend and roadie Bruce Berry also died of an overdose. Neil's live shows became like funeral rites – spooky, bluesy, musical wakes where he confronted the demons that the deaths of his friends had unleashed. And in the middle of the turmoil with his band, friends, and music, his first two children were born with developmental disabilities.

Neil Young was in a dark place. It was no wonder that he released those albums and why "Revolution Blues" was written at the height of his disillusionment.

I got the revolution blues,
I see bloody fountains,
And ten million dune buggies coming down the mountains.
Well, I hear that Laurel Canyon is full of famous stars,
But I hate them worse than lepers,
And I'll kill them in their cars.

"REVOLUTION BLUES" WAS THE FIRST OF THREE SONGS on the album that has "blues" in the title. The others are "Vampire Blues," which is about the oil industry, and the tired but hopeful closer, "Ambulance Blues."

"Revolution Blues" was built around a simple guitar riff played by David Crosby and a rhythm section featuring Levon Helm and Rick Danko from The Band. Young sings it with a snarl in his voice and plays the lead guitar between verses since there is no chorus. Oddly syncopated with irregular stanzas, the lyrics are sung from the point of view of a Manson-like criminal and would-be revolutionary who is disgusted by the rich and anxious to bring on the apocalypse. Young's tenor – right out of the "high lonesome" Appalachian genre – sounds ruthless, filled with resentment, and desperate for chaos. The effect is made even more chilling because he sounds like he means every word. It leaves the listener wondering if this is a facet of Neil Young — an inner Charlie Manson — that we might not want to see.

Initially, David Crosby wanted nothing to do with the song. When Young played it for him, he immediately said, "Don't sing about that. That's not funny." Crosby was a friend of Terry Melcher and was deeply spooked by the murders and had a fear of overzealous, drugged-out fans because of it.

When Young wrote "Revolution Blues," friends like David Crosby wanted nothing to do with it.

This seemed like inviting trouble.

Crosby also knew that Young had known Manson. He'd met him at Dennis Wilson's house in 1969 and had been impressed enough by his music to recommend him to a record executive. Young later recalled, "Manson's songs were off-the-cuff things he made up as he went along. And they were never the same twice in a row, Kind of like Dylan, but different because it was hard to glimpse a true message in them. But the songs were fascinating."

Manson's music was divisive, even then. Later, it would be scrutinized because of his infamy, which makes the quality of it challenging to agree on since so many of his "fans" have obvious and usually arrested-adolescent agendas of their own. The songs he pitched in the late '60s — now available online, of course — are largely forgettable. They are less inspired by folk and blues than by the radio crooners from Charlie's youth, like Perry Como and Nat King Cole. The most compelling aspects of his songs are the sometimes morbid or psychotic-sounding lyrics, which consequently means that it's novelty music that's suited only for his "fans" and the curious.

"Charlie never had a musical bone in his body," Dennis Wilson said two years after adapting one of his better songs for the Beach Boys.

But maybe Young was on to something. Manson was at his best — such as it was -- when he was at his most free form, the way that Neil heard him in 1969. Without the constraints of a studio, Family backup singers, and the need for commercial songs, Manson found a sinister, controlling groove in mostly improvised songs that were driven purely by his own secret motivations.

By the mid-1970s, most of Charlie's followers had denounced him, and those who weren't in prison had gone off the grid. The exceptions were Lynette "Squeaky" Fromme and Sandra Good. Manson was now preoccupied with man's abuse of the Earth, and the pair passionately spread the word for him, writing press releases and calling out corporate polluters for their abuses. They also became pioneering eco-terrorists, sending threatening letters to CEOs – a federal offense that landed Sandra Good in prison.

Lynette "Squeaky" Fromme at the time of her arrest in 1975.

The final Family incident occurred on September 4, 1975, when Squeaky, dressed in a flowing scarlet gown and matching pixie hat, pointed a .45-caliber automatic at Gerald Ford in a Sacramento crowd. The gun failed to fire because, even though the magazine was loaded, she'd failed to chamber a bullet. This led some to believe that her assassination attempt was a bluff and a desperate attempt to bring some of the dwindling media attention back to Manson and his cause.

"Every girl should have a daddy just like Charlie," Squeaky had once said.

FROM THAT POINT, THE ROAD BETWEEN "REVOLUTION Blues" and our other Manson song, "Death Valley '69," is easily navigated. The Manson murders had brought about the symbolic death of the 1960s but had cast a long shadow on the cynical decade that followed. For those who were the product of both eras, like Neil Young, the 1970s must have seemed like purgatory – a drug-fueled hangover of disorder and decay with the flower children reborn as junkies, whores, and coked-up record executives.

And when your faith is gone, only nihilism remains. As Young sang on another track from *On the Beach*, "Though your confidence may be shattered, it doesn't matter."

The counterculture had fallen, the '70s had consumed it, and the 1980s brought spectacle, escapism, and a government that became the opposition. In the middle of all that, punk rock appeared, which, more than any other musician of his generation, Neil Young welcomed and understood.

Birthed by punk was a quartet of New York art-school types whose noisy, experimental rock seemed doomed to the margins of pop culture during the heyday of Michael Jackson, New Wave, and Madonna.

They called themselves Sonic Youth, and in 1985, their first recording of note – a creepy-looking LP with a burning jack-o-lantern-headed scarecrow on its cover – was released into the bins at the cooler record stores of the U.S. Titled *Bad Moon Rising*, it was a dark soundscape of out-of-tune guitars and stream-of-consciousness lyrics that starts quietly and finishes with a bang. It was a bad-vibes document of Regan-era uneasiness filtered through layers of feedback and uncaring detachment.

The one song that seems to engage the band more than others is "Death Valley '69," which is about the Manson murders.

Coming down,
Sadie, I love it.
Now, now, now,
Death Valley '69.

Many years after the release of *Bad Moon Rising*, it's become common knowledge that Sonic Youth helped to give birth to a musical movement. While redefining what noise meant within rock-n-roll – and what success meant for a bad with experimental roots – they became one of the most influential and popular acts to emerge from underground music. Their use of alternative tunings, dissonance, and feedback, combined with the intensity of hardcore punk and the performance art aesthetic of New York's art world, made an impact that has lasted for decades.

What they created was for a generation born too late for 1960s rock or 1970s punk but who were eager to forge rebellious sounds of their own in a decade filled with glitzy materialism and right-wing politics. First called post-punk, then indie, and finally alternative, the burgeoning genre had to accompany everything from the aggressions of Black Flag and the

Sonic Youth 1985

moody jangle-pop of R.E.M., then finally reaching critical mass when Nirvana toppled the old-school hair metal bands like Guns n' Roses. The new music was smarter, darker, more inventive, uglier, and certainly more nihilistic than most anything that had come before.

However, Sonic Youth's future acclaim seemed unthinkable when guitarists and vocalists Thurston Moore and Lee Ranaldo, as well as bassist and vocalist Kim Gordon, formed the band in 1981. The trio arrived in New York during the start of the New York-based post-punk movement. Moore grew up in Bethel, Connecticut; Ranaldo was from Long Island; and Gordon was an art student and musician from California.

After Moore's band, The Coachman, broke up, he began playing with CKM and met Gordon, who was also a member of the short-lived group. The pair became romantic and creative partners – they married in 1984 -- and soon settled on the name Sonic Youth when they started their project in the summer of 1981. That June, they helped stage the Noise Festival, where the band made their debut.

Soon after, they added a third member to the group when Moore saw Ranaldo performing with an ensemble created by avant-garde composer Glen Branca. He invited Ranaldo to join Sonic Youth. At the time, the group also featured keyboardist Anne DeMarinis and drummer Richard Edson. DeMarinis left before their first album was recorded with Glen Branca's Neutral Records label. Their first self-titled EP was released in 1982 and had a more straightforward post-punk sound than the music they would make in the near future.

When Edson left Sonic Youth to pursue an acting career, he was replaced by Bob Bert. However, "creative differences" between Bert and the rest of the band while they were on tour led to his firing. It was Jim Sclavunos who played most of the drums on Sonic Youth's debut album,

Confusion is Sex, which was released in February 1983 and introduced the abrasive approach that defined most of the band's early work.

A few months later, Sclavunos quit, and Bert rejoined Sonic Youth in time to record the *Kill Yr Idols* EP for a label in Germany. Early in 1984, Moore tried to land a contract for the band with the British label Doublevision, but the demos were rejected. However, Paul Smith, one of the owners of Doublevision, formed Blast First Records so that he could release the band's music. They also made a deal with U.K. indie label Rought Trade, giving them their first label with strong distribution.

And then came their *Bad Moon Rising* album. For this second album, Sonic Youth worked with Martin Biel and expanded on improvised pieces they played in between songs while in concert. It was released in March 1985 and earned strong reviews from the underground music press, thanks to its combination of dissonant, feedback-drenched experiments with relatively straightforward pop song structures.

The theme of the album drew on the shadowy side of Americana and reflected on the state of the nation in the mid-1980s. It was easy to parallel the album with William Burroughs' lines from *Naked Lunch* when he wrote:

America is not a young land; it is old and dirty and evil before the settlers, before the Indians. The evil is there waiting.

The band addressed that evil in "Death Valley '69," which remains as the high-water mark for post-punk's fascination with Charles Manson as a symbol of brutality and violence – a toxic antidote to the shiny, happy people and phony nostalgia of Reagan's America in the 1980s.

The iconography of Manson – hated by conservatives as a sex-and-drugs-and-rock-n-roll degenerate – was also appropriated by Lydia Lunch, Black Flag, and artist Raymond Pettibon. At one point, the SST label considered releasing an album of Manson's prison recordings, and Henry Rollins had a brief correspondence with him.

Thurston Moore once said in an interview about Manson:

I think Rollins's correspondence was its own thing and was really nothing to do with what we were up to, which had much more literary aspects to it. It was never meant to be any kind of endorsement. A direct connection to Manson was something we had no interest in.

Living in New York we were meeting up with people like Lydia Lunch who were expressing this very sort of nefarious imagery in a way, going back and re-evaluating Manson's iconic images.

Older than many of their contemporaries, the band members had actual memories of the 1960s. They also had a Manson connection – Kim Gordon, who grew up in Los Angeles, had an older brother, Keller, who was invited to Spahn Ranch, where the Family lived for a couple of years, by Manson acolyte Bobby Beausoleil. The girl that Keller was dating was later abducted and stabbed to death, and many suspect that the Family murdered her.

This close encounter, combined with the interest in Manson going on at the time, likely spawned "Death Valley '69." While the band had no interest in a direct connection with Manson, Kim and Thurston became so fascinated with the subject that they named their house pets after various members of the Family.

The band was skeptical of the escapist tendencies of the 1960s, represented by Charlie Manson, though, and also with what Lee Ranaldo called "flowers and unicorns and rainbows." While other bands were looking back at that era with bitter resolve, like post-punk folkies, "Death Valley '69" – the explosive final track on the album – wallows in the seediness and grime that Manson represented. It's a manic song, a bit of musical overkill, that offers a perverse mix of taste and tastelessness, a tense art-vs-trash dynamic that gives way to the sheer force of the song.

It's a subversive tune, but the structure is traditional, with a long, taut midsection that's bookended by a thrashy power-cord chorus. It delivers the kind of purge that the rest of the album promises. Lyrically, it strings together quotes and phrases related to the murders, evoking their horror through suggestion and misdirection. There's even a mention of "Sadie" in the first verse, which was the name given to Susan Atkins by Manson when she joined the Family.

Coming down
Sadie, I love it,
Now, now, now
Death Valley '69

You're right, I was on the wrong track,
We're deep in the valley, and now in the canyon,
And in the gulley.

She started to holler, she started to holler,
I didn't wanna, I didn't wanna,
I didn't wanna, I didn't wanna,
So I had to hit it,
Hit it, hit it, hit it

    Sung by Thurston Moore and guest vocalist Lydia Lunch – who was then a fixture of the New York underground and a pioneer of the city's style of noise as rock – the song's shrill singing splits listeners into separate love-it-or-hate-it camps. Lunch sings self-consciously in a flat tone on the album, which threatens the art-trash balance of the song. Likely for just that reason, Kim Gordon took Lunch's part when the band sang it live, and her husky-voiced sexiness becomes a less abrasive counterpoint to Moore.

    After all these years, "Death Valley '69" remains a relic of the art-rock era, but in the best way – as a dark poem of layered guitars, throbbing drums, and passionate vocals about a faraway time and place.

18. "THE BEST IS YET TO COME" & "CALIFORNICATION"

THE RISE AND FALL OF DOROTHY STRATTEN

"I DIDN'T PUT MY BEST EFFORT INTO THE PERFORMANCE," that's what songwriter and musician Jim Vallance said about the piano track that he performed for a song that he had co-written with his friend, Bryan Adams. They were laying down tracks for what would be Bryan's 1983 album, *Cuts Like a Knife*, and Jim had been asked to play piano as a "guide track" that would be replaced later by keyboardist Tommy Mandel.

But a month or two later, Bryan told him that he'd decided to keep the piano track. Jim begged him for another shot at it, knowing that he could've played better, but the song had already been mixed, and it was too late. Years later, Jim would say, "I know where the mistakes are, and I still cringe every time I hear it on the radio."

But I think that's what makes this song so poignant and melancholy. It's not perfect, just like the woman who inspired it. And when you learn her story, the song becomes even more heartbreaking than it already is.

> *Just a small-town girl who had it made,*
> *Or so the story goes.*
> *She had it there then it slipped away,*

Oh - how was she to know?

DOROTHY RUTH HOOGSTRATEN WAS BORN ON February 28, 1960, in Vancouver, British Columbia. Her parents, Simon and Nelly, had come to Canada from the Netherlands. Dorothy grew up with two younger siblings, John and Louise. By the time she was in high school, there was no mistaking just how beautiful she was – something that Dorothy never really seemed to see for herself.

Dorothy attended Centennial High School in Coquitlam and worked part-time at a local Dairy Queen to help her mother with bills. One day in 1977, while she was working one of her shifts, she met a 26-year-old Vancouver club promoter and pimp named Paul Snider. He took immediate notice of Dorothy and began grooming her for the romantic relationship that began when she turned 18. He even went so far as to take her to her high school prom – which, yes, is as creepy as it sounds.

Paul was convinced that he could turn Dorothy into a star and, of course, ride her coattails to his own fame and fortune. He convinced Dorothy to have nude photographs taken by a professional photographer, and he sent them to *Playboy* magazine in the summer of 1978. Since she was under 19 – the legal adult age in Canada – her mother had to be persuaded to sign the model release form.

Even when still in high school, Dorothy was already beautiful.

As soon as editors at *Playboy* received the photos, they immediately wanted to see more pictures of her. Dorothy flew to Los Angeles, where she met *Playboy* founder Hugh Hefner, who naturally took an immediate interest in her becoming a Playmate.

Dorothy moved to Los Angeles in August 1978, when she was chosen as a finalist for the 25th Anniversary Great Playmate Hunt. She was soon signed to *Playboy* and was featured in the 1979 calendar spread as "Miss August." In addition, Hefner hired her to work in the *Playboy* mansion,

Dorothy Stratten
Miss August 1979

serving drinks to guests and acting as "arm candy" during the many parties held at the mansion.

Unfortunately, many people who crossed paths with Dorothy at parties and during work had to deal with Paul Snider, too. He had followed Dorothy to L.A. in October and slithered his way even more deeply into her life. He began trying to control every aspect of her life and started calling himself her manager. He was obsessed with Dorothy becoming a big star, controlling her finances and business decisions, and deciding who Dorothy needed to sleep with to advance her career.

Paul constantly manipulated her, convincing Dorothy that because he had discovered her at that Dairy Queen and was the first person to tell her she had star potential, she owed all her success to him in some way. He told her this so many times that eventually, she started to believe it.

Once Paul was living in L.A. with Dorothy full-time, he went with her everywhere, much to the dismay of most of the staff at *Playboy*. He tried to ingratiate himself with Hugh Hefner, executives at the magazine, and the celebrities who came to parties at Hefner's mansion. No one was interested in dealing with the pushy and annoying former pimp. Many of the staff at *Playboy* – including Hefner himself – tried to warn Dorothy about Paul but she wasn't listening. She had been convinced that she owed everything to him.

In 1979, during a party that Paul attended at the mansion without his girlfriend, a secretary discovered Paul having sex with another woman in the water grotto. After that, he was banned from the *Playboy* Mansion unless Dorothy escorted him.

Dorothy made her next mistake with Paul Snider in June 1979 – she married him. Nearly all of Dorothy's friends – again, including Hefner – were opposed to the marriage. By now, Dorothy was making enough money so that she could have easily found a real manager, but Paul would never allow it, even if she were brave enough to ask.

But soon, Dorothy's star was going to rise higher than she could have imagined – so high that Paul was going to be left behind.

Dorothy's popularity as a model – especially at *Playboy* – continued to thrive, and soon, she had a budding acting career, too. She made her television debut when she appeared in *Playboy's Roller Disco and Pajama Party* on ABC in late 1979. Then, she started landing minor roles in television shows like *Fantasy Island* and *Buck Rogers in the 25th Century.*

Dorothy with her husband and manager, Paul Snider

Her career hit a major milestone when she was named 1980 Playmate of the Year and landed her first major role in a sci-fi comedy film called *Galexina*.

Now that Dorothy was becoming a familiar face in Hollywood, new opportunities began to open for her, and she made a lot of new acquaintances. One of them was filmmaker Peter Bogdanovich, who had recently ended his last relationship. Peter started hanging around at the Playboy Mansion between projects, which is where he met Dorothy – and promptly fell in love with her. He became so smitten with her that he wrote a role for her in his upcoming film, *They All Laughed,* which was going to start filming in New York in March. In the film, she would play the unhappily married love interest of John Ritter, who would also star in the film. Bogdanovich later admitted that he'd written the backstory of Dorothy's character based on what he'd learned about her marriage to Paul Snider.

Dorothy spent the first two and a half months of 1980 in Los Angeles, completing her Playmate of the Year shoot and finishing her work on *Galexina*. Paul was still acting as his wife's driver, manager, and acting

coach, and his near-constant presence, as well as his criticisms and daily arguments, caused Dorothy so much stress that her co-workers at *Playboy* and on the *Galexina* set all noticed the tension in their relationship.

As the date got closer for Dorothy to leave for New York, Paul started making plans to accompany her to the set. However, Dorothy knew the problems his presence would cause on set, and she wanted to pursue her relationship with Bogdanovich. So, Dorothy managed to convince him to remain in L.A., explaining that the director had decided to close the set of the new film to all but the immediate cast and crew.

This was the first time that Dorothy had stood up to her domineering husband and won. She was growing into herself, becoming more confident and independent, and no longer needed to lean on Paul. She had already started to consider separating from him and felt that her time in New York would give her the distance she needed to follow through with her plan.

Dorothy arrived in New York on March 22, 1980, and as production began on the set, Bogdanovich confessed his feelings for her, and the two began a discreet affair.

In April, Dorothy briefly returned to L.A. to prepare for her upcoming introduction as the new Playmate of the Year and take part in a short publicity tour. She still had several months of filming for *They All Laughed*, so this short trip home was the last time that she would live with Paul in their California home.

On April 30, an event was held on the *Playboy* Mansion grounds where Dorothy was presented to the entertainment press as the 1980 Playmate of the Year. In his introductory remarks, Hugh Hefner spoke about Dorothy's charming combination of beauty, intelligence, and sensitivity and added that, to those who knew her, "she was something rather special." After Dorothy came onstage, she thanked Mario Casilli, who had photographed her, several *Playboy* executives, and finally, Hefner, whom she announced, "has made me probably the happiest girl in the world today."

There was no mention of her husband, Paul Snider.

Later that evening, Dorothy appeared as a guest on *The Tonight Show* with Johnny Carson and then began a two-week promotional tour. With no events over her first weekend of the tour, she flew to New York to surprise Peter.

She also surprised Paul that same weekend when he received a letter from her asking for more freedom in their marriage. With his wife out of his immediate control and fearing the worst, Paul called Bogdanovich in New York and was enraged when Dorothy answered the phone. It was a short call.

Dorothy's tour was arranged to end in Vancouver so that she might visit her family for a few days before returning to New York. However, Paul showed up there and coerced her into spending some of her time off making appearances at several local nightclubs. Since Paul personally knew the club owners, he negotiated and collected Dorothy's appearance fees, all of which he pocketed when Dorothy flew back to New York.

In the days and weeks after Paul returned to Los Angeles, he found it increasingly difficult to get in touch with Dorothy. He knew that she was slipping further and further out of his reach. This was especially difficult for him because their marriage was the only thing legally keeping him in California. If they were to divorce, Paul would be forced to return to Canada. He was nothing without Dorothy and her success, and he knew it.

In late June, Paul's worst nightmare about losing control of Dorothy came true when he received a letter in the mail from attorneys that Dorothy had hired. The letter made it clear that they were now officially and financially separated. Paul had several responses to the letter – he emptied the couple's joint bank account, had a brief affair with an old girlfriend, and hired a private detective named Marc Goldstein to gather evidence of his wife's infidelity with Bogdanovich.

Dorothy with her co-tar, John Ritter, and director, Peter Bogdanovich

Once Paul was separated from Dorothy, he desperately scrambled to stay in Hollywood – and pay his bills. Since he was a foreign national without a green card, he was unable to get a job, and so, without regular income, he had to rely on Dorothy, through her new business manager, to pay the household bills. Anxious, he began selling off the gifts that Dorothy had been given when she was named Playmate of the Year for quick cash, including a Jaguar sportscar.

He also attempted grooming another young girl into modeling for *Playboy*, 17-year-old Patti Laurman. He moved her into the house that he'd once shared with Dorothy and even trained her to walk and pose like Dorothy. He endlessly promoted her to *Playboy*, but Hefner and the magazine's staff wanted nothing to do with him.

Paul's last chance was an upcoming project that he and Dorothy had started planning a year earlier, just before they were married. Paul collaborated with photographer friends Bill and Susan Lachasse, who had taken photos of Dorothy on ice skates in a French-cut skating outfit. They planned to have a poster printed of the photo, sell one million copies, and net about $300,000 each from the project.

But Dorothy had turned down the final project.

Paul managed to convince Bill and Susan to try to get Dorothy to change her mind, and they went to New York to see her. The film's production office sent them to Peter's suite at the Plaza Hotel, but when

Dorothy opened the door in her pajamas, they were not invited inside. She turned down the poster project again, and Paul's last hope of staying in L.A. was gone.

Confused, angry, and unsure what to do next, Paul began trying to get a gun. He borrowed a .38-caliber revolver from a friend, but the friend, uneasy, wisely asked for it back. So, Paul found one on his own – a 12-gauge shotgun that he picked up from a store on August 13, 1980.

PRINCIPAL PHOTOGRAPHY WAS COMPLETED FOR *They All Laughed* in mid-July, and the New York production was wrapped. Dorothy and Peter went on a 10-day trip to England, and then the pair returned to Los Angeles on July 30. Dorothy's official address was a newly rented apartment in Beverly Hills, but she had actually quietly moved into Peter's house in Bel Air.

The house that Dorothy had shared with Paul in Los Angeles.

On August 8, Dorothy and Paul saw each other for the first time in nearly three months at the house they had once shared. Still convinced he was responsible for all his wife's success, Paul was confident that he could persuade Dorothy to take him back. But any hopes he had for reconciliation were dashed when Dorothy told him that she was in love with Bogdanovich and wanted to finalize their separation.

Paul was shattered by her decision, he told her. He wasn't sure how he could live without her, but Dorothy couldn't be swayed. It was over.

Then, on August 14, Dorothy agreed to return to the house and meet with Paul to discuss some kind of financial settlement. Dorothy knew that she had been the one who'd earned the money, but after years of Paul's manipulation, guilt nagged at her. She believed that she could pay Paul off and he'd go away – but she was wrong.

Dorothy parked her car outside of her former home around noon. She had spent the morning with her business manager, and one of the topics they discussed was a property settlement that she could offer Paul that afternoon. The police later found $1,100 in cash among Dorothy's belongings, which she'd apparently brought as a downpayment. Just as the meeting was ending, her business manager noted that Dorothy could spend less time with her estranged husband by handing off the separation and divorce negotiations to her lawyers. But Dorothy replied that the process would go easier if she dealt with Paul personally. She believed he'd be nicer that way and finally added, "I'd like to remain his friend."

Shortly after Dorothy arrived at the house, the private investigator that Paul had previously hired, Marc Goldstein, gave him a call and asked how things were going. Paul said that things were fine. Goldstein had reason to be concerned – Paul had tried to get him to buy a gun for him a few weeks earlier, but Goldstein had refused.

Later that afternoon, Goldstein tried to call back several times but never got an answer or a return call. Aside from Paul and Dorothy, the first person to enter the house that day was Patti Laurman, around 5:00 P.M. She quickly stopped by the house with a friend and noticed that the door to Paul's room was closed and the house was quiet. Patti assumed he wanted some privacy.

The two teenagers left to go skating and returned to the house around 7:00 P.M. Neither she nor Goldstein had heard from Paul all afternoon. The next time Goldstein called the house, around 11:00 P.M., Patti answered, and he asked her to knock on Paul's bedroom door. She refused and asked a friend who was also staying in the house to check on him instead. When he knocked on Paul's door, there was no response, so he opened the door.

He was greeted with a scene out of a slaughterhouse.

Dorothy was lying nude on the bedroom floor. She had been shot in the face, obliterating her features. Paul's body was propped up against the wall a few feet away, with the shotgun lying across his bare legs. He had shot himself in the head, spraying blood and brains all over the wall behind him.

It was later determined that he had raped and then killed Dorothy within an hour after she'd arrived at the house. Paul had killed himself less than an hour later.

Dorothy's body had bloody handprints and smears on her body, suggesting she'd been moved. Paul had strands of Dorothy's blond hair clenched in his right first. According to his friends, Paul always said he would rather die than ever go to jail.

News of the murder and suicide spread like wildfire through Hollywood. Marc Goldstein called Hugh Hefner and delivered the terrible news. A friend would always say, "Hef was never the same after that. Part of him died, too." Hefner called Bogdanovich, who collapsed and had to be sedated after the call.

Many of Dorothy's friends and loved ones said that Dorothy's only real weakness was her kindness

After Dorothy's murder, a friend said, "Hef was never the same after that." But Peter Bogdanovich later blamed Hefner and *Playboy* for Dorothy's death.

and her habit of always finding the good in others. Even after she had grown apart from Paul – whom so many had advised her not to marry – she was still kind to him and hoped to have a friendly relationship with her after they divorced.

Once news of Dorothy's murder spread, many people – including Peter Bogdanovich – were quick to blame the environment at *Playboy* as the catalyst for the tragedy. Dorothy was a symbol of a publication where women were seen as objects that could be possessed by men, which had twisted Paul's mind.

But in truth, the murder-suicide was the fault of Paul Snider alone. He didn't want to lose his meal ticket or his control over Dorothy. He was a manipulator and an abuser, and if he couldn't have Dorothy, no one could.

THE LOSS OF DOROTHY STRATTEN RIPPED A HOLE IN the heart of everyone who knew and loved her, especially her family and Peter Bogdanovich – who simply couldn't let her go.

In August 1981, a year after Dorothy's death, her last film, the romantic comedy *They All Laughed,* had its U.S. release. It bombed. After a disappointing limited run in a handful of theaters, the film was quietly shelved.

Devastated that what would be his only project with Dorothy didn't have a nationwide release, Peter bought the theatrical rights to it. Out of his own pocket, he paid for a re-release of the movie in nearly a dozen large markets across the country, but despite generally favorable reviews,

Peter Bogdanovich later released the film he made with Dorothy — and wrote a biography about her — but it was unsuccessful.

it simply didn't find an audience. Peter spent more than $5 million trying to promote and distribute the movie and eventually declared bankruptcy in 1985.

To make matters worse, negative reviews savaged a biography that he wrote about Dorothy around this same time and cost him his friendship with Hugh Hefner. The book called *The Killing of the Unicorn* was not only about Dorothy's life and death, but it was also a scathing attack on Hefner, *Playboy*, and the hedonistic lifestyle that he promoted with his magazine. The most controversial section of the book was Bogdanovich's claim that Hefner had sexually assaulted Dorothy in August 1978. When the book came out, he used the word "seduced" to describe Hefner's behavior but had initially used the word "raped" in his manuscript. The publisher changed the wording after Hefner and his attorneys threatened a lawsuit.

It gets a little weirder after that. In 1988, when Bogdanovich was 49, he married Dorothy's younger sister, Louise, who was 20. Peter had been paying for her to attend private school and take modeling classes since she was a teenager. They divorced in 2001, after being married for 13 years, but remained friends and continued to work on projects together for many years.

After Dorothy's death, her body was cremated, and Peter had her remains interred at the Westwood Village Memorial Park in Los Angeles. The epitaph on her marker includes a passage, chosen by Peter, from Ernest Hemingway's novel *A Farewell to Arms:*

> *If people bring so much courage to this world the world has to kill them to break them, so of course it kills them... It kills the very good and the very gentle and the very brave impartially. If you are none of these, you can be sure it will kill you too but there will be no special hurry.*

When Bogdanovich died in 2022, he was interred next to her, bringing an end to more than 40 years of grief.

THERE WERE TWO FILMS RELEASED ABOUT THE SHORT life and tragic death of Dorothy Stratten – *Death of a Centerfold* in 1981, starring Jamie Lee Curtis, and *Star 80* in 1983, which starred Mariel Hemingway as Dorothy and Eric Roberts as Paul Snider. Both came and went to little acclaim, and only *Star 80* is remembered by most fans today.

It would be in song that Dorothy's story truly lived on.

In 1983, Canadian singer Bryan Adams released his breakout album, *Cuts Like a Knife*. It was his third album, but it was the first that featured singles that rose to the tops of U.S. charts. Although he'd toured widely after his second album, *You Want It You Got It*, it would be this album that made him a headliner.

Bryan Adams 1983

Bryan had been born on November 5, 1959, in Kingston, Ontario. His parents, Elizabeth and Conrad, had come to Canada from England in the 1950s. His father was an officer in the British Army, joined the Canadian Army, and later worked for the United Nations as a peacekeeping observer and Canadian foreign service diplomat. He was largely raised in Ottawa, but then Bryan, his mother, and younger brother, Bruce, moved to Vancouver while his father was posted abroad.

This was while Dorothy Stratten was also growing up nearby, although Bryan never met her.

He bought his first guitar when he was 10 – yes, during the summer of 1969 – and later dropped out of school to join a band, using the money his parents had saved for his college fund to finance his dreams. He played with several bands and recorded on a few albums before meeting Jim Vallance in 1978, thanks to a mutual friend who worked at a record store. Jim was a drummer and songwriter for a Vancouver band called Prism but had recently dropped out of it to focus on his writing. This was the start of a partnership that became prolific throughout the 1980s. In

Jim Vallance and Bryan Adams

addition to writing songs for Bryan, Jim also wrote for artists like Tina Turner, Bonnie Raitt, Rod Stewart, Loverboy, and Neil Diamond.

Later that same year, Bryan was signed to A&M Records for the grand sum of $1. No one knew what to do with an 18-year-old kid with a guitar and a gravelly voice – until his records slowly started to sell.

In January 1983, *Cuts Like a Knife* was released, and the first single, "Straight from the Heart," reached number 10 on the Billboard charts. It was followed by the title cut, "Cuts Like a Knife," and "This Time," which also made the charts. By the time his next album, *Reckless*, came out in 1984, Bryan Adams had become a household name. A string of hits followed -- including "Run to You," "Somebody," and "Heaven" – and he became a go-to musician when catchy songs were needed for a movie soundtrack.

But it had been the final track on the *Cuts Like a Knife* album that Bryan and Jim Vallance had written in memory of Dorothy. It was the tenth song on the record, and aside from "Straight from the Heart," it was the only song that heavily featured a piano and a slow ballad-like tempo.

Both Bryan and Jim had been aware of Dorothy's sudden rise and brutal fall just two years before the song was written. Dorothy was a small-town girl, growing up and working at the Dairy Queen, which was not far from where both of them had been teenagers.

It's the only sad song on the album, telling the story of a young woman who seemed to have everything going for her, dreaming of the good things still to come in her life, but then it all slips away. The piano in the song was a throwaway by Jim Vallance. He dashed it off, believing it was going to be replaced.

It wasn't – unlike Dorothy, who died a terrible death and yet was quickly replaced by other blonds, other models, and other actresses, reducing her story to a footnote in the history of the "almost famous."

*Even through her tears
I never saw her come undone.
Ain't it funny how time flies,
When the best was yet to come?*

*What's so good about goodbye,
When the best was yet to come?*

IN 1999, DOROTHY WOULD BE REFERENCED AGAIN IN SONG BY The Red Hot Chili Peppers in their song "Californication," a dark and jaded tune about the seamy side of Los Angeles – a side that Dorothy became familiar with, thanks to Paul Snider.

The band was formed in Los Angeles in 1982 as Tony Flow and the Miraculously Majestic Masters of Mayhem by singer Anthony Kiedis, guitarist Hillel Slovak, bassist Flea, and drummer Jack Irons, all of whom were classmates at Fairfax High School.

Red Hot Chili Peppers – the early days

They began playing gigs and soon dropped their mouthful of a name for something a little simpler – The Red Hot Chili Peppers. They started playing in larger venues around L.A., and by November, their manager had gotten them a record deal with EMI America and Enigma Records. When Slovak and Irons dropped out to focus on another band, Flea and Kiedis recruited drummer Cliff Martinez and guitarist Jack Sherman.

The band's first album was self-titled and released in August 1984. Airplay on college radio and MTV helped build a fan base, but the band was unhappy with the record, believing the producer had made it sound too polished.

This also marked the start of an ever-changing line-up for the band, with members coming and going, and included DeWayne McKnight, D.H.

Peligro, Dave Navarro, John Frusciante, and Chad Smith, who has remained with Flea and Kiedis since December 1988.

The second Chili Peppers album, *Freaky Styley*, came out in 1985 and was produced by George Clinton, who introduced elements of punk and funk into the band's sound. Although the band was pleased with it, the album wasn't successful, which is why they attempted to hire Rick Rubin to produce their next record. He declined, though, thanks to the band's increasing drug problems.

Early attempts to record the album were halted thanks to Kiedis' addictions, and he was briefly fired. After the Chili Peppers were named "band of the year" by *LA Weekly*, though, he checked into rehab and got clean. He rejoined the recording sessions with new enthusiasm, but it didn't last. The recording process was difficult because, after 50 days of sobriety, Kiedis decided to get high to celebrate their new music. He frequently disappeared from the studio to buy drugs.

Their third album, *The Uplift Mofo Party Plan*, was finally released in September 1987, and the band immediately started a two-and-a-half-month North American tour to promote its release. Both Kiedis and Hillel Slovak were now suffering from intense drug addiction and often disappeared for days at a time. Slovak died from a heroin overdose on June 25, 1988, soon after the conclusion of the tour. Kiedis fled the city and didn't attend the funeral. Drummer Jack Irons, troubled by the death, left the band and, after years of depression, became a member of Pearl Jam in 1994.

DeWayne McKnight joined the Chili Peppers as guitarist a short time later, as did drummer D.H. Peligro of Dead Kennedys. Three dates into the next tour, though, McKnight was fired because of his lack of chemistry with the rest of the band. He was so pissed off that he threatened to burn down Anthony Kiedis' house.

Kiedis, meanwhile, had returned to rehab, finally confronting his grief over Slovak's death. He had just gotten out when Peligro introduced Kiedis and Flea to 18-year-old guitarist John Frusciante, a fan of the band. The band went on tour, during which they fired Peligro, who was now dealing with his own drug and alcohol problems. After some open auditions, they hired Chad Smith, who later recalled, "We started playing, and right away we hit it off musically."

The Chili Peppers began work on their next album in late 1988. Unlike last time, the recording went smoothly, and when *Mother's Milk* was released the following year, it produced several hit singles and was certified gold.

In 1990, after the success of *Mother's Milk*, the band left EMI and signed with Warner Bros. Records. They were now able to hire Rick Rubin, who'd turned them down before because of drug problems within the band. The songwriting went well, and at Rubin's suggestion, the next album was recorded at The Mansion in Laurel Canyon, a studio in a house once owned by magician Harry Houdini.

In September 1991, they released *Blood Sugar Sex Magik* with "Give It Away" as the first single. It became their first number one, followed by "Under the Bridge." The album sold over 12 million copies and achieved international fame for the band. The tour that followed featured Pearl Jam, Nirvana, and Smashing Pumpkins as opening acts.

The Chili Peppers finally had the fame they'd been working toward, but not all of them were happy about this turn of events. John Frusciante, unsettled by the attention, had a falling out with Kiedis. He isolated himself and developed a secret heroin addiction. When the band performed on Saturday Night Live, he played off-key, prompting Kiedis to believe he'd deliberately sabotaged their performance. He quit the band while they were on tour in May 1992 and returned to Los Angeles. He spent the next several years living in squalor and struggling with his heroin addiction.

The Chili Peppers contacted Dave Navarro to replace Frusciante. He had just split from Janes's Addiction, but he had drug problems of his own. After several failed auditions, they hired Arik Marshall, and he was with the band when they headlined Lollapalooza in 1992. He also appeared with them in several award-winning videos, including when the Chili Peppers won their first Grammy Award. But he was soon fired from the group, and the search for a guitarist was on again. At this point, Dave Navarro said he was ready to join the band.

Navarro first appeared with the Chili Peppers at Woodstock '94, followed by a brief tour, two festivals, and two performances as an opening act for The Rolling Stones. That was all it took for Navarro's relationship with the rest of the band to start falling apart.

Worse, Kiedis had relapsed into heroin addiction following a dental procedure in which an addictive sedative was used, though the band wouldn't discover this until later.

At the same time, the band was working to put together songs for their next album, which proved more difficult without Frusciante and with Dave Navarro. After several delays, *One Hot Minute* was released in September 1995. It was a departure from the Chili Peppers' earlier music, with Navarro bringing in heavy metal and psychedelic riffs. The band always described it as a "darker, sadder record." Kiedis' lyrics addressed addiction and the deaths of Kurt Cobain and River Phoenix. Although it received mixed reviews, it sold more than eight million copies.

The Chili Peppers went on tour to support the release in 1995, although it was temporarily postponed after Smith broke his wrist. In 1997, several shows were canceled because of injuries, disagreements within the band, and drug problems for Navarro and Kiedis. In April 1998, Navarro was gone. He claimed his departure was due to creative differences, but reports at the time stated that he was too high and strung out to rehearse one too many times.

With no guitarist, the Chili Peppers were on the verge of breaking up. In the years since John Frusciante had departed, his heroin addiction had left him in poverty, and once nearly died. His drug use left him with scarring on his arms and other parts of his body, and he'd later be forced to have his nose restructured and get dental implants due to the loss of teeth from infection. Flea convinced John to enter rehab, and when Flea visited him after his recovery, he asked him to return to the band. Frusciante began sobbing and told him that nothing would make him happier.

In June 1999, after more than a year in production, the band released *Californication*, their seventh studio album. It sold over 16 million copies, becoming their most successful album. It received strong reviews and produced three number-one hits – "Scar Tissue," "Otherside," and "Californication."

The album was supported by a two-year international tour and included the closing show at the infamous Woodstock 1999. During their set, a small fire escalated into vandalism, violence, and a small-scale riot. The band was blamed in the media for inciting the riots after performing a cover of the Jimi Hendrix song "Fire." However, Anthony Kiedis had his own explanation for what happened: "It was clear that this situation had nothing to do with Woodstock anymore. It wasn't symbolic of peace and love, but of greed and cashing in."

Although Woodstock 1999 – an event that ranks with the Rolling Stones at the Altamont Raceway in 1969 as one of the worst concert disasters in American history – happened after the Chili Peppers had written and recorded their *Californication* album, it certainly could have influenced what became their third single from the album.

By the time "Californication" was written, the band had seen the side of Los Angeles that was very different from the sun, sand, surf, movie stars, and the Hollywood image that was portrayed in films, books, magazines,

The Red Hot Chili Peppers had reached the pinnacle of their success in 1999 with the release of *Californication*.

and ads that beckoned to tourists from all over the world. They'd dealt with drug addiction, violence, threats, poverty, and the dark and superficial side of their hometown. It became a song about the underbelly of L.A. and, by extension, the rest of America. There was deceit, desperation, and death under the gilded face of the California dream, and Los Angeles represented those extremes – the elaborate, gold-plated nature of the city and the darkness that was rotting underneath.

When the band – Kiedis, Smith, Flea, and Frusciante – saw down to write the song, they presented their message through a string of clever allusions and metaphors, showing the listener what was going on instead of just telling them about it.

The opening verse touches on the broad reach that California has, luring people from everywhere to its streets, and it takes a jab at the disappointment that greets so many of them when they arrive. Hollywood sells the idea of California, they explain, and it depends on people believing that it's the place that people know from the movies. In truth, L.A. is filled with people who are never what they seem, even in appearance.

The third verse delves into how sex is glorified by hiding the reality of it:

> *A teenage bride with a baby inside,*
> *Getting high on information.*

Kiedis later explained this line in detail, saying, "I met a young mother at a meeting. She was living in a YWCA with her baby girl, trying to get sober but failing miserably. The beauty and sadness and tragedy and glory, all wrapped into one, of this mother and daughter relationship was evoked by the vibe of that music."

The fourth verse then takes the listener into the depths of popular culture with references to *Star Trek, Star Wars*, Kurt Cobain, and then finally, Dorothy Stratten.

First born unicorn
Hardcore soft porn,
Dream of Californication

The reference to "First Born Unicorn" hints at Dorothy being the oldest child in her family and at the book Peter Bogdanovich wrote after her murder, *The Killing of the Unicorn*. "Hardcore soft porn" really speaks for itself. As Bogdanovich stated in his book, even if softcore pornography is acceptable to many people, it's still hardcore in a sense because of the damage that it can do.

It's not a message that is spelled out clearly in the song, but it gets the point across when you begin unraveling the various references that "Californication" makes.

Dorothy, perhaps more than most, would've certainly been able to understand what the Chili Peppers were trying to say with their warnings about the evil that lurks beneath the shiny veneer of LA.

It's just too bad that the warning came much too late to save her.

285 | "Don't You Wish You Were Dead?"

BIBLIOGRAPHY

Allen, William - *Starkweather: Inside the Mind of a Teenage Killer*, New York, NY, Emmis Books, 2004

American Songwriter, Savage Ventures, 2025

Apter, Jeff -- *Fornication: The Red Hot Chili Peppers Story*, New York, NY, Omnibus Press, 2004

Austerlitz, Saul – *Just A Shot Away*, New York, NY, St. Martin's Press, 2018

Bailey, F. Lee - *The Defense Never Rests*, New York, NY, Stein and Day, 1971

Bebergal, Peter – *Season of the Witch*, New York, NY, Penguin Books, 2014

Bogdanovich, Peter -- *The Killing of the Unicorn: Dorothy Stratten 1960-1980*. New York, NY, William Morrow and Company, 1984

Breskin, David – "Cult Killing: Kids in the Dark," *Rolling Stone*, November 22, 1984

Brown, Cecil – *Stagolee Shot Billy*, Boston, MA, Harvard University Press, 2003
------------------ - *We Did Them Wrong: The Ballad of Frankie and Albert*, New York, NY, W.W. Norton & Co., 2005

Brownstein, Ronald – *Rock Me on the Water*, New York, NY, Harper Collins, 2021

Bugliosi, Vincent and Curt Gentry – *Helter Skelter: The True Story of the Manson Murders*, New York, NY, Bantam Books, 1995

Burt, Olive Woolley – *American Murder Ballads and Their Stories*, New York, NY, Oxford University Press, 1958

Carlson, Peter – "A Regular Old Southern Maryland Boy" *Washington Post Magazine*, August 4, 1991

Casstevens, Frances H. – *Death in North Carolina's Piedmont*, Charleston, SC, History Press, 2006

Cohen, Anne B. – *Poor Pearl, Poor Girl! The Murdered Girl Stereotype in Ballad*, Austin, TX, University of Texas Press, 1973

Didion, Joan – *The White Album*, New York, NY, Farrar, Straus and Giroux, 1979

Dunstan, William E. – *Nell Cropsey and Jim Wilcox*, Independently Published, 2019

Dylan, Bob – *Chronicles: Volume One*, New York, NY, Simon & Schuster, 2004

Eliot, Marc – *To The Limit*, Boston, MA, Da Capo Press, 1998

Felton, David and David Dalton – "Charles Manson: The Incredible Story of the Most Dangerous Man Alive," *Rolling Stone*, June 25, 1970

Frank, Gerold - *The Boston Strangler*, New York, NY, Penguin Publishing Group, 1967

Friedman, Albert – *The Viking Book of Folk Ballads of the English-Speaking World*, New York, NY, Viking Press, 1956

"Full Moon, Dark Heart: Eddie Noack's "Psycho" - Singout.org. - November 6, 2017

Gardner, Rufus – *Tom Dooley: The Eternal Triangle*, Rufus Gardner, 1960

Gilmore, John – *Garbage People*, Los Angeles, CA, Amok Books, 2000
------------------ - *L.A. Despair: A Landscape of Crimes & Bad Times*, Los Angeles, CA, Amok Books, 2005

Gollmar, Robert H. - *Edward Gein: America's Most Bizarre Murderer*, Delavan, WI, C. Hallberg, 1981

Gribben, Mark – "Poor Pearl" from *The Malefactor's Register*

Guinn, Jeff – *Manson: The Life and Times of Charles Manson*, New York, NY, Simon & Schuster, 2013

Guralnick, Peter – *Feel Like Going Home*, New York, NY, Random House, 1971

Herman, Gary – *Rock-N-Roll Babylon*, London, UK, Plexus Books, 2008

Heylin, Clinton – *Bob Dylan: Behind the Shades*, New York, NY, 2000

Holbrook, Stewart H. – *Murder Out Yonder*, New York, NY, MacMillan, 1941

Hopkins, Jerry and Danny Sugerman – *No One Here Gets Out Alive*, New York, Grand Central Publishing, 1980

Hoskyns, Barney – *Hotel California*, Hoboken, NJ, John Wiley & Sons, 2006
--------------------- - *Waiting for the Sun*, Milwaukee, WI, Backbeat Books, 1996

Hunt, N Leigh - *I Don't Like Mondays: The True Story Behind America's First Modern School Shooting*, Wild Blue Press, 2022

Jones, Stephen L. – *Murder Ballads Old & New*, Port Townsend, WA, Feral House, 2023

Katz, Gary J. – *Death by Rock & Roll*, New York, NY, Citadel Books, 1995

Kelly, Susan - *The Boston Stranglers: The Public Conviction of Albert Desalvo and the True Story of Eleven Shocking Murders*, New York, NY, Citadel, 1995

Kiedis, Anthony and Larry Sloman -- *Scar Tissue*, New York, NY, Hyperion, 2004

Krajicek, David J. – *Charles Manson: The Man Who Murdered the Sixties*, London, UK, Arcturus Holdings Limited, 2019

Kreps, Daniel – "Grant Hart, Hüsker Dü' Drummer and Singer, Dead at 56," *Rolling Stone*, September 14, 2017

Kriek, Erik – *In the Pines: Five Murder Ballads*, Amsterdam, Scratch Books, 2016

Kunheim, Anthony – *The Pearl Bryan Murder Story,* Alexandria, KY, Campbell County Historical and Genealogical Society, 1996

Lachman, Gary – *Turn Off Your Mind*, New York, NY, Disinformation Co. Ltd., 2001

Lomax, John and Alan – *Folk Song USA*, New York, NY, Duell, Sloan & Pierce, 1946

MacDara, Conroy – "Grant Hart – All of My Old Friends are Assholes," *Thumped*, December 2, 2012

Marcus, Greil – *Mystery Train: Images of America in Rock-n-Roll Music*, New York, NY, Faber & Faber, 1975

Marsh, Dave - *The Heart of Rock & Soul: The 1001 Greatest Singles Ever Made.*, New York, NY Plume, 1989

McClure, Dudley – "The Real Story of Frankie and Johnny," *Daring Detective*, June 1935

Melnick, Jeffrey – *Creepy Crawling: Charles Manson and the Many Lives of America's Most Infamous Family*, New York, NY, Arcade Publishing, 2018

Mysterious Murder of Pearl Bryan, or The Headless Horror, Cincinnati, OH, Barclay & Co., 1897

Nelson, Donald Lee – "The Lawson Family Murder, *JEMF Quarterly*, University of California, 1973

Newton, Michael -- *Waste Land: The Savage Odyssey of Charles Starkweather and Caril Ann Fugate*, New York, NY, Pocket Books, 1998

O'Neill, Tom and Dan Piepenbring – *Chaos: Charles Manson, the CIA, and the Secret History of the Sixties*, New York, NY, Little, Brown & Co., 2019

Parish, James Robert -- *The Hollywood Book of Death: The Bizarre, Often Sordid, Passings of More than 125 American Movie and TV Idols*, New York, NY, McGraw-Hill, 2001

Patterson, R. Gary – *Take A Walk on the Dark Side*, New York, NY, Simon & Schuster, 2004

Polenberg, Richard - *Hear My Sad Story: The True Tales That Inspired "Stagolee," "John Henry," and Other Traditional American Folk Songs*, Ithaca, NY, Cornell University Press, 2015

Pollak, Jesse – *The Acid King*, New York, NY, Simon and Schuster, 2018

Poock, L.D. – *Headless, Yet Identified: A Story of the Solution of the Pearl Bryan or Fort Thomas Mystery Through the Shoes,* Columbus, OH, Hann & Adair Printers, 1897

Public Domain Music – "Meaning of the Song Sudden Impact by Big Audio Dynamite," PD Music, 2025

Riley, James – *The Bad Trip*, London, UK, Icon Books Ltd., 2019

Rucker, James – *The Story of the Ballad of Tom Dooley*, Appalachian Heritage Winter 2008 edition, University of North Carolina Press

Sanders, Ed – *The Family*, New York, NY, Signet Books, 1989

Schechter, Harold – *Deviant: The Shocking True Story of Ed Gein*, New York, NY, Pocket Books, 1989
---------------------- - –*Psycho USA: Famous American Killers You Never Heard Of*, New York, NY, Ballantine Books, 2012

Selvin, Joel – *Hollywood Eden*, Canada, Anansi Books, 2021

Simon, David – "A Lonesome Death," *New Yorker*, January 26, 2009

Slade, Paul – *Unprepared to Die: America's Greatest Murder Ballads and the True Crime Stories that Inspired Them*, London, UK, Soundcheck Books, 2015

Smith, Trudy J. -- *The Meaning of Our Tears: The Lawson Family Murders of Christmas Day 1929*, Upwards Publishing, 2006

Sounes, Howard – *27: A History of the 27 Club*, Boston, MA, Da Capo Press, 2013
--------------------- - *Down the Highway: The Life of Bob Dylan*, New York, NY Doubleday, 2001

St. Clair, David – "*Say You Love Satan*," New York, NY, Dell Books, 1987

St. James, Izabella - *Bunny Tales: Behind Closed Doors at the Playboy Mansion*, New York, NY, Running Press Adult, 2006

Strand, Ginger -- *Killer on the Road: Violence and the American Interstate*, Austin, TX, University of Texas Press, 2012

Taylor, Troy – *A Song of Dance and Death*, Jacksonville, IL, American Hauntings Ink, 2019
----------------- - *Suffer the Children*, Jacksonville, IL, American Hauntings Ink, 2018

Thompson, Dave -- *Red Hot Chili Peppers – By the Way: The Biography*, New York, NY, Virgin Books, 2004

Townsend, Henry – *A Blues Life*, Champaign, IL, University of Illinois Press, 1999

Vallance, Jim – Songs, jimvallance.com

Walker, Michael – *Laurel Canyon: The Inside Story of Rock-n-Rolls Legendary Neighborhood*, New York, NY, Farrar, Straus & Giroux, 2006

Wall, Mick – *Life in the Fast Lane*, New York, NY, Diversion Books, 2023

Watts, Steven - *Mr. Playboy: Hugh Hefner and the American Dream*, Hoboken, NJ, John Wiley & Sons, 2008

West, John Foster – *Lift Up Your Head, Tom Dooley*, Down Home Press, 1993

Young, Andrew – *Unwanted: A Murder Mystery of the Gilded Age*, Yardley, PA, Westholme Publishing, 2016

NEWSPAPERS

Afro-American (1963 editions)
Baltimore Sun
Burlington Weekly Free Press (VT)
Charlotte Observer (NC)
Daily Capital-Journal
Daily Dispatch (NC)
Danbury Reporter (CT)
Decatur Daily Review (IL)
Fort Wayne Journal-Gazette (IN)
Harrisburg Telegraph (PA)
Indianapolis Star
Kansas City Globe
Lakeland Ledger (FL)
Lubbock Morning Advertiser (TX)
Medford Mail Tribune (MA)
New York Herald
New York Times
Oregon Statesman
Ottawa Journal
Portland Daily Press (ME)
Salt Lake Tribune
St. Louis Globe-Democrat
St. Louis Star
Statesville American
Washington Post
Winston-Salem Journal (NC)

SONG LICENSING ACKNOWLEDGEMENTS

Revolution Blues
Words and Music by Neal Young
Copyright © 1974 Hipgnosis Side A and Silver Fiddle Music Copyright Renewed.
All Rights Administered by Hipgnosis Songs Group All Rights Reserved Used by Permission Reprinted by Permission of Hal Leonard LLC

Thanks to songwriters no longer with us whose work is part of the public domain, as well as Bruce Springsteen, Rolling Stones, Bob Dylan, and others.

SPECIAL THANKS TO

April Slaughter: Cover Design
Becky Ray: Editing
Samantha Smith
Athena & the "Aunts" - Sue, Carmen & Rocky
Orrin and Rachel Taylor
Rene Kruse
Rachael Horath
Bethany Horath
Elyse and Thomas Reihner
John Winterbauer
Cody Beck
Trey Schrader
Tom and Michelle Bonadurer
Lydia Rhoades
Cheryl Stamp and Sheryel Williams-Staab
Joelle Leitschuh and Tonya Leitschuh
Scott and Hannah Rob
Victoria & Reese Welch
And the entire crew of American Hauntings

ABOUT THE AUTHOR

Troy Taylor is the author of books on ghosts, hauntings, true crime, the unexplained, and the supernatural in America. He is the founder of American Hauntings Ink, which offers books, ghost tours, events, and the Haunted America Conference, as well as the creator of the American Oddities Museum in Alton, Illinois.

He was born and raised in the Midwest and divides his time between Alton, Illinois and wherever the wind decides to take him. See Troy's other titles at: www.americanhauntingsink.

www.ingramcontent.com/pod-product-compliance
Lightning Source LLC
Chambersburg PA
CBHW070047100426
42734CB00040B/2568